The Cambridge Companion to Postmodernism

The Cambridge Companion to Postmodernism offers a comprehensive introduction to postmodernism. The Companion examines the different aspects of
postmodernist thought and culture that have had a significant impact on contemporary cultural production and thinking. Topics discussed by experts in the
field include postmodernism's relation to modernity, and its significance and
relevance to literature, film, law, philosophy, architecture, religion, and modern
cultural studies. The volume also includes a useful guide to further reading and
a chronology. This is an essential aid for students and teachers from a range of
disciplines interested in postmodernism in all its incarnations. Accessible and
comprehensive, this *Companion* addresses the many issues surrounding this
elusive, enigmatic, and often controversial topic.

D1355017

THE CAMBRIDGE
COMPANION TO
POSTMODERNISM

EDITED BY
STEVEN CONNOR

CAMBRIDGE
UNIVERSITY PRESS

PUBLISHED BY THE PRESS SYNDICATE OF THE UNIVERSITY OF CAMBRIDGE
The Pitt Building, Trumpington Street, Cambridge, United Kingdom

CAMBRIDGE UNIVERSITY PRESS
The Edinburgh Building, Cambridge CB2 2RU, UK
40 West 20th Street, New York NY 10011-4211, USA
477 Williamstown Road, Port Melbourne, VIC 3207, Australia
Ruiz de Alarcón 13, 28014 Madrid, Spain
Dock House, The Waterfront, Cape Town 8001, South Africa

http://www.cambridge.org

First published 2004
Reprinted 2005

Printed in the United Kingdom at the University Press, Cambridge

Typeface Sabon 10/13 pt   *System* LATEX 2$_\varepsilon$ [TB]

A catalogue record for this book is available from the British Library

ISBN 0 521 64052 0 hardback
ISBN 0 521 64840 8 paperback

CONTENTS

Contents

NOTES ON CONTRIBUTORS

PHILIP AUSLANDER is Professor in the School of Literature, Communication, and Culture of the Georgia Institute of Technology. He holds the PhD in Theatre from Cornell University. At Georgia Tech, Professor Auslander teaches in the areas of Performance Studies, Cultural Studies, and Media Studies. He is a contributing editor to both the US-based *TDR: The Journal of Performance Studies* and the UK-based *Performance Research*. He contributes regularly to these and other journals, and his books include *Presence and Resistance: Postmodernism and Cultural Politics in Contemporary American Performance*; *From Acting to Performance: Essays in Modernism and Postmodernism*; and *Liveness: Performance in a Mediatized Culture*. He received the 2000 Callaway Prize for the Best Book in Theatre or Drama for *Liveness*. He recently edited *Performance: Critical Concepts*, a collection of eighty-nine essays in four volumes. His next book project as an author will be *All the Young Dudes: Glam Rock and the Discourse of Authenticity in Popular Music*. In addition to his scholarly work on performance, Professor Auslander writes art criticism for *ArtForum* in New York City and *Art Papers* in Atlanta.

PHILIPPA BERRY is a Fellow and Director of Studies in English at King's College, University of Cambridge. She combines interdisciplinary research in English and European Renaissance culture with work on feminist and postmodern theory. She is the author of *Of Chastity and Power: Elizabethan Literature and the Unmarried Queen*, and of *Shakespeare's Feminine Endings: Disfiguring Death in the Tragedies*, and co-editor of *Shadow of Spirit: Postmodernism and Religion* and *Textures of Renaissance Knowledge*. She is currently writing a study of Shakespeare's comedies, to be entitled *Phenomenal Shakespeare*.

STEVEN CONNOR is Professor of Modern Literature and Theory in the School of English and Humanities at Birkbeck College, London, and Director of the London Consortium Programme in Humanities and Cultural Studies.

He is the author of books on Dickens, Joyce, Beckett, and postwar fiction, as well as of *Postmodernist Culture: An Introduction to Theories of the Contemporary; Theory and Cultural Value; Dumbstruck: A Cultural History of Ventriloquism*; and *The Book of Skin*. Other unpublished works and works in progress are to be found on his website at <www.bbk.ac.uk/eh/skc>

CATHERINE CONSTABLE is a senior lecturer in Film Studies at Sheffield Hallam University, where she specializes in philosophy and film theory. She has written articles on postmodernism, philosophy, and film and has co-edited a special issue of *Hypatia* (vol. 15, no. 2) on Australian feminist philosophy, which was published in Spring 2000. She is currently completing a book for the British Film Institute that is provisionally entitled *Thinking in Images: Feminist Philosophy, Film Theory and Marlene Dietrich* and due to be published in 2004.

COSTAS DOUZINAS is Professor of Law at Birkbeck College, London, and a Visiting Professor at the University of Athens. Educated in Athens, London, and Strasbourg, he has taught at the Universities of Middlesex, Lancaster, Prague, Thessaloniki, Griffith, Cardozo, Nanjing, and Beijing. He is the managing editor of *Law and Critique: The International Journal of Critical Legal Thought* and of the Birkbeck Law Press. He specializes in jurisprudence, human rights, and critical thought. His books include (with Ronnie Warrington) *Postmodern Jurisprudence: The Law of Text in the Texts of Law*; (with Ronnie Warrington) *Justice Miscarried: Ethics and Aesthetics in Law*; (with Ronnie Warrington) *The Logos of Nomos: Interpretation, Ethics and Aesthetics in the Law; The End of Human Rights: Critical Legal Thought at the Turn of the Century*; (with Lynda Nead) *Law and the Image: The Authority of Art and the Aesthetics of Law*; and *Critical Jurisprudence*; and *Postmodern Just Wars* (forthcoming). His work has been translated into five languages.

ROBERT EAGLESTONE works on contemporary and twentieth-century literature, literary theory, and philosophy and teaches at Royal Holloway, University of London. His publications include *Ethical Criticism: Reading after Levinas; Doing English: A Guide for Literature Students; Postmodernism and Holocaust Denial*; and articles on contemporary European philosophy, Samuel Beckett, Angela Carter, ethics, science, the Holocaust, archaeology, and historiography. He is a Literary Advisor to the British Council and on the Executive of the Forum for European Philosophy. He is the academic series editor of Routledge Critical Thinkers.

URSULA K. HEISE is Associate Professor of English and Comparative Literature at Columbia University and the author of *Chronoschisms: Time,*

Narrative and Postmodernism, as well as many essays on literature, science, and postmodernism. She is currently working on a book project entitled *Ecology, Technology, and the Posthuman: Postmodern Literature and the Challenge of the Environment*.

STEPHEN MELVILLE is Professor of the History of Art at Ohio State University and was Leverhulme Visiting Professor in the Department of Art History and Theory at the University of Essex during 2002–3. He is the author of *Philosophy Beside Itself: On Deconstruction and Modernism* and *Seams: Art as a Philosophical Context*; co-author, with Philip Armstrong and Laura Lisbon, of *As Painting: Division and Displacement*; and co-editor, with Bill Readings, of *Vision and Textuality*. He has written widely on contemporary art and theory.

JULIAN MURPHET has taught at the Universities of Cambridge, Oxford, and California at Berkeley, and presently is a lecturer in the Department of English, University of Sydney. He has published widely in the field of postmodernism, most substantially in his book *Literature and Race in Los Angeles*. He is also the author of *Bret Easton Ellis's "American Psycho": A Reader's Guide*. Currently he is preparing a book on the impact of cinema on literary production in America.

PAUL SHEEHAN is a Research Fellow at Macquarie University, Sydney. He has published in the areas of narrative poetics and the philosophy of literature, including articles on Dickens and Beckett. He is also the author of *Modernism, Narrative and Humanism* and the editor of *Becoming Human: New Perspectives on the Inhuman Condition*.

CHRONOLOGY

1972 Robert Venturi and Denise Scott-Brown, *Learning From La Vegas*
   Demolition of Pruitt-Igoe, failed modernist housing project in
   St Louis

1973 Establishment of ARPANET (Advanced Research and Projects
   Network), forerunner of the internet, linking together universities
   of Stanford, UCSB, UCLA, and Utah

1973 Thomas Pynchon, *Gravity's Rainbow*

1974 President Nixon resigns over Watergate scandal after break-in at
   Democratic Party headquarters

1975 Appearance of first personal computer
   Philip Glass, *Einstein on the Beach*

1976 *October* begins publication

1977 Charles Jencks, *The Language of Post-Modern Architecture*
   Punk rock

1979 First cellular phone released in Tokyo

1979 Jean-François Lyotard, *La condition postmoderne*

1980 Michael Graves, Portland Building, Portland, Oregon
   Salman Rushdie, *Midnight's Children*
   Gilles Deleuze and Félix Guattari, *Milles plateaux*

1981 Richard Serra, *Tilted Arc*
   New York Times reports on appearance of AIDS

1982 Ridley Scott, *Blade Runner*

1983 Jean Baudrillard, *Simulations*

1984 English translation of Lyotard's *The Postmodern Condition*

1984 William Gibson, *Neuromancer*
   Fredric Jameson, *Postmodernism, or, The Cultural Logic of Late
   Capitalism*
   Michel Foucault dies

1985 Donna Haraway, "A Cyborg Manifesto"
   Don DeLillo, *White Noise*
   David Lynch, *Blue Velvet*
   Live Aid, world's first global concert, held simultaneously in
   London and Philadelphia

1986 Space shuttle *Challenger* explodes shortly after take-off, killing
   all seven crew members

1988 Dennis Potter, *The Singing Detective* broadcast

1989 Tiananmen Square protest and massacre in Beijing. Fall of Berlin
   Wall
   Tim Berners-Lee develops concept of World Wide Web
   David Lynch's *Twin Peaks* begins broadcasting

1990 *Postmodern Culture*, an online journal, founded

STEVEN CONNOR

Introduction

"Finished, it's finished, nearly finished, it must be nearly finished," Clov promises himself at the beginning of Beckett's *Endgame*.[1] Surely, the first thing to be said about postmodernism, at this hour, after three decades of furious business and ringing tills, is that it must be nearly at an end. But in chess, from which Beckett's play takes its title, the endgame is not the end of the game, but the game of ending that forms part of it and may be looked towards from the beginning. Playing the game may become identical with playing the game out. There are strategies for managing the end of the game, including ways of deferring that ending, which come not after the game but in the thick of it. One is compelled to begin almost any synoptic account of postmodernism with such sunset thoughts, even as, in the very midst of one's good riddance, one senses that the sweet sorrow of taking leave of postmodernism may be prolonged for some time yet.

For postmodernism has indeed shown an extraordinary capacity to renew itself in the conflagration of its demise. One might almost say that the derivative character of postmodernism, the name of which indicates that it comes after something else – modernism, modernity, or the modern – guarantees it an extended tenure that the naming of itself as an *ex nihilo* beginning might not. You can credibly inaugurate a new beginning only for a short so long, whereas you can carry on succeeding upon something almost indefinitely, catching continuing success from your predecessor's surcease. Like Shelley's famous fading coal of inspiration, the weakening of postmodernism itself can be turned into the same kind of regenerative resource as the weakening of modernism itself. Might postmodernism have solved the problem of eternal life? We should remember from Swift's Struldbrugs that eternal life is a monstrosity without the promise of eternal youth.

I will here distinguish four different stages in the development of post-modernism: accumulation; synthesis; autonomy; and dissipation. In the first stage, which extends through the 1970s and the early part of the 1980s, the hypothesis of postmodernism was under development on a number of different fronts. Daniel Bell and Jean Baudrillard were offering new accounts of consumer society, Jean-François Lyotard was formulating his views about the waning of metanarratives, Charles Jencks was issuing his powerful manifestos on behalf of architectural postmodernism, and Ihab Hassan was characterizing a new sensibility in postwar writing, all of them, apart from Baudrillard, more or less programmatically employing the rubric "postmodernism." I will not consume the limited space I have at my disposal here in trying to characterize their ideas and arguments in detail, especially since so many serviceable introductions to their work already exist.[2]

At this stage, it was a genuine puzzle for anyone trying to get a secure fix on the term "postmodern" to make the different sorts of argument applied to different kinds of object line up. Perhaps the principal problem was how to synchronize the arguments of those who claimed that the societies of the advanced West had undergone fundamental changes in their organization, and who therefore seemed to be characterizing a shift from modernity to postmodernity, with the arguments of those who thought that they discerned a shift in the arts and culture of these societies from a distinctively modernist phase to a distinctively – or indistinctly – postmodernist phase.

From the middle of the 1980s onwards, these separate accounts began to be clustered together – most notably in the superb synopsis and synthesis provided in Fredric Jameson's landmark essay "The Cultural Logic of Late Capitalism."[3] Gradually, what came to seem important was not so much the aptness of the explanations of particular varieties of postmodernism as the increasingly powerful rhymes that different accounts of the postmodern formed with each other. Indeed, it seemed to be a feature of the postmodern itself that parallelism became more important and interesting than causation. This was also the period of the most vigorous syncretism in thinking of the postmodern. Jameson's essay opened the way for a number of synthesizing guides and introductions, which were followed in the early 1990s by a wave of anthologies of postmodern writing.[4]

The effect of this was that, by the beginning of the 1990s, the concept of the "postmodern" was ceasing to be used principally in the analysis of particular objects or cultural areas and had become a general horizon or hypothesis. I was an amateur astronomer as a boy and I remember being told that the way to make out the elusive color of a faint star was not to look directly at it, but to look just to its side, since this allowed the image to fall on a part of the retina that is more sensitive to color. I don't know if this is true of star-observation (it certainly never worked for me), but it seems to have begun to be true for spotters of the postmodern during this second period, when it seemed that, if one wanted to pin down the postmodernist features of some unlikely object of analysis – war, say, or prostitution, or circus – the thing to do was to look directly not at your target but at what lay in its periphery. Postmodernism was the practice of critical distraction (literally being "drawn aside"). Postmodernism arose from the amalgamation of these many deflections or diagonal gazes. It evoked a horizontal lattice-work of connections between different postmodernisms, rather than a discontinuous series of "vertical" diagnoses of specific postmodernisms. As kinship patterns among postmodernists became more important than patterns of descent, "analogical" postmodernism took the place of "genealogical" postmodernisms.[5]

But synthesis brought its own problems. Postmodernist theory responded to the sense that important changes had taken place in politics, economics, and social life, changes that could broadly be characterized by the two words *delegitimation* and *dedifferentiation*. Authority and legitimacy were no longer so powerfully concentrated in the centers they had previously occupied; and the differentiations – for example, those between what had been called "centers" and "margins," but also between classes, regions, and cultural levels (high culture and low culture) – were being eroded or complicated. Centrist or absolutist notions of the state, nourished by the idea of the uniform movement of history towards a single outcome, were beginning to weaken. It was no longer clear who had the authority to speak on behalf of history. The rise of an economy driven from its peripheries by patterns of consumption rather than from its center by the needs of production generated much more volatile and unstable economic conditions. These erosions of authority were accompanied by a breakdown of the hitherto unbridgeable distinctions between centers and peripheries, between classes and countries. Given these changes, it seemed to many reasonable to assume that equivalent changes would take place in the spheres of art and culture.

The problem was that this very assumption drew from a model in which there was enough of a difference between the spheres of politics, economics, and society on the one hand and art and culture on the other for the spark of a specifiable relation to be able to jump between them. During the early twentieth century, relations between the two spheres were thought of as tense, if not downright antagonistic, with many assuming that art and culture needed to be protected from the "culture industry," and both traditional and Marxist critics agreeing on the need for art to maintain an antagonistic distance from the market and prevailing norms.

Some accounts of postmodernism depended on the argument that not only had the conditions of social and economic organization changed, but so, as an effect of those changes, had the relations between the social and economic and the artistic-cultural. Drawing on the early work of Baudrillard, Fredric Jameson saw that, rather than subsisting in a state of fidgety internal exile, the sphere of culture was in fact undergoing a prodigious expansion in an economy driven by sign, style, and spectacle rather than by the production of goods. The plucky attempts of commentators to legislate terminologically between these realms, insisting, as I myself attempted to do in my book *Postmodernist Culture*, on the difference between "postmodernity" on the one hand and "postmodernism" on the other, were in fact mistakenly tidy-minded responses to a more fundamental coalescence, in which politics and economy had become culturized, art and culture sociologized, and postmodernity had itself become postmodernist. It is perhaps for this reason that the 1980s saw such a proliferation of variants in the words used to describe the phenomena under discussion. How one capitalized or hyphenated – "post-modern," "Post-Modern," "postmodern," or "Postmodern" – seemed to many to matter a great deal, along with whether one chose to refer to "postmodernism," "postmodernity," or simply "the postmodern."

During this second, syncretic phase, another subtle shift began to take place in the word "postmodernism." This word was now a name not only for the way in which new attitudes and practices had evolved in particular areas of society and culture – in architecture, in literature, in patterns of economic or political organization – but also for the characteristic discourse in which such things were discussed. "Postmodernism" named all those writers who gave house-room to the postmodern hypothesis and all the writing they did about it. At this period, it did not seem possible even to discuss the existence of the postmodern without being drawn into its discourse. Genealogies of specific postmodernisms in politics, society, and the arts were followed by genealogies of the discourse of postmodernism, such as Hans Bertens's *The Idea of the Postmodern* (1995).[6]

By the middle of the 1990s, a third stage had evolved, as the "post" idea had achieved a kind of autonomy from its objects. At this point, the argument about whether there really was such a thing as postmodernism, which had driven earlier discussions of the subject, started to evaporate, since the mere fact that there was discourse at all about the subject was now sufficient proof of the existence of postmodernism – but as idiom rather than actuality. Postmodernism became the name for the activity of writing about postmodernism. John Frow declared roundly in 1997 that the word "postmodernism" "can be taken as nothing more and nothing less than a genre of theoretical writing."[7] The postmodern became a kind of data-cloud, a fog of discourse, that showed up on the radar even more conspicuously than what it was supposed to be about. Thus postmodernism had passed from the stage of accumulation into its more autonomous phase. No longer a form of cultural barometer, postmodernism had itself become an entire climate.

Having expanded its range and dominion hugely during the first period of separate accumulation in the 1970s and the syncretic period of the 1980s, the idea of the postmodern began for the first time to slow its rate of expansion during the 1990s. In this decade, "postmodernism" slowly but inexorably ceased to be a condition of things in the world, whether the world of art, culture, economics, politics, religion, or war, and became a philosophical disposition, an all-too-easily recognizable (and increasingly dismissable) style of thought and talk. By this time, "postmodernism" had also entered the popular lexicon to signify a loose, sometimes dangerously loose, relativism. Now, its dominant associations were with postcolonialism, multiculturalism and identity politics. So, whereas postmodernism had expanded its reach in academic discussion, it had shrunk down into a casual term of abuse in more popular discourse. Postmodernism had become autonomous from its objects.

So far, I have been describing postmodernism as though it were itself merely a descriptive project, the attempt simply to get the measure of the new prevailing conditions in art, society, and culture. But, from its beginning, postmodernism has always been more than a cartographic enterprise; it has also been a *project*, an effort of renewal and transformation. The questions raised by postmodernism were always questions of value.

One of the earliest commentators on postmodernism, Daniel Bell, made the suggestion that something like a postmodern condition arose when the utopian ideals and lifestyles associated with modern artists began to be diffused among populations as fashion, lifestyle and consumer "choice." It is common to construe some kinds of artistic postmodernism as a reaction against the canonization of modernism, in institutions such as the Museum of Modern Art in New York. There were many in the 1980s who welcomed the loosening of the grip of modernism in favor of a more popular sensibility, and for a period postmodernism was strongly identified with what were thought of as the leveling tendencies of cultural studies, with its emphasis on popular culture. This was in conflict with the view held by many early formulators of postmodernism. Rather, they were inclined to emphasize the difficulty, the challenge, and the provocation of postmodernist art. Lyotard's argument that the postmodern represented the acknowledgment of unrepresentability without the retreat into the consolation of form could easily be read as a confirmation of modernist principles. Indeed, Lyotard was inclined to see postmodernism as the reactivation of principles that had flared up first in modernism.

The well-known tendency of many of the thinkers and theorists associated with postmodernism to focus on modernists (Lacan on Joyce, Derrida on Mallarmé, Foucault on Roussel) might have offered support for the view

that early postmodernist formulations were attempting to reinstate something like the heroic refusal of modern life that constituted artistic modernism. Whereas the modernity refused by modernists was the modernity of
urban transformation, mass production, and speed of transport and communications, the modernity refused by postmodernists was that of consumer
capitalism, in which the world, forcibly wrenched into new material forms
by modernity, was being transformed by being immaterialized, transformed
into various kinds of spectacle.

As postmodern studies began to proliferate, more complex relations began to arise between description and allegiance, or between postmodernism
conceived as a condition and postmodernism conceived as a project. During
the 1980s, it was still possible to separate out the question of whether there
was such a thing as postmodernism from the question of whether one was
or was not generally for it. The work of Fredric Jameson may be seen as
maintaining the fragile equilibrium between description and recommenda-
tion, which is why that work has been read in so many different ways: as a
stern critique of postmodernism; as a subtle preservation of the project of
the modern through strategic accommodation to the postmodern; and as a
full-scale capitulation to postmodernism.

Fredric Jameson once amused himself and his readers with a diagram that
permutated the ways in which being pro- or anti-modernism could be combined with being pro- or anti-postmodernist.[8] One might adopt his strategy
here and permutate the possibilities according to which the credence and ap-
proval accorded to the idea of the postmodern can be combined. The range
of possibilities would be as follows. (1) One could believe in postmodernism
and be all for it. This was the position adopted by propagandists for postmodernism, such as Charles Jencks and Jean-François Lyotard. In fact, most
of those who wrote about postmodern condition in the 1970s were broadly in
favor of it, or at least saw the postmodern as an irresistible necessity. (2) One
could believe in postmodernism but nevertheless recoil from or be opposed
to it. This was the position influentially dramatized in David Harvey's *The
Condition of Postmodernity* (1980)[9] and carried forward recently by critics
such as Paul Virilio. (3) One could not believe in postmodernism and (one
supposes for that very reason) not be for it. This was the position occupied
by most of the early critics of the "postmodern turn," as well as of Marxist
cultural critics who believed that postmodernism was a snare and a delusion that mystified the real bases of domination and gave up prematurely
on modernity, identified as this latter can be with the project inaugurated in
the Enlightenment of human emancipation from error and oppression. The
most influential proponent of this view was Jürgen Habermas, in his *The
Philosophical Discourse of Modernity* (1987).[10]

An interesting feature of such permutations is that they often generate a seemingly abstract possibility, which is required for the logical integrity of the model but cannot reasonably be expected to have any real-world existence – a sort of $\sqrt{-1}$ or similar mathematical fiction. In the case of this model, the phantom position is that which would both dispute the possibility of postmodernism and yet be in favor of it. But even this Carrollian contortion seems to have found an exponent. In *We Have Never Been Modern*, Bruno Latour argues that modernity, which he prefers to call "The Modern Constitution,"[11] arises from the coordination of two absolutisms: (1) the absolute separation of human culture from nonhuman nature, and (2) the absolute separation of present from past. The Modern Constitution arises out of the sense of the sharp separation of nature and culture, and out of the forms of knowledge they produce and are addressed by. Nature produces science, the knowledge of how things are in themselves. Culture (language, society, politics) produces the social sciences and the discourses of morality, politics, psychology, etc. Modernity is characterized by the belief that there is no relation between these two kinds of object or between these two kinds of knowledge; indeed, by the requirement that they should be kept rigorously distinct. Modernity thus "invents a separation between the scientific power charged with representing things and the political power charged with representing subjects" (p. 29). We might recognize here a version of the distinction between the spheres marked out earlier, albeit unreliably, as modernity and modernism, postmodernity and postmodernism.

The originality of Latour's argument is that the very moment at which modernity invents this distinction and starts to hold itself in being by means of it (the beginning of the "scientific revolution" in the seventeenth century) is the moment at which the middle ground – of objects and forms and ideas and practices, lying between the inhuman realm of nature and the human realm of culture – begins to proliferate. More and more "things" get drawn into social life, which will become more and more dependent upon and liable to be transformed by what it draws from and does with nature. Whereas modernity supposes a stark division between subjects and objects, cultures and natures, Latour proposes that we pay attention to what (borrowing a phrase from Michel Serres) he calls "quasi-objects," which crowd into, and then start to crowd out, the space between nonhuman nature and human culture.

Latour then re-angles his argument to address the question of temporality. He shows that the first absolutism, the absolute separation between inhuman things and human cultures, is mapped on to a second, the absolute temporal distinction between past and present. *"The asymmetry between nature and culture then becomes an asymmetry between past and future. The past was the confusion of things and men; the future is what will no longer confuse them*" (p. 71, italics original). Despite their many antagonisms, modernism (let's say, free love and free indirect style) and modernization (telegrams and tanks) depend upon two principles: the sense of the uniform passing of time and the sense of the homogeneity of the present moment, or the self-identity of the "now." "Modernizing progress is thinkable only on condition that all the elements that are contemporary according to the calendar belong to the same time" (p. 73), Latour declares.

But the multiplication of quasi-objects produces a temporal turbulence, a multiplication of times:

> No one can now categorize actors that belong to the "same time" in a single coherent group. No one knows any longer whether the reintroduction of the bear in Pyrenees, kolkhozes, aerosols, the Green Revolution, the anti-smallpox vaccine, Star Wars, the Muslim religion, partridge hunting, the French Revolution, service industries, labour unions, cold fusion, Bolshevism, relativity, Slovak nationalism, commercial sailboats, and so on, are outmoded, up to date, futuristic, atemporal, nonexistent, or permanent . . . (p. 74)

Latour's argument is that, since modern society has not in fact purified itself of nature, but implicated itself ever more deeply within it, there is no distinction to be made between modern and premodern cultures. Indeed, there is no such thing as a "culture": "the very notion of culture is an artifact created by bracketing Nature off. Cultures – different or universal – do not exist, any more than Nature does. There are only natures-cultures" (p. 104). Furthermore, there never have been any cultures in the sense of wholly self-inventing, non-natural phenomena. Hence, since the idea of the modern depends upon the claim that we have freed ourselves, or will free ourselves, from nature, "we have never been modern." Postmodernism apprehends the unevenness of times, the mingling of old and new that belongs to the premodern or amodern apprehension, but, clinging to the habits of modern thinking, sees it as a new development in the flow of time, a new kind of "now." Our present condition does not represent a postmodern break with ideas of progress. Latour acknowledges that his own "amodernist" attitudes overlap considerably with those of "the postmoderns" (they are clearly supposed to know who they are as well as Latour does), but attempts also to distance himself from them.

> The postmoderns are right about the dispersion; every contemporary assembly is polytemporal. But they are wrong to retain the framework and to keep on believing in the requirement of continual novelty that modernism demanded. By mixing elements of the past together in the form of collages and citations, the postmoderns recognize to what extent these citations are truly outdated.

Moreover, it is because they are outmoded that the postmoderns dig them up, in order to shock the former "modernist" avant-gardes who no longer know at what altar to worship. But it is a long way from a provocative quotation extracted out of a truly finished past to a reprise, repetition or revisiting of a past that has never disappeared. (p. 74)

Latour's objection to postmodernism is that it turns the standing impossibility of being modern into a postmodern value. This is perhaps the most lasting problem of postmodernism. The more compelling postmodernism seems as an hypothesis, the more it seems that it might be a condition rather than an imperative, and the more beside the point seems the question of how or whether one chooses to be postmodernist. Choosing to be postmodernist then starts to look like choosing to embrace contingency, when the point about contingency is that it chooses you, for its own (non)reasons.

The most striking difference between modernism and postmodernism is that, though both depend upon forms of publicity, few guides or introductions to modernism appeared until it was felt to be over. Modernism was built out of prophecy rather than retrospect. What the incendiary manifesto was to modernism, the firefighting "guide" or "introduction" has been to postmodernism. The guide appears more democratic than the manifesto, in that it attempts to meet the reader on his or her own ground; but, in the pedagogic relation it assumes and establishes, it can also work to maintain a privative distinction between those in the know and those not yet so. The structure of books such as my own *Postmodernist Culture* (1989, 1996), which tracked the emergence of different kinds of postmodernism from different kinds of modernism, encouraged readers to feel that, in order to understand and participate in the postmodernist break, it was necessary for them to undergo a kind of apprenticeship in modernism. The seemingly paradoxical fact that the affirmation of the postmodern break required such extensive reprise of modernism does not seem so paradoxical after all, if postmodernist theory is seen as having the same uneasy relation to its public as modernism did to its public, and if postmodernism is seen as driven by some of the same resentful desire for privilege as modernism. It should therefore not seem so surprising that the postmodernist transformation should have brought about so remarkable and extensive a revival of interest and research in modernism on all fronts.

Modernism had shocked sensibilities and assaulted senses with sex, speed, noise, and nonsense. Postmodernist artists have carried on relentlessly shocking and assaulting and provoking, as they had done for nearly a century, but they added to their repertoire the kinds of defensive attack represented by postmodernist theory. Modernist work was shock requiring later analysis.

As T. S. Eliot wrote, referring to something else altogether: "We had the experience but missed the meaning."[12] Postmodernist work attempts to draw experience and meaning, shock, and analysis into synchrony. Being modernist always meant not quite realizing that you were so. Being postmodernist always involved the awareness that you were so.

But, if Bell is right when he says that modernism is surpassed by being diffused, so postmodernism may also be suffering the same fate. We have reached a situation in which the idea of postmodernism has both broadened and become simplified. The late 1990s were characterized by a different kind of guide, which pays attention to postmodernism as a general and popular sensibility. A recent example might be Ziauddin Sardar's *A – Z of Postmodern Life* (2002).[13] Cristopher Nash's *The Unravelling of the Postmodern Mind* (2002), though much less of a pop guide, nevertheless assumes that postmodernism is a sensibility or state of mind, rather than the result of rigorous philosophical or cultural-political deliberation.[14]

As postmodernism became generalized during its third phase in the 1990s, so the force of postmodernism as an ideal, or a necessary premonition of the good, seems also to have begun to dissipate. Perhaps the very acceptance, grudging or resigned, of the existence of a widespread postmodern condition in society, culture, and politics and a postmodern disposition in the arts and culture has meant that it has become more difficult to see postmodernism as something to be invented, or as a project towards which one must bend one's best efforts. We can now, it seems, be postmodernist without knowing it, and without ever having had to get good grades in modernism.

Postmodernism shares with modernism a kind of presentism. Other literary-cultural periods in the past have come about when cultures have looked elsewhere, with a renewing attention to other periods, other cultures: the Renaissance and antiquity, Romanticism with its native archaisms and exoticisms, even modernism with its strange mixture of primitivism and zippy contemporaneity. Postmodernism, by contrast, is concerned almost exclusively with the nature of its own presentness. Indeed, one definition of postmodernism might be: that condition in which for the first time, and as a result of technologies that allow large-scale storage, access, and reproduction of records of the past, the past appears to be included in the present, or at the present's disposal, and in which the ratio between present and past has therefore changed.

Of course, postmodernism shares with modernism its concern with the present, as well as its sense of the long or enduring present. But modernism's present was undefinable, a vertigo or velocity rather than a habitat. The presentness to which modernism was drawn was a hair-tigger affair, always on the brink of futurity. By contrast, the perpetual present of postmodernism is mapped, scheduled, dense with retrospection and forecast. The present (as of old) is all there is, but now it includes all time. There is nothing absent from this present, which makes it curiously spectral. This means in its turn that the present can start to age, to become old before its time. The present of postmodernism has come to seem like a stalled present, an agitated but idle meanwhile.

Perhaps the most extraordinary example of the generalization of postmodernist thinking in the rich cultures of the North is in the area of sexuality. If, as Jameson suggests, the world has been taken over by "culture," then there is a more recent assimilation of culture in general to the culture of sex. Sex used to be proclaimed to be the secret, forbidden truth of human life. It is now the most manifest, ubiquitous, and compulsory truth. Sex can no longer be stopped or avoided. From being the accessory that assisted the packaging and consumption of a range of commodities, sex has become the product that other commodities exist to sell. Sex has come into its own, because sex wants to be more than sex. This is why everything is sex – because sex has become the form and the name of transcendence. Sex has become the only and ultimate quality. Eros has become life. Sex has been subject to economic transaction, to buying and selling as a commodity, for centuries. But what seems to have come about in the last couple of decades is a situation in which sex becomes the very medium in which other exchanges take place. You do not pay for sex with money; you pay for everything in the currency of sex.

And yet, because it is so triumphant, sex may also be forced to be on guard. Because sex has become so ubiquitous, so polymorphously perverse, so mixed-up and mingled with everything else, it fears – we fear – it may lose its meaning. In previous eras, sex had struggled against repression, and it was repression that made it a looming, irrepressible "it," a force gathering itself beneath and behind repression. Now, having either defeated repression, or recruited it to its own cause, sex may face a larger battle, a battle against an enemy that it itself produces: indifference. Repression energizes and recharges sex: indifference depletes it. Sex could never be defeated while there was repression. Now that it has won, it stands to lose everything in the face of disaffection.

If it is true that something like a "sex culture" is in the process of arising, this may suggest that, though sexuality has certainly featured centrally in many discussions of the postmodern, it may now itself have achieved a kind of autonomy from it. This in its turn suggests that, having been progressively more generalized over the thirty or so years during which it has been under development, postmodern discourse may now be entering a new phase of productive dissipation, in which some of the very cultural themes and phenomena that it has made its concern are now themselves achieving a kind of autonomy. Rather than embarking on a new round of synthesizing, this collection attempts to register the mass and velocity of some of these new areas of growth to which postmodernism has undoubtedly given rise. They may not continue to operate indefinitely within the horizon of postmodernist studies, but may nevertheless prolong postmodernism by breaking with it.

Postmodernism has been represented through its different stages by different disciplines and cultural areas. The essays in this collection represent a very different range of subject-areas from those that might have appeared in such a volume had it been published in 1970, 1980, or 1990. In 1970, the talk would all have been of postmodernist literature. In 1980, a sort of heyday of postmodernism, architecture would perhaps have slipped into the position of dominant discipline, supplying, as it seemed, a fund of language and arguments for the other areas of postmodernism. By 1990, after the break-up of the Soviet Union and the revolutions across Europe had both confirmed the hypothesis of the unsustainability of historical grand narratives (or their appropriation on behalf of states) and brought to the surface new problems of ethnic and religious diversity, postmodernism became centered not on any one cultural form but in the problems attaching to the plurality of cultures. The postmodern condition no longer seemed a possible future, to be adumbrated allegorically by literary texts, buildings, or other works, but had become a real and urgent predicament.

Now, at the beginning of the new millennium, there remain disciplines and intellectual areas that are central to the definition of postmodernism and continue to throw up questions and challenges. The essays on philosophy, film, literature, and art included in this collection focus in different ways on how the "old" postmodernism that has become part of the landscape and equipment of a discipline continues to develop. In all these essays, postmodernism is seen as a relation not just to a preceding modernism, as might have seemed to be the case a couple of decades ago, but to the very condition of postmodernism's persistence and success in the discipline in question. The newness of postmodernism in these areas is in part to be found in responses to the relative oldness of the postmodern hypothesis.

But, as well as reporting on survivals and mutations in some of the most important host or home disciplines of postmodernism, this collection also reflects the most significant shifts of emphasis that have been taking place in postmodern studies over the last decade, especially in the areas of most rapid growth, namely law, religion, science, and technology. Sometimes, these new formations can throw up problems and provocations that do not so readily come to light in postmodernism's more settled provinces.

A good example of this is the field of legal studies, which are considered in the essay by Costas Douzinas. It seems clear that the new development that one can call postmodern legal studies represents not just a form of legal theory arising from the deforming entry into the field of law of a body of ideas from elsewhere, but also a series of claims now radiating outwards from law and the disciplines with which it is affiliating itself – art, literature, film – that may make the whole field of postmodern studies begin to resonate at a different frequency. In allowing the unsettling question of justice to breach the closure of a modernist legal theory that had concerned itself almost exclusively with the problem of making law consistent with itself rather than justly responsive to the world within which it functions, postmodern legal theory also makes the question of justice newly compelling in many other areas of postmodern thinking. As much a polemical example of a new way of conceiving law as a review of the changes it has undergone as a result of the pressure of postmodern questioning, Costas Douzinas's essay will repay the close attention it may require from those not accustomed to thinking of legal questions alongside cultural and artistic ones.

Another area of reciprocal influence is in religious studies, or the field of spirituality. Philippa Berry's essay shows how theologians and other writers on religion have responded to what she calls "the haunting of our secular culture by something like yet unlike religion" (p. 173). In one sense a post-modern skepticism about the grand narrative of increasing secularism makes postmodern theory a natural resource for those concerned to interpret the many different forms of religious belief and practice as something more than survival or regression to the premodern. In another sense, the very fact that writers on questions of religion and spirituality have been able to draw so tellingly on the work of philosophers and theorists such as Georges Bataille, Hélène Cixous, Michel de Certeau, Luce Irigaray, and, most importantly, Emmanuel Levinas and Jacques Derrida discloses the fact that the question of religion has been at work in powerful but unarticulated ways in the discourse of postmodernism for much longer than may have appeared. Post-modernism's characteristic mode of the "post-," the manner of its "after-thought," provides a model for what Berry would have us see as "post-religion" – a kind of spirituality that both comes after and persists in being religion.

Something similar can be seen in the field of performance studies, here discussed by Philip Auslander. In one sense, the performing arts can be seen as simply another area in which postmodernism has come to have an im-portant influence – though the slight dislocation of drama and other per-forming arts, such as dance, from the mainstream of modernist development at the beginning of the twentieth century has led to odd anachronisms and anomalies in the development of postmodern theories in those areas. For instance, since the characteristic of much modern drama is its heightened and scandalizing realism (Ibsen, Strindberg), one sign of postmodernism in drama is an antirealism (Brecht, Beckett) that actually makes it seem similar to what was happening in arts such as painting in their modernist phase. Dance seems clearly to have its modernist moment, in the break made by dancers and choreographers such as Isadora Duncan and Martha Graham from the traditions of classical ballet; but even the most authoritative exponent of postmodernism in dance, Sally Banes, seems to acknowledge that there have been two very different kinds of postmodernism in dance. The first, described in her book *Terpsichore in Sneakers*, is a postmodernism by subtraction, which deliberately strips dance down to its basic principles (and thus confusingly resembles the analytic mode of modernist painting celebrated by Clement Greenberg).[15] But her more recent book, *Writing Dancing in the Age of Postmodernism*, shows that this analytic period has been followed by the much more opulent, richly combinative forms of dance that proliferated during the 1980s and 1990s, which have sought to enlarge the scope of dance rather than to clarify its essence.[16] Auslander makes it clear, however, that the importance of performance to postmodernism lies not so much in the adjustment of the postmodernist paradigm to existing areas of the performing arts as in much further-reaching resonance between postmodernism and the idea of performance. This is brought to a focus by the example of what is variously called "live art," "performance art," and simply "performance," which seems so intrinsically a postmodern form that there is no question of there ever having been modernist or premodernist variants of it. In something of the way that the emergence of post-religion allows the retrieval of the force of religious concerns within postmodern thought, so the emergence of postmodern "performance" allows a delayed recognition of the origin of postmodernism in the apprehension that "everything performs;" that, rather than simply resting serenely in being, art, politics, identity, all act themselves out.

It is through the work of one of the most influential of anticipatory thinkers, Emmanuel Levinas, that law, philosophy, and religion are drawn together in what one might call, if not exactly a new discipline, then at least a powerful cross-disciplinary "attractor" or center of gravity. Emmanuel Levinas represents for the postmodernism of the 1990s and beyond what Mikhail Bakhtin was for the postmodernism of the 1980s. Bakhtin's theory of the crowding of every apparently singular voice by a multiplicity of competing or qualifying voices quickly spread from literary studies into film, art history, philosophy and politics. Polyphonic plenitude, the searching out and affirmation of the plurality of different voices, became the leading and defining principle of postmodernism's cultural politics. Just as Goethe is said to have died with the Enlightenment slogan "Mehr Licht!" ("More Light!")

on his lips, so at one point one might have imagined postmodernism going ungently into its goodnight uttering the defiant cry, "More Voices!"

But the 1990s also saw an unexpected swerve away from this celebratory or festival mood, as a number of writers in different areas began to ask whether the ethical questions that postmodernist thought had been so very good at setting aside, dissolving, or transcending might not still have a claim. The question being asked in a number of quarters was: could it be possible to found postmodernism not just on the negative claim to go beyond the narrowness of particular value systems but in some more positive value-claim of its own? Postmodernism had proved extremely resourceful in showing the socially constructed nature of systems of values; but writers in the late 1990s began to ask whether it might not be possible to imagine a postmodernism that would be not just constructionist but itself "constructive."[17]

The remarkable turn, or turn back, to the ethical was accomplished almost entirely through an engagement with Levinas, the importance of whom is explained in Robert Eaglestone's essay on postmodern ethics. For Levinas, ethics is not a matter of rules of behavior; it is a matter of a condition of exposure to others. Postmodern ethics is not a repertoire; it is a (positive) predicament. In encountering "the other," that exotic creature whose sightings have been reported in so many of the travelers' tales of philosophy from Hegel onwards, there is always a painful intimacy, which nevertheless prevents the other from being taken to be simply a reflection of the ego. The other represents a kind of immediate demand on the self, a demand for recognition and response. Although this demand is ethical, it also demands not to be formalized into structures of knowledge and policies of action, which turn the other into an object of knowledge. It is the attempt to remain responsive to the claims of the other without resorting to the violence of formalization and objectification that characterizes postmodern ethics. Indeed, Eaglestone suggests, the ethical turn may reveal a sort of ethical concern that is originary in postmodernism. Just as Levinas declared that ethics is "first philosophy," so, writes Eaglestone, "postmodernism, implicitly or explicitly, is about ethics before it is anything else" (p. 183). In the light of this claim, Lyotard's influential account of the different kinds of exposure before and response to the sublime enacted by modernist and postmodernist works of art might thus become legible as a differential ethics; the modernist work reduces the other to a theme, while postmodernism attempts to preserve the infinity or unapproachability of the other. In recent years the word "ethics" has come to have the same authority and reach as the word "text" had during the 1970s and 1980s. Eaglestone's account of Levinas is as demanding as it is rich; but it is a measure of the current and continuing importance of Levinas to postmodernism that discussions of his work are prominent not just in Eaglestone's essay, but also in the discussions of philosophy, law, and religion to be found in this volume.

Although postmodern ethics is not a new discipline, it brings about a new coherence or configuration among disciplines, in the same way that women's studies and gender studies and postmodernism itself had done previously. There is no more powerful example of the way in which arguments prompted by the postmodern debate have been generalized beyond postmodernism itself than in the heightened awareness of science and technology during the 1990s. For a decade or so, Jean-François Lyotard's *Postmodern Condition* was read as though it were a manifesto on behalf of avant-garde art, when in fact most of its pages are taken up with questions about the relations between science and society.[18] This is easy to understand. Despite its passing references to fractals and chaos theory, the field of science as treated by Lyotard remains curiously without content. As Ursula Heise's essay in this collection demonstrates, the 1980s and 1990s saw an explosion into visibility of the sciences of information and computing, of genetics and reproduction, and of ecology. Where Lyotard's arguments had assisted the view that scientific optimism fed the most totalitarian strains of modern thinking, the unignorable mood of exhilaration regarding the development and reach of these new sciences has forced a more complex kind of response to science. Indeed, one might say that postmodernism has been defined increasingly in terms of a complex conjuncture of scientific optimism and more traditional critique of science. A postmodern rejection of modern scientific rationality has been complicated by the emergence of what might be called "postmodern sciences" – of information, cybernetics, and ecology – which are based on the relatedness of the human and the natural rather than on the stark antagonism assumed by the Enlightenment and the nineteenth century. As science has become culturized, it has become less and less plausible to look in any simple way to the restoring or survival effects of culture against science.

Naturally, there are areas of postmodernism that are not reported on in this volume. It would have seemed necessary in the 1980s for a volume of this kind to include some account of the treatment of popular culture within postmodernism. That popular culture no longer seems the issue it was is perhaps due partly to the simultaneous growth and convergence of electronic media, led of course by the development of the internet. The previous distinctions between elite and popular forms had much to do with the material forms and contexts in which they were produced and circulated, but the "immediatization" of the contemporary world means that both high and popular culture circulate indifferently within a kind of unified field. The relative decline, or at least slowing of growth, of popular-culture studies may also have to do with the fact that the discipline of "cultural studies," which had centered on the study of contemporary popular culture, has achieved hegemony through diversification rather than through consolidation, and through the many different forms in which it has transformed itself and the disciplines in which it has taken root. As cultural studies has become less identified with the study of popular culture, so the assertion of the value of popular culture against high or elite culture has become less important as a principle of postmodernism.

Given the conspicuous role that music had in the formation of modernism, one might have expected a stronger conception of postmodernism to have taken root in music studies. The relative conservatism and autonomy of the world of academic music study may account for its long resistance to postmodernist formulations and arguments. Even where there is a willingness to explore the applicability of postmodernist concepts to concert music, it has taken a conservative form. The recent collection *Postmodern Music/Postmodern Thought* seems to represent the most conservative kind of extension of postmodernism's range.[19] The essays are concerned to establish analogies and continuities between postmodern discourse and the discussion of concert music. Scarcely anywhere in the collection is there acknowledgment of the difference made by the enormous reconfiguration not only of the sphere of music in general, but even of the terms and conditions of concert music. It would be possible to characterize the postmodernism of music not in terms of the stylistic changes and changes to musical language that take place in scores and in concert halls, but in terms of the explosion of collaborations and fusions, and the many ways in which the gap between classical and popular music has been narrowed. As yet, these two ways of bringing postmodern concepts and categories to bear have not been combined. The strange absence of a mature postmodernist discourse within music studies, rather than the absence of potential fields in which it might be brought to bear, is the reason that musical postmodernism is not one of the areas reported on in this current collection.

The great difficulty for expositors of the postmodern is that there are so many separate histories of postmodernism that are internal to different disciplines and areas of culture, even as, from its beginning, postmodernism has consistently acted to knock individual disciplines off centre. Postmodernism was always a phenomenon of cultural interference, the crossing or conjugation of ideas and values. A "companion" seems a particularly appropriate name for a volume of this kind, which aims to show the "accompanied" nature of all postmodernist thinking. At the same time, the essays collected here seem to register the flaring-up of something like a new disciplinary dispensation, even this late in postmodernism's long career, in which the great decentering force of postmodernism is turned against itself, to form new centers of interest and alternative forms of organization. As Beckett has put it, there is nothing like breathing your last to put new life into you.

NOTES

1. Samuel Beckett, *Endgame*, in *The Complete Dramatic Works* (London: Faber, 1986), p. 93.
2. Recent examples might include Malcolm Waters, *Daniel Bell* (London: Routledge, 1996); Simon Malpas, *Jean-François Lyotard* (London: Routledge, 2002); Chris Horrocks, *Introducing Baudrillard* (Duxford: Icon, 1996); Adam Roberts, *Fredric Jameson* (London: Routledge, 2000). Charles Jencks's *The Language of Post-Modern Architecture* first appeared in 1977 and has been reissued in enlarged and updated editions ever since, most recently in *The New Paradigm in Architecture: The Language of Post-Modernism* (New Haven, CT, and London: Yale University Press, 2002).
3. Fredric Jameson, "The Cultural Logic of Late Capitalism," *Postmodernism, or, The Cultural Logic of Late Capitalism* (London: Verso, 1991), pp. 1–54.
4. See, for example, Thomas Docherty (ed.), *Postmodernism: A Reader* (New York and London: Harvester Wheatsheaf, 1992); Patricia Waugh (ed.), *Postmodernism: A Reader* (London: Edward Arnold, 1992); Charles Jencks (ed.), *The Post-Modern Reader* (London: Academy Editions, 1992); Joseph Natoli and Linda Hutcheon (eds.), *A Postmodern Reader* (Albany, NY: State University of New York Press, 1993).
5. See my *Postmodernist Culture: An Introduction to Theories of the Contemporary*, 2nd edn. (Oxford: Blackwell, 1996), p. vii.
6. Hans Bertens, *The Idea of the Postmodern: A History* (London: Routledge, 1995).
7. John Frow, "What Was Postmodernism?," *Time and Commodity Culture: Essays in Cultural Theory and Postmodernity* (Oxford: Clarendon, 1997), p. 15.
8. Jameson, *Postmodernism*, p. 61.
9. David Harvey, *The Condition of Postmodernity: An Inquiry Into the Origins of Social Change* (Oxford: Blackwell, 1980).
10. Jürgen Habermas, *The Philosophical Discourse of Modernity: Twelve Lectures*, trans. Frederick Lawrence (Cambridge, MA: MIT Press, 1987). See too Alex Callinicos, *Against Postmodernism: A Marxist Critique* (Cambridge: Polity, 1989).
11. Bruno Latour, *We Have Never Been Modern*, trans. Catherine Porter (New York and London: Harvester Wheatsheaf, 1993), p. 13. References hereafter in the text.
12. T. S. Eliot, "The Dry Salvages," *Four Quartets, The Complete Poems and Plays of T. S. Eliot* (London: Faber, 1969), p. 186.
13. Ziauddin Sardar, *The A – Z of Postmodern Life: Essays on Global Culture in the Noughties* (London: Vision, 2002).
14. Cristopher Nash, *The Unravelling of the Postmodern Mind* (Edinburgh: Edinburgh University Press, 2001).
15. Sally Banes, *Terpsichore in Sneakers: Postmodern Dance* (Middletown, CT: Wesleyan University Press, 1987).
16. Sally Banes, *Writing Dancing in the Age of Postmodernism* (Hanover, NH: Wesleyan University Press/University Press of New England, 1994).

17. Martin Schiralli, *Constructive Postmodernism: Toward Renewal in Cultural and Literary Studies* (Westport, CT, and London: Bergin and Garvey, 1999); Donald L. Gelpi, *Varieties of Transcendental Experience: A Study in Constructive Postmodernism* (Collegeville, MO: Liturgical, 2000).
18. Jean-François Lyotard, *The Postmodern Condition: A Report on Knowledge*, trans. Geoff Bennington and Brian Massumi (Manchester: Manchester University Press, 1984).
19. Judy Lochhead and Joseph Auner (eds.), *Postmodern Music/Postmodern Thought* (New York and London: Routledge, 2002).

I

PAUL SHEEHAN

Postmodernism and philosophy

This is the end

Postmodernist thinking has typically reacted with suspicion to the notion of origins. As first cause or foundation, an origin – a transcendental ground to which all subsequent phenomena must pay obeisance – resurrects the deity that the "death of God" supposedly vanquished. This resistance to origins is matched by a much messier obsession with "ends." Postmodernist endings are not so neat as the term suggests, however. They are thorny and recalcitrant, at the very least placing certain practices or instruments of thought off-limits; at most, the latter are rendered fallacious, untenable, "no longer possible."

An abiding example of this temper is the seemingly suicidal declamation of the end of philosophy. Where philosophy has engaged directly with postmodernism – let us call the result, for the moment, post-Nietzschean continental philosophy – it has produced a kind of thinking that cleaves to the shadow of its own mortality, compulsively rehearsing its own demise. But unlike other postmodernist annulments – the "ends" of authorial presence and ideology, for example – philosophy's reprieve was granted in the same breath as its death sentence was pronounced. Which is to say, accompanying the termination was the possibility of renewal, ways of finding new uses for philosophical thinking. In fixating upon the conditions of its own abolition, then, philosophy turned those conditions into a kind of negative capability.

Postwar French philosophers have generally repudiated the notion of the end of philosophy. Luce Irigaray derided it as one of the "status quo values."[1] Gilles Deleuze and Félix Guattari declared that "the overcoming of philosophy has never been a problem for us: it is just tiresome, idle chatter."[2] Even more categorically, Jacques Derrida has stated, "I do not at all believe in what today is so easily called the death of philosophy (nor, moreover, in the simple death of whatever – the book, man, or god, especially since, as we all know, what is dead wields a very specific power)."[3] Derrida illustrates this in his discussion of "The End of the Book and the Beginning of Writing." He describes the book as the idea of a totality, an idea that is "profoundly alien to the sense of writing." It is necessary to recognize the monolithic, encyclopedic, theological character of the book, he declares, in order to countermand it with the dispersive, "aphoristic energy" of writing.[4] But what takes place is not a mere replacement or taking-up; it is a superposition of one with the other, so that neither writing nor book can be said truly to begin or end. Derrida posits the *closure* of the idea of the book, permitting its indefinite continuation, rather than the more definitive *end*.[5]

It is not so much a process of completion, then, as a complex maneuvering between ending and renewal. To carry out this maneuver, philosophical postmodernism has performed a comprehensive demolition job on western orthodoxies. Knowledge is deemed questionable, and it is no longer the job of philosophy to provide it. The human subject is dispossessed until it seems no longer to exist (perhaps it never did), and its philosophical corollary, humanism, is unmasked as a form of covert oppression. Narrative logic is broken down, removing one of the central organizing principles of western thought. The notion of the "real world" is permanently encased in quotation marks, and even such an (apparently) uncomplicated matter as sexual difference is rendered illegitimate and misleading, while newer, more difficult ways of theorizing gender are opened up.

What all of the above share is a resistance to totality (in particular, the philosophical systems comprising the western tradition), to teleology (the notion that those systems might be going somewhere in particular) and to closure of any kind – narrative, conceptual, metaphysical. Within the philosophical tradition, the two chief advocates of the above are Descartes, whose method of radical scepticism led to the foundationalist claim that a correct beginning could finally be made; and Hegel, whose synthetic approach first of all organized the entire tradition into a purposive and dialectical whole, and then assumed that it had reached its apogee, with no further work to be done. The rest of this essay will examine the postmodernist reaction to this legacy – the major philosophical attempts to reveal its gaps, inconsistencies, and shortcomings, and the efforts made to bring it to an end.

Any account of postmodernism and philosophy must deal with the problem of naming. Put simply, the two terms cannot stay separate for long. Philosophy slides into "theory," which combines philosophical reflection with elements of sociology, historiography, psychoanalysis, politics, anthropology, mythology, and literature. And postmodernism mutates into "poststructuralism," the term most associated with the above-mentioned mélange. It is prudent to note, therefore, that, once the theme of the "end of philosophy" has been invoked, the discussion cannot be restricted to (as it were) philosophical concerns – as those concerns have generally been recognized and understood, within the western tradition. The theme has also given rise to a form of writing that signifies a revolution at the level of style. Indeed, it amounts to the overthrow of yet another "orthodoxy": the notion that philosophical thinking can be conveyed in the language of proposition and logical argument. More so than in, say, the novel or the poem, the post-modernist influence on philosophy brings to mind the difficult, disorienting, obsessive stylistics of literary modernism.

Language turns: the end of metaphysics

After the problem of naming, the next difficulty posed by the "end of philos-ophy" thematic is one of scope. How can something so broad and diverse as philosophy, with branches in countless other disciplines (philosophies of sci-ence, language, history, law, religion, and so on) be comprehensively closed down? Such a titanic feat would surely require a number of different strikes, from different strategic positions, to achieve its end. In fact, it is one key aspect of the philosophical tradition that is negated, and from this the whole tradition is disabled. That aspect is the method of metaphysical speculation and argument. Immanuel Kant proffered a critique of this tradition in his *Critique of Pure Reason* (1781); to some extent, then, philosophical post-modernism is operating in a post-Kantian context, driven by the urge to find new ways of resisting what Kant carefully circumscribed and confined.[6]

As a term, "metaphysics" was originally coined simply to indicate that which could not be explained by the physical sciences. Yet by the twenti-eth century it had accreted a whole range of meanings, indemnifying man's (supposed) separation from nature, and fortifying the project of orthodox humanism. It also provided the linking factor between Cartesian founda-tionalism and Hegelian synthesis. Descartes famously pictured knowledge as a tree, with metaphysics as the root; by metaphysics, then, he meant largely epistemology. Similarly, Hegel's *Phenomenology of Mind* was envis-aged as a journey towards "absolute knowledge," where mind realizes that the knowledge it has been seeking is self-knowledge, mind knowing itself as mind. Metaphysical humanism is thus characterized by the urge to *know*, yet this apparently noble impulse has a dubious underside – it can just as readily devolve into the desire to possess and master, to convert otherness and difference into sameness.

The postmodernist rejection of metaphysics was impelled by the turn to-wards language. In philosophical terms, this comes from two sources, usually regarded as antithetical. From within the analytical tradition, the late philos-ophy of Ludwig Wittgenstein bequeathed a new way of thinking and a new terminology – "language games," "family resemblance," "forms of life," the "private language argument" – that philosophical postmodernism has assimilated and reworked in its own image. And across the philosophical divide, in the continental tradition, Martin Heidegger saw one of the antidotes to the modern spiritual malaise as *poiesis* – creativity, in the broadest sense, but also the language of poetry, especially as manifested in a few key German poets (Hölderlin, Rilke, Georg Trakl). Both philosophers, therefore, were proponents of the "linguistic turn" in philosophy, albeit in very different ways. In the analytical tradition, the linguistic turn contended that the limits of philosophy, and of what was understood to be "reality," could manifest themselves only within language. It was a turn from ideas to words, from an idealist philosophical focus to a language-centered one – a reversal, in short, of what Descartes had inaugurated with his inward turn towards ideas and the contents of the mind. For analytical philosophers, the ultimate facts were seen to be those of language. In keeping with this conviction, they concentrated on the kinds of human practices that grow from language and make it possible in the first place.[7]

Wittgenstein's posthumous *Philosophical Investigations* mounted a critique of his earlier project (in the *Tractatus*) of seeking objective structures for language; instead, he came to see it as a purely human product and attempted to define the limits thereof.[8] The focus was thus on the social perspective of linguistic analysis, and the ways in which everyday communication takes place. This has led to the description of his later philosophy (like the linguistic turn of analytical philosophy in general) as "anthropocentric."[9]

A different state of affairs obtains in continental philosophy, and in the postmodernist theory evolving out of it. The linguistic turn here is based on the belief that, because language is riven with figuration – a "mobile army of metaphors, metonyms, and anthropomorphisms," to borrow Nietzsche's phrase[10] – it cannot represent the world with any degree of accuracy, let alone in the immediate, undistorted way that some theories of mind have claimed. This could be simplified to say that words depend on *other* words for their meaning, rather than on reference to some extra-linguistic reality. From this comes the postmodernist dictum that language constructs human identity, rather than vice versa. Heidegger writes: "Man acts as though *he* were the shaper and master of language, while in fact *language* remains the master of man."[11] The linguistic turn associated with the postmodern condition is thus quite explicitly antihumanist, denying human beings the instrumental command of language that supports the belief in "metaphysical man."

In "The End of Philosophy and the Task of Thinking," Heidegger describes how philosophy has lost its way. Philosophy's end is nigh, he claims, because it has evolved into all those things smuggled in by metaphysics – logic, science, technology, cybernetics, and forgetfulness (of Being). The end or "completion" of metaphysics, however, does not take the form of "perfection" towards which, Hegel declared, the tradition was moving, but rather harks back to the older sense of "place": "The end of philosophy is the place, that place in which the whole of philosophy's history is gathered in its uttermost possibility."[12] Heidegger's response to metaphysics is "thinking," a task "that can be neither metaphysics nor science."[13] Such an activity will be an unassuming one, dedicated to awakening possibilities; yet it must also be resolutely present-based, rather than speculative.[14] If "thinking" cannot undo the changes wrought by metaphysics, it can nevertheless help to alleviate the spiritually impoverished character of modernity.

The two currents of Wittgenstein and Heidegger converge in the neo-pragmatism of Richard Rorty (who also draws on the ur-pragmatism of John Dewey). For Rorty, the post-Kantian shape of western philosophy has been determined by epistemology, out of which metaphysics emerges (rather than vice versa, as in Descartes's roots-and-trunk metaphor); philosophical modernity has thus been recast as a "theory of knowledge." Seeking to overturn this state of affairs, Rorty's version of the "end of philosophy" is directed towards the end of epistemology.

Philosophy's transformation into a theory of knowledge was made possible by a theory of representation – the mind's ability to "mirror" the external world, thereby establishing a certain congruence, or "fit," between mind and world. Knowledge, says Rorty, is not about congruence so much as about social acceptance; it is what receives communal support or assent from one's peers. With the loss of the "mirror of nature" idea, then, epistemology effectively *ends*.[15] What replaces it? Rorty suggests that philosophers should abandon knowledge-seeking strategies for "edification," a conversation that is always open to improvement. Edification is "this project of finding new, better, more interesting, more fruitful ways of speaking . . . edifying discourse is *supposed* to be abnormal, to take us out of our old selves by the power of strangeness, to aid us in becoming new beings."[16] Despite the laid-back manner of his writing, Rorty's "post-philosophical" project is a genuine anomaly, seeking humanist ends (ethical improvement) through counter-humanist means (discourse rather than knowledge).

If Rorty sees epistemology as more fundamental than metaphysics, and censures it with the ethical, inter-subjective notion of "edification," Heidegger's one-time follower Emmanuel Levinas finds ethical reasons for *preserving* metaphysics – or at least for reworking it. Before metaphysics is anything, he declares, it is *ethics*. Levinas sees the philosophical systems of the West as having exercised, in the guise of ontology, a deep-seated suppression of otherness. Countering this, he conceives of the ethical as non-foundational and prior to those systems ("ontology," he writes, "pre-supposes metaphysics").[17] The ethical encounter, the face-to-face relation to the other, is the originary instance of metaphysics, its primordial enactment. In keeping with this attitude, Levinas has described the ends of humanism and metaphysics, and the death of God and of man, as "apocalyptic ideas or slogans of intellectual high society," brought on by "the tyranny of the latest fashion."[18]

Yet whether it is celebrated, substituted, or excoriated, the "end of meta-physics" thesis is a powerful current within philosophical postmodernism. In fact, it almost assumes the status of a metanarrative, an organizational paradigm to which even the most diverse "endist" attempt must inevitably refer, no matter how obliquely, to give its argument historical credence. The following sections demonstrate the scope and depth of this reliance.

Deregulated subjects: the end(s) of man

The metaphysical subject was an early casualty of philosophical postmod-ernism. In the western tradition, man has been the measure of all things and the maker of all meanings – and the autonomous, transcendental subject the "site" where meaning is incarnated. The strict separation of human and natural orders could be maintained by asserting that man was inherently "metaphysical," a truth-hungry being who yearned for self-enlightenment. Equipped with this metaphysical optic, man was able to transform experi-ence into knowledge, and his involvements in the world – no longer blind and present-based – into the material for human empowerment.

In the French philosophy of the 1960s, the subject lost its metaphysical aura.[19] The temper of the times is apparent from the widespread eagerness to embrace the "death of the subject" – a diktat which became, as Perry Anderson noted, "the slogan of the decade."[20] The proclamation filtered through the various disciplines associated with structuralist theory. In the anthropology of Claude Lévi-Strauss, man was reduced to an empty space, a mere vantage point where the codes and conventions of language and culture happened to coincide. Lacanian psychoanalysis saw the subject as subsequent to language, and always dependent on it for its existence. And in Louis Althusser's post-Marxist suppositions, human subjectivity was considered an effect of ideology.[21]

But the most sustained and influential pronouncement of the "end of man" came from the historical discourse analysis of Michel Foucault. His anti-humanist spirit is made manifest in a single expression: man, he declares, is as an "empirico-transcendental doublet." This strange entity arose because of the human sciences, whose tendency to situate man as both origin (transcendental) and evaluative limit (empirical) placed him in a position that was unintelligible. As Dreyfus and Rabinow write, "Modernity begins with the incredible and ultimately unworkable idea of a being who is sovereign precisely by virtue of being enslaved, a being whose very finitude allows him to take the place of God."[22]

Taking stock of the scientific contradictions of the past 160 years that have made man the sacred being that he is, Foucault issues a bold declaration: "If those arrangements were to disappear as they appeared, then one can certainly wager that man would be erased, like a face drawn in sand at the edge of the sea."[23] The figure of "man" is but a dim notation at the edge of the shore, awaiting the incoming tide of history, and with it his liquidation. For that tide will reveal man in his true aspect: not as a timeless, godlike being possessed of an immortal soul, but as an accidental, provisional creature, precariously poised between the "epistemological regions" of economics, biology, and philology.

The above debates about anthropocentrism have never been more than peripheral concerns in the mainstream of the anglophone world. (Not so in France, however, where the "philosopher king" is accorded a great deal of popular attention and even some measure of celebrity.) A more pressing debate here, which has infiltrated the media as well as the academy, concerns the relationships between human beings and the natural world, and between human beings and animals. Environmental anxieties, Green politics and debates about "speciesism" have decreased the sovereignty of the human animal more thoroughly than any number of structuralist–humanist debates could ever have done. What they share with the "death of the subject" thesis is the anti-anthropocentric conviction that man is no longer the measure of all things, but something to be measured, like anything else in the world. Whether as abstruse theoretical polemic or populist concern over ecological ruin, man's dethronement continues.

Yet philosophical postmodernism still has something to contribute to these more pressing forms of "anthropological deregulation" – albeit couched in language and postulates rebarbative to a mainstream readership. The most prominent strand of postmodern ecological theory derives from Heidegger's animadversions on nature. His antipathy to human action lies in the danger of the "will to will," the infinite desire to master nature and dominate the earth. This craving for mastery, manifested through man's technological command, is what lies behind the ruinous environmental practices of the twentieth century. Advocates of Green politics and radical environmentalism have used Heideggerian arguments to urge the adoption of a more benign and harmonious attitude towards the nonhuman world.[24]

There is much less concern with harmony and restraint, or with human integration within nature, in the collaborative writing of Deleuze and Guattari. They state their position plainly, in the early pages of *Anti-Oedipus*:

> We make no distinction between man and nature: the human essence of nature and the natural essence of man become one within nature in the form of production or industry, just as they do within the life of man as a species . . . man and nature are not like two opposite terms confronting one another . . . rather, they are one and the same essential reality, the producer-product.[25]

In a later work, the monumental, multifaceted *Thousand Plateaus*, they impugn the "arborescent" model of thought, the model of organic growth and stolidity that makes the western tradition seem so implacable. (Descartes's metaphor is the obvious target here.) Deleuze and Guattari adopt instead the "rhizome," a multi-linked network which "operates by variation, expansion, conquest, capture, offshoots . . . an acentred, nonhierarchical, nonsignifying system . . . defined solely by a circulation of states."[26] To fasten such a diverse, multidisciplinary work to specific theses is a hopeless task. Yet one of the things this transformative text gestures towards is a new ecological understanding, a dynamic, nonhierarchical relationship between human beings and the natural environmental (plants and animals) that curbs human dominion and narcissism in a tour de force of ceaseless reinvention.[27]

If ecology is only an interstitial concern in Deleuze and Guattari's many-chambered book, it is at the forefront of Michel Serres's *The Natural Contract*. He posits an alarmist view of our contemporary condition: "Global history enters nature; global nature enters history: this is something utterly new in philosophy."[28] The violence of ownership has defined the modern era, the twofold desire for "war and property." But interhuman conflict is being overshadowed by a different kind of violence, where man wages war on the world; indeed, Serres estimates that the combined effect of environmental disasters is equivalent to another world war.[29] He regards human despoliation of the natural environment as a form of ownership claim, akin to an animal marking its territory: "Thus the sullied world reveals the mark of humanity, the mark of its dominators, the found stamp of their hold and their appropriation."[30] In the past, the social contract has conditioned and contained the waging of war; another kind of agreement is necessary, then, for this new type of warfare, a "natural contract."

Counteracting Cartesian mastery, Serres emphasizes the need for a new, non-anthropocentric ecological schema. The natural contract he proposes is "metaphysical," in that it goes beyond the physical. The latter, he suggests, is limited in its scope to the local and immediate; to think in global terms, and of the furthest consequences of one's actions, is to think in metaphysical terms. Just as the social contract has united the immediate with the universal, so must the natural contract: "Together these laws [i.e. social and natural] ask each of us to pass from the local to the global, a difficult and badly marked trail, but one that we must blaze."[31] Serres's impassioned argument has a further "doubleness": it pertains as much to everyday life – that is, to the living habits of individuals – as it is does to the elite realms of political assembly, where government legislation is drafted.

Police matters: the end of narrative

As should be clear, the end of human sovereignty is an ongoing project for philosophical postmodernism. Closely related to this is the questioning of another human-related practice. Alasdair MacIntyre raises the issue with his claim that "man is in his actions and practice, as well as in his fictions, essentially a story-telling animal."[32] If this is so, then the interrogation of the human must extend to the ruses and machinations of narrative logic. In Roland Barthes's words, the past tense of narrative "is the ideal instrument for every construction of a world; it is the unreal time of cosmogonies, myth, History and Novels . . . The world is not unexplained since it is told like a story."[33]

This is the disposition that Jean-François Lyotard seeks to unsettle in *The Postmodern Condition*. He mounts two related arguments about narrative. The first concerns "narrative knowledge," and its putative other, "scientific knowledge." The former, in the guise of storytelling, does not require "proof" beyond its own internal consistency and rules of procedure; beyond, that is to say, its heterogeneous status as a particular language game. Scientific knowledge, by contrast, has for centuries laid claim to being universal and authoritative, transcendent of all other language games. Science has traditionally regarded narrative knowledge with scorn, says Lyotard, yet despite this has used narrative to justify itself and its operations.[34]

Lyotard also claims to be presenting a "report on knowledge." Knowledge requires legitimation, and it is here that his second argument about narrative takes shape. Two "grand narratives" have determined western self-understanding – the Enlightenment story of progress and political emancipation, and the Hegelian narrative of the manifestation of scientific reason. Both of these have foundered, he declares, along with every other meta-discursive attempt at organizing modernity's immense sprawl into something coherent and socially useful.[35] Postmodernity, by contrast, recognizes the impossibility of this undertaking and its need for legitimation, and recoils from it: "Simplifying to the extreme, I define *postmodern* as incredulity towards metanarratives."[36] In postmodernity, legitimation does not stand outside social practices, but is "plural, local, and immanent." In other words, the language game of narrative has become a model for *every* kind of legitimation, no longer playing second fiddle to scientific "transcendence." The death of the grand narrative thus heralds the birth of the local narrative, with its emphasis on diversity and heterogeneity.[37]

Lyotard subsequently concretized his argument with examples of historical contradiction – Auschwitz confutes the Hegelian belief that history is "rational," Stalin subverts the possibility of a proletarian revolution, crises in capitalist societies undermine the feasibility of the free-market economy.[38] Gianni Vattimo questions the thesis behind these claims in "The End of (Hi)story," centering his argument on the problem of postmodernity. "If this notion has a meaning at all, it has to be described in terms of the end of history." The implication of Lyotard's conviction that metanarratives have ended is that "history itself has become impossible."[39] And yet, as Vattimo argues, because Lyotard is using history to legitimate his thesis (in the examples above) he is, in effect, drawing on the organizing powers of a metanarrative.

There is a wider allusion, in Vattimo's critique, to the subtle power of narrative to insinuate itself into historical discourse, an explicatory method that is almost a kind of "default setting." By way of response, he cites Heidegger's awareness that metaphysics is not something easily abandoned, since to do so would mean perpetuating its methods and structures.[40] We must acknowledge, then, that the "only way we have to argue in favor of postmodernist philosophy is still an appeal to history . . . only if we tell explicitly, again and again, the story of the end of history, shall we be able to change, distort, *verwinden*, its metaphysical significance."[41]

Hayden White, however, has warned that it is not just historical metanarratives that pose problems but *any* fully realized historical narrative, no matter how "local" or limited. White mobilizes Hegel's argument that "historicality" is unthinkable without a system of law, which in turn presupposes (and constitutes) a "legal subject." He then suggests that the historical consciousness that looks to narrative logic as a way of (re)presenting the past will always use story in its *allegorical* mode; that is, it will make it a distinctly moral undertaking: "it seems possible to conclude that every historical narrative has as its latent or manifest purpose the desire to *moralize* the events of which it treats."[42] (Derrida expressed this more pungently when he declared that "all organized narration is 'a matter for the police,' even before its genre (mystery novel, cop story) has been determined.")[43]

But if Lyotard, Vattimo, and White suggest that narrative has become an intractable problem for philosophy, that is not (as it were) the whole story. American pragmatism has embraced the possibilities of narrative knowledge, as MacIntyre's remark above indicates. In the postmodern pragmatism of Richard Rorty, a similar endorsement is made. Through "genres such as ethnography, the journalist's report, the comic book, the docudrama, and, especially, the novel," Rorty envisages "a general turn against theory and toward narrative." The kinds of narratives he has in mind would "connect the present with the past, on the one hand, and with utopian futures, on the other."[44] Rorty is unconcerned with the side-effects of storytelling practices; in the ongoing conversation of mankind, narrative logic is a resource to be harnessed. As a form of discourse it can edify and hence assist the post-philosophical project of the future in reducing the amount of cruelty and suffering in the world. That there *is* a world beyond narrative discourse is not disputed; other thinkers of philosophical postmodernism are less certain, as the next section illustrates.

Real simulations: the end of the world

In a typically caustic and condensed section of *Twilight of the Idols*, Nietzsche seeks to show "How the 'Real World' Became a Fable." In six short moves the "real world" – the metaphysical realm of truth persisting beyond the ephemeral world of appearance – escapes human grasp. First it is attainable, then successively promised, consolatory, unknowable, and refutable. Once refuted, this "real world" disappears – along with its "apparent world" double.[45] The two worlds, clearly, are codependent. Because the world of appearance is somehow anchored by its deeper, "truer" metaphysical complement, dismissing the senior partner means dissolving the entire relationship.

A continuation of this line of thinking was undertaken by Jean Baudrillard in the 1980s. Attending to the postmodern condition of media saturation, Baudrillard charted the disappearance of a different kind of "real world": the concrete, material foundation to which human systems of signification point. Thus, instead of the couple sign/object, with its promise of a substantive "ground" beneath the various forms of cultural representation – something to anchor those representations, like Nietzsche's "real world" of metaphysical verity – there are only the representations themselves, mere "simulations" of concrete reality. Abandoning the metaphysical couple of surface/depth, and the notion of a transcendental "inner" realm, thus prefigures a loss of referentiality. Pursuing this further, Baudrillard sets out in four moves what Nietzsche did in six. Initially referring to a material reality beyond itself, the sign then distorts, disguises, and finally replaces that reality.[46] Baudrillard's catalogue of disappearances cuts across Saussurean linguistics (signified/referent), Marxist economics (exchange-value/use-value) and religious idolatory (icon/deity).[47]

In the absence of the "real," there is only the "hyperreal." As Baudrillard describes it in ". . . Or the End of the Social," the hyperreal is not a heightening or distortion of the real, but a "meticulous reduplication," executed with such "macroscopic hyperfidelity" as to efface all signs of its counterfeit status.[48] It is the abolition of distance between the real and its representational double that produces the hyperreal, eliminating referentiality in the process. The social contract, as Michel Serres noted, has a distancing function; it maintains civility by organizing social relations around legal codes. When the social relation becomes hyperreal, however, the "hypersocial" is produced and distanciation is lost.[49]

There is a historical component to Baudrillard's argument. The hyperreal has displaced the real because one thing has made it possible: technology. Baudrillard's most notorious move was to apply his philosophy of disappearance to the first Gulf War. After a "hot war" and a "cold war," the (techno)logical next step, he argued, was a "virtual war."[50] Foreshadowed by his analysis of Nixon's bombing of Hanoi,[51] Baudrillard asserts that whatever it was that took place in the Persian Gulf – a CNN simulation of a Hollywood blockbuster, a hyperreal video game, an exercise in New World Order police tactics – it bore no resemblance to any kind of "war." (Hence his title, *The Gulf War Did Not Take Place*, with its witty echo of a play by Jean Giraudoux.)[52]

Baudrillard's polemic provides a scaffold for Christopher Norris to identify (in the words of an earlier indictment) what's wrong with postmodernism.[53] As Norris sees it, Baudrillard claimed that the Gulf War took place on *no* fronts, but only on the depthless, ephemeral plane of the CNN broadcasts. Norris then makes the counter-claim that it actually took place on *two* fronts. The Iraqi targets in Baghdad and Kuwait, with their casualties and collateral damage, constituted the first front; and the postmodern affectations of scepticism and cynicism, and accompanying talk of "simulacra" and "hyperreality," amounted to a second, equally treacherous war zone. Norris positions himself as a latter-day Orwell-in-Catalonia, anxious lest the truth about the war get hijacked by the forces of acquiescence. Because postmodern nihilism is powerless to unmask media disinformation, says Norris, it is unwittingly complicit with the manufacturers of consensus.

The need for "critical resistance" is not lost on Baudrillard: "Be more virtual than the events themselves, do not seek to re-establish the truth, we do not have the means, but do not be duped . . . Turn deterrence back against itself."[54] For Norris this knowing complicity, this immanent insurgency, is doubly dangerous. First, from Norris's standpoint no critical resistance can be properly mounted without critical distance; second, and more damagingly, in aspiring to be, as it were, more virtual than the virtual, Baudrillard further erodes the distinction between truth and falsehood that Norris is so anxious to maintain, on which he has staked his entire critical stock. Yet despite this, Baudrillard's position evinces a clear-eyed awareness of one thing: that our postmodern condition is precisely that, a *condition*, and not (as Norris would insist) a figment of a decadent, nihilistic intellectual imagination. To deny this condition is, ironically, to disqualify in advance – or at least to curtail considerably – the possibility of resistance. Philosophers of postmodernism have taken up this possibility in different ways, such as we have already seen in the debates about ecology. The next section demonstrates an equally concerted challenge to consensus thinking.

Identity crisis: the end of "man"

Thus far we have seen philosophical postmodernism described as postmetaphysical, anti-anthropocentric, counter-humanist, non-narrative and hyperrealist. Postmodern feminist philosophy provides a crossroads where all these critiques meet. As Linda Hutcheon has argued, feminist practices have shaped to a large extent the emergence and development of postmodernist styles of thought (though she is careful not to conflate feminism with postmodernism).[55] In the field of philosophy, feminist thinkers such as Irigaray have seen the tradition as a site of ceaseless conflict: "The philosophical order is indeed the one that has to be questioned, and *disturbed*, inasmuch as it covers over sexual difference."[56]

Central to this order is the question of subjectivity. But rather than subscribing to the 1960s' "death of the subject" scenario – which culminates in Foucault's pronouncement of the "end of man" – feminist philosophy in the 1970s considered the question on its own terms. The constructed nature of subjectivity was not an occasion for anguish and loss (as Lacan describes the shift from being to meaning) or for false consciousness (Althusser's theory of "interpellation"). Rather, the subaltern status of women meant that subjectivity was a privilege consistently and determinedly withheld from them. As Irigaray put it, "Any theory of the subject is always appropriated by the masculine."[57] But in repudiating the disembodied, metaphysical "reasoning subject," whose role in western culture has been to protect and promote male ideals, feminists were not abandoning the subject *tout entier*.[58] Julia Kristeva, for example, has deployed the notion of the "speaking subject" – a process, rather than a result, where contradiction and change are not problems but givens.[59]

At root in western metaphysics is the logocentric nature of patriarchy, or *phallogocentrism*. Kristeva writes: "The very dichotomy man/woman as an opposition between two rival entities may be understood as belonging to

metaphysics. What can 'identity', even 'sexual identity,' mean in a new theoretical and scientific space where the very notion of identity is challenged?"[60]
If phallogocentric practices suppress difference in favor of identity – in particular, the self-identity conferred by oneness, autonomy, and integrity, coextensive with notions of (male) subjectivity – then the philosophical cen-
suring of metaphysics issues a bold challenge to the logic of identity.

Irigaray has both contested the notion of identity and advocated a specific
female identity. Her argument turns on the distinction between *identity* and
identification. The futural, as-yet-unrealized female identity she advances
will not be based on sameness; it will not be an identity enabling its bearer
to *identify* with the static, fixed attributes of a particular order. The project of
developing a women's identity will therefore be a transformative one, altering
the very nature and meaning of "identity."[61] Bringing this new, undetermined identity into being presupposes a fundamental restructuring of the
symbolic economy. There is some similarity here with Baudrillard's strategy
of disruptive immanence, of being "more virtual than the virtual." Irigaray's
feminine metaphysics works against conventional metaphysics, bypassing
absolute truths for the modes and workings of concepts and discourse.

Cutting the ground out from (Cartesian) foundationalism and dispersing
(Hegelian) synthesis, Irigaray argues that female subjectivity, identity, and
essence are projects to be realized rather than pillars on which to build,
and are resistant to the imposition of a teleology. She writes: "In order to
become, it is essential to have a gender or an essence (consequently a sexuate
essence) as *horizon*. Otherwise, becoming remains partial and subject to the
subject . . . To become means fulfilling the wholeness of what we are capable
of being. Obviously, this road never ends."[62] A horizon is not a "goal" as
such; where a goal can be attained, a horizon cannot be reached without its
ceasing to be a horizon. Similarly, a metaphysical becoming can strive for
"wholeness" without congealing into a fixed or final identity. As Christine
Battersby notes, "Flow, flux, becoming do not always have to be envisaged
in terms of a movement that is alien to persisting identity or to metaphysics
itself."[63]

Attempting to rework the metaphysics of identity is misguided and my-
opic, counters Judith Butler. The term "women," she argues, "marks a dense
intersection of social relations that cannot be summarized through the terms
of identity."[64] The error is compounded by treating the signifying economy
as if it were monolithic and masculinist – a totalizing gesture that is a form
of "epistemological imperialism." Butler writes: "The effort to identify the
enemy as singular in form is a reverse-discourse that uncritically mimics
the strategy of the oppressor instead of offering a different set of terms."[65]
Though Irigaray does see the philosophical order as cohesive and monolithic,

her interrogation of it is tireless and punctilious, and her writing style bristles with provocation. Further, in the horizon constituted by sexual difference – one that is "more fecund than any known to date – at least in the West" – Irigaray imagines there might be space for the "creation of a new *poetics*."[66]

The nature of Irigaray's "horizon" is also problematic for Butler, however, who is more concerned with the behavioral notion of gender than with embodied notions of sexual difference. Gender, she declares, is not an inert category with fixed attributes, but a contingent *doing*, a "stylized repetition of acts."[67] It points towards a destabilization of identity: "There is no gender identity behind the expressions of gender; that identity is performatively constituted by the very 'expressions' that are said to be its results."[68] Gender attributes, then, do not express a stable identity preceding the act of performance and enduring through time. Instead, they consist in a provisional repertoire depending on reiteration for its existence, and hence are potentially fluid and variable.

In the absence of fixed identities, the fixity of identity politics is also abandoned. If gender roles are variable, fluid, and multiple, they lend themselves to oppositional strategies, principally in the form of parodic subversion. Such strategies are, however, restricted to individual gender "performances." Butler's reluctance to see the symbolic economy as unitary means that collective resistance to it, in the guise of political reform or universal panacea, is also untenable. The "metaphysical" contract that Serres proposes, with its movement from the local to the global, is not an option in Butler's all-out war against stable identity.

From the point of view of language, identity is also invoked through "presence": if words and their meanings are congruent, if they can be mapped without remainder or deficit, then there is perfect, self-present *identity*. Resisting (or reworking) the metaphysics of identity leads then, perhaps inevitably, to the search for a new discourse, and to a form of writing that might convey it adequately. Irigaray makes reference to a "feminine syntax," exemplified in "more and more texts written by women in which another writing is beginning to assert itself."[69]

Within postmodern feminism, the writing alluded to here goes by the name of *écriture féminine*, a writing of the female body that "will always surpass the discourse that regulates the phallocentric system."[70] Much has been written about its potential for disruption, liberation, and pleasure, its manifesting in literary terms many of the claims made above for sexual difference. (Indeed, before it was a theory of gender, performativity was a theory of language.)[71] Though there is some doubt as to whether or not it matches the claims made for it by theorists, it might be seen as underwriting Linda Hutcheon's affirmation above about the profound influence of feminism on postmodernism. Gayatri Spivak writes: "In a certain sense the definitive characteristic of the French feminist project of founding a woman's discourse reflects a coalition with the continuing tradition of the French avant-garde."[72]

This "continuing tradition," I suggest, abides in philosophical postmodernism, which is above all a powerful and original form of *writing*. Its fugitive, elliptical nature still arouses heated debate, suggesting that the full measure of its textual stylistics has yet to be taken. If such a thing as an aesthetics of theory were possible, it might consider the difficult, self-conscious nature of much theoretical writing, particularly as it has developed in France; the way its assertions are conveyed through codes of association and abrupt transition, resisting the logic of causal development; its use of ludic, performative language in noninstrumental ways, incorporating sly puns, audacious juxtapositions, and eccentric allusions; and the general resistance it presents to distillation, paraphrase, and quotation.

Furthermore, its sheer stylistic brio – often operating at the outermost edge of coherence – is equally at odds with the prose conventions of critical exposition as it is with the tradition of philosophical proposition and elaboration. I suggested earlier that the elusive quality of this writing had much in common with literary modernism. It is both broader and narrower than that. As a mode of articulation, rather than as a specific linguistic practice, post-Nietzschean continental philosophy leans towards the condition of poetry – but a poetry of compaction and intensity, effectively revitalizing the stylistic pact of the early twentieth-century avant-garde.

After the end: towards posthuman becoming

"The whole problem of speaking about the end (particularly the end of history) is that you have to speak of what lies beyond the end and also, at the same time, of the impossibility of ending."[73] As Jean Baudrillard makes clear, once the discourse of "endism" is entered into, it becomes impossible to escape the aporetic bind of termination-and-reprieve. But if the situation now is no longer so pressing or disabling, it is because the various forms of endism have, for the most part, ended. In fact, it was Jacques Derrida (a resolute anti-endist from the start, as we have seen) who in 1983 launched a critique of the portentous rhetoric that has accreted around the "end of philosophy." Even Kant, in his day, Derrida argued, denounced the "apocalyptic" claims that philosophy was at an end – at the same time as he "freed another wave of eschatological discourses in his philosophy." (Endism as a form of negative capability was extant even in the eighteenth century.)[74]

The move away from endist thinking is reflected in the shift from theoretical and philosophical antihumanism – whose tenets were all in place by

1968 – to what might be termed technological posthumanism. Drawing on the cybernetic advancements of the last three decades, which have threatened to disfigure the integrated physical nature of human being, the balance of ending-and-renewal shifts decisively towards the latter. For thinkers of the posthuman, it is a moot point whether the human is obsolete or not; it will be technologically upgraded, and its anticipated successor avidly pursued, even if the old model still prospers. Philosophical inquiry implements a powerful metaphorical paradigm for this in the condition of endless becoming, where origins and ends are negated by a process of metamorphic perpetuity with no (final) result.

The feminist focus on the body, the transgression of boundaries, and the disruption of identity merge with the philosophical concerns of the post-human. The rapprochement can be seen in Irigaray's feminist praxis ("The goal that is most valuable is to go on *becoming*, infinitely")[75] and in But-ler's assertion that *"woman* itself is a term in process, a becoming, a con-structing that cannot rightfully be said to originate or end."[76] The source of this orientation, once again, is Nietzsche – though its philosophical an-cestry stretches back to Hegel, for whom becoming was envisaged as the unity of being and nothing; and to Heraclitus, who famously viewed ex-istence, not as a condition of stable being, but as a process of continual change and conflict. The Nietzschean cosmos, accordingly, is conceived as a ceaseless becoming, without aim or achievement, progress, or destiny. Be-cause becoming must be justified at every moment, it reveals itself in eternal recurrence ("Everything becomes and recurs eternally") and will to power ("Regarded mechanistically, the energy of the totality of becoming remains constant").[77]

Taking up this line of thought, Deleuze fashions a tool to break apart temporal unity. Becomings are above all *creative*, escaping the present with its orderly demarcations of before and after, past and future: "Becomings belong to geography, they are orientations, directions, entries and exits."[78] The rhizome illustrates this by linking up all points with one another, in contrast to the "arborescent" model and its method of contiguous connec-tion. Becoming takes place through a line or block without beginning or end, origin or destination. A line of becoming has only a middle: it "is neither one nor two, nor the relation of the two; it is the in-between."[79] Deleuzean becoming thus defies any kind of stability – physical, conceptual, spatio-temporal. It is a plateau of thought that aims to unleash a force of pure transgression, to realize a permanent revolution in social relations (or what Deleuze would term "becoming-revolutionary"). It operates not through re-semblance, imitation, or identification, nor via correspondence or filiation, but only through *alliance*. Thus, the becoming is real, even if what the human becomes – animal, woman, child, girl – is not. Neither can it lend itself to the production of identity or meaning: "Becoming produces nothing other than itself."[80]

As I have suggested, philosophical becoming is the primary condition of possibility for thinking the posthuman. Perhaps its most influential application is the model of the cyborg – a "becoming" that is neither human nor posthuman, but a threshold leading from one to the other.[81] In "A Cyborg Manifesto," Donna Haraway complicates easy divisions between the human and the natural, showing the former's fusion with animals and machines.[82] For Haraway, the cyborg is an ironic, perverse creature, beyond gender and without origin (i.e. a myth of unity and fullness). It is an imaginative resource out of (feminist) science fiction, the postmodern dream of hybridity realized as a technocultural fantasy. Haraway uses the cyborg as a multiple disrupter of categories and identities and, like Deleuzean becoming, as a form of alliance: "One is too few, but two are too many."[83] Divisions between the physical and the nonphysical also cannot be maintained. Thus, cyborgs do not exist as such – they are "ether, quintessence" – yet are all too real: "in short, we are cyborgs."[84]

Haraway uses the figuration in two ways. First, the primary cyborg alliance is with women, whose identities are similarly nonexistent, borrowed, incomplete, and "other." And second, it inveighs against feminist theories of embodiment that have demonized technological freedom, favoring bodies over minds, nature over culture, biology over technology. Rather than reversing these dichotomies, cyborg feminism demonstrates how unsustainable they are. "The machine is us, our processes, an aspect of our embodiment."[85] Haraway's cybernetic antihumanism is not unequivocal; she recognizes its potential for domination and subjugation, as well as for emancipation. But the conceptual distinctions she attempts to elide raise difficult questions about ethical responsibility and political efficacy.[86]

These questions are implicitly addressed in the dystopian prognostications of Paul Virilio. Unlike the advocates of technological posthumanism, Virilio's work in the 1990s attended more to "ending" than to "renewal." In *Open Sky* he approaches human–mechanical convergence through alienating teletechnology (action at a distance) and invasive nanotechnology (miniaturized components that "explore" the human metabolism). Between them they have precipitated the "pollution of the life-size," or "the unperceived pollution of the distances that organize our relationships with others, and also with the world of sense experience."[87] The absolute speed of immediacy and instantaneity creates a blurring of subject and object, a form of technological embodiment that bodes ill for individual self-realization. "Interactivity," warns Virilio, is as dangerous for human well-being as "radioactivity."[88]

The gloomiest implication of the new technologies is that they are manufacturing the interactive means to wipe out temporality itself. Virilio's master-theme is the "general accident,"[89] a vague yet all-encompassing occurrence whose main feature will be an "unprecedented temporal breakdown." Time itself will crash, duration will freeze, and there will be only perpetual present;[90] or, in the book's epigrammatic announcement: "One day / the day will come / when the day won't come." The general accident foretells a narrative about the end of narrative, where temporal difference is liquidated and time becomes "self-identical." Its eschatological purport is matched by an earlier alarmist tract against absolute speed:

> In these conditions, how can one fail to see the role of the *last vehicle*, whose non-travelling traveller, non-passing passenger, would be the ultimate stranger, a deserter from himself, an exile both from the external world (the real space of vanishing geophysical extension) and from the internal world, alien to his animal body, whose mass would be as fragile as the body of the planet already is as it undergoes advanced extermination?[91]

Ecological calamity and human self-estrangement are run together here, just as the general accident anticipates narrative foreclosure and the suspension of history.

What are we to make of these dire pronouncements? At the very least, they describe humankind as being entirely unequipped for the arrival of the posthuman. But Virilio's doomsday scenarios could also be read as a metacommentary on the philosophy of ends itself. The collapse of distance on which the hyperreal and the cyborg are predicated, and the more general yearning for immanence – the desire for dissolution, disruption, and disintegration, for a condition where hierarchy and identity no longer prevail – are figured as bleak and malevolent prospects. Even ecological schemas such as Serres proposes, where concern is shifted from the local to the global, are no solution; it was the speed of global communication that produced the psychosocial torpor of "polar inertia" in the first place. Virilio is the last endist, recuperating the most abiding concern of philosophical postmodernism, even as he shows its ominous determinations and potentially hazardous consequences for life in the twenty-first century.

NOTES

1. Luce Irigaray, *An Ethics of Sexual Difference*, trans. Carolyn Burke and Gillian C. Gill (Ithaca, NY: Cornell University Press, 1993), p. 5.
2. Gilles Deleuze and Félix Guattari, *What is Philosophy?*, trans. Hugh Tomlinson and Graham Burchell (New York: Columbia University Press, 1994), p. 9.
3. Jacques Derrida, *Positions*, trans. Alan Bass (London: Athlone, 1972), p. 6.

4. Jacques Derrida, *Of Grammatology*, trans. Gayatri Chakravorty Spivak (Baltimore, MD, and London: Johns Hopkins University Press, 1976), p. 18.
5. Ibid., p. 4.
6. Though dissociating deconstruction from postmodernism in general, Christopher Norris has stressed this aspect of Jacques Derrida's philosophy: "the issues [Derrida] raises belong within the tradition of Kantian enlightened critique, even while pressing that tradition to the limits (and beyond) of its own self-legitimizing claims." See *Derrida* (London: Fontana, 1987), p. 167. See also pp. 94–5, 147–50.
7. Analytical philosophy may have denounced metaphysics, but it nevertheless lends it covert support through its faith in science. Derrida, for example, has referred to "the classical notion of science, whose projects, concepts and norms are fundamentally and systematically tied to metaphysics." See his *Positions*, p. 13.
8. Crucial in this regard is Wittgenstein's notion of "language games," different modes of utterance corresponding to different social institutions, each following its own set of rules. See his *Philosophical Investigations*, trans. G. E. M. Anscombe (Oxford: Blackwell, 1958), p. 5. For examples, see p. 11.
9. See David Pears, *Wittgenstein* (London: Fontana, 1971), p. 103. This has not prevented Jean-François Lyotard from using Wittgenstein's philosophy for antihumanist ends. See Lyotard, *The Postmodern Condition: A Report on Knowledge*, trans. Geoff Bennington and Brian Massumi (Manchester: Manchester University Press, 1984), pp. 9–11.
10. Friedrich Nietzsche, "On Truth and Lie in an Extra-Moral Sense," in Walter Kaufmann (ed.), *The Portable Nietzsche* (New York: Random House, 1980), p. 46.
11. Martin Heidegger, *Basic Writings*, ed. David Farrell Krell (London: Routledge, 1978), p. 348.
12. Ibid., p. 433.
13. Ibid., p. 436.
14. Ibid., p. 437.
15. Richard Rorty, *Philosophy and the Mirror of Nature* (Oxford: Blackwell, 1980), ch. 6.
16. Ibid., p. 360.
17. Emmanuel Levinas, *Totality and Infinity: An Essay on Exteriority*, trans. Alphonso Lingis (The Hague: Martinus Nijhoff, 1979), p. 48.
18. Emmanuel Levinas, *Humanisme de l'autre homme* (Montpellier: Fata Morgana, 1972), p. 95. Quoted in Colin Davis, *Levinas: An Introduction* (Cambridge: Polity, 1996), p. 124.
19. See Luc Ferry and Alain Renaut, *French Philosophy of the Sixties: An Essay On Antihumanism* (Amherst, MA: University of Massachusetts Press, 1990), p. 8.
20. Perry Anderson, *In the Tracks of Historical Materialism* (London: Verso, 1983), p. 37.
21. See Claude Lévi-Strauss, *The Savage Mind* (London: Weidenfeld and Nicolson, 1966); Jacques Lacan, *Ecrits: Selections*, trans. Alan Sheridan (London: Routledge, 1989); Louis Althusser, *Lenin and Philosophy and Other Essays*, trans. Ben Brewster (London: New Left Books, 1971), p. 160.
22. Hubert L. Dreyfus and Paul Rabinow, *Michel Foucault: Beyond Structuralism and Hermeneutics* (Brighton: Harvester, 1982), p. 30.

23. Michel Foucault, *The Order of Things: An Archaeology of the Human Sciences* (London: Routledge, 1970), p. 387.

24. See, for example, Michael E. Zimmerman, "Rethinking the Heidegger-Deep Ecology Relation," *Environmental Ethics* 15 (1993), pp. 195–224; Charles Taylor, "Heidegger, Language and Ecology," in Hubert L. Dreyfus and Harrison Hall (eds.), *Heidegger: A Critical Reader* (Oxford: Blackwell, 1992); David Michael Levin, *The Opening of Vision: Nihilism and the Postmodern Situation* (New York and London: Routledge, 1988).

25. Gilles Deleuze and Félix Guattari, *Anti-Oedipus*, trans. Robert Hurley, Mark Seem, and Helen R. Lane (Minneapolis, MN: University of Minnesota Press, 1983), pp. 4–5.

26. Gilles Deleuze and Félix Guattari, *A Thousand Plateaus*, trans. Brian Massumi (Minneapolis, MN, and London: University of Minnesota Press, 1987), p. 21.

27. Philip Goodchild suggests that "Deleuze and Guattari have constructed the first ethic appropriate to such an ecological vision of the world." See *Deleuze and Guattari: An Introduction to the Politics of Desire* (London: Sage, 1996), pp. 211–13. Guattari himself produced an essay exploring the "social ecology" of life under capitalism, wherein he developed a context for thinking beyond exploitative power relations known as "ecosophy." See his *The Three Ecologies*, trans. Ian Pindar and Paul Sutton (London: Athlone, 2001).

28. Michel Serres, *The Natural Contract*, trans. Elizabeth MacArthur and William Paulson (Ann Arbor, MI: University of Michigan Press, 1995), p. 4.

29. Ibid., p. 32.

30. Ibid., p. 33.

31. Ibid., p. 50.

32. Alasdair MacIntyre, *After Virtue: A Study in Moral Theory* (London: Duckworth, 1981), p. 201.

33. Roland Barthes, *Writing Degree Zero*, trans. Annette Lavers and Colin Smith (London: Jonathan Cape, 1967), p. 30.

34. Lyotard, *Postmodern Condition*, pp. 27–9.

35. Ibid., pp. 31–7.

36. Ibid., p. xxvi.

37. Ibid., p. 30.

38. Jean-François Lyotard, "Histoire universelle et différences culturelles," *Critique* 456 (May 1985), p. 561.

39. Gianni Vattimo, "The End of (Hi)story," in Ingeborg Hoesterey (ed.), *Zeitgeist in Babel* (Bloomington and Indianapolis, IN: Indiana University Press, 1991), p. 134.

40. Ibid., p. 136.

41. Ibid., p. 139.

42. Hayden White, "The Value of Narrativity in the Representation of Reality," in W. J. T. Mitchell (ed.), *On Narrative* (Chicago, IL, and London: University of Chicago Press, 1981), p. 14.

43. Jacques Derrida, "Living On: Borderlines," in Harold Bloom *et al.*, *Deconstruction and Criticism* (London and Henley: Routledge & Kegan Paul, 1979), p. 105.

44. Richard Rorty, *Contingency, Irony, and Solidarity* (Cambridge: Cambridge University Press, 1989), p. xvi.

45. Friedrich Nietzsche, *Twilight of the Idols* and *The Anti-Christ*, trans. R. J. Hollingdale (Harmondsworth: Penguin, 1968), pp. 40–1.

46. Jean Baudrillard, *Simulations* (New York: Semiotext(e), 1983), p. 10.

47. See Baudrillard, *The Mirror of Production* (St Louis, MO: Telos, 1975) and *Simulations*.

48. Jean Baudrillard, *In the Shadow of the Silent Majorities . . . Or the End of the Social* (New York: Semiotext(e), 1983), p. 85.

49. Ibid.

50. Jean Baudrillard, *The Gulf War Did Not Take Place*, trans. Paul Patton (Sydney: Power, 1995).

51. See Baudrillard, *Simulations*, p. 69.

52. *La guerre de Troie n'aura pas lieu* (1935). Baudrillard, in a later piece, points out the "many analogies between the Trojan and Gulf wars." See his *The Illusion of the End*, trans. Chris Turner (Cambridge: Polity, 1994), p. 64.

53. Christopher Norris, *Uncritical Theory: Postmodernism, Intellectuals and the Gulf War* (London: Lawrence and Wishart, 1992).

54. Baudrillard, *Gulf War*, pp. 66–7.

55. Linda Hutcheon, *The Politics of Postmodernism* (London: Routledge, 1989), p. 142.

56. Luce Irigaray, *This Sex Which Is Not One*, trans. Catherine Porter and Carolyn Burke (Ithaca, NY: Cornell University Press, 1985), p. 159.

57. Luce Irigaray, *Speculum of the Other Woman*, trans. Gillian C. Gill (Ithaca, NY: Cornell University Press, 1985).

58. For an account of female "subjecthood," and the necessity of renewing the Enlightenment contract of human agency and emancipation, see Nancy Hartsock, "Foucault on Power: A Theory for Women?," in Linda Nicholson (ed.), *Feminism/Postmodernism* (New York: Routledge, 1990), pp. 157–75.

59. See Julia Kristeva, "The System and the Speaking Subject," in Toril Moi (ed.), *The Kristeva Reader* (Oxford: Blackwell, 1986), pp. 25–6.

60. Julia Kristeva, "Women's Time," *Kristeva Reader*, p. 209.

61. See Margaret Whitford, *Luce Irigaray: Philosophy in the Feminine* (New York and London: Routledge, 1991), p. 136.

62. Luce Irigaray, *Sexes and Genealogies*, trans. Gillian C. Gill (New York: Columbia University Press), p. 61.

63. Christine Battersby, *The Phenomenal Woman: Feminist Metaphysics and the Patterns of Identity* (Cambridge: Polity, 1998), p. 101.

64. Judith Butler, *Bodies that Matter: On the Discursive Limits of "Sex"* (New York and London: Routledge, 1993), p. 218.

65. Judith Butler, *Gender Trouble: Feminism and the Subversion of Identity* (New York and London: Routledge, 1990), p. 13. Battersby gives credence to this aspect of Butler's critique: "For Irigaray, the history of western philosophy remains the expression of a seamless masculine imaginary." See *Phenomenal Woman*, p. 56.

66. Irigaray, *Ethics of Sexual Difference*, p. 5.

67. Butler, *Gender Trouble*, p. 140.

68. Ibid., p. 25.

69. Irigaray, *This Sex Which Is Not One*, p. 134.

70. Hélène Cixous, "The Laugh of the Medusa", in Elaine Marks and Isabelle de Courtivron (eds.), *New French Feminisms* (Brighton: Harvester, 1981), p. 253.

71. See J. L. Austin, *How to Do Things with Words* (London: Oxford University Press, 1962).

72. Gayatri Chakravorty Spivak, "French Feminism in an International Frame," *Yale French Studies* 62 (1981), p. 166.

73. Baudrillard, *Illusion of the End*, p. 110.

74. Jacques Derrida, "On a Newly Arisen Apocalyptic Tone in Philosophy," trans. John Leavey, Jr., in Peter Fenves (ed.), *Raising the Tone of Philosophy: Late Essays by Immanuel Kant, Transformative Critique by Jacques Derrida* (Baltimore, MD, and London: Johns Hopkins University Press, 1993), p. 144.

75. Irigaray, *Sexes and Genealogies*, p. 61.

76. Butler, *Gender Trouble*, p. 35.

77. Friedrich Nietzsche, *The Will to Power*, trans. Walter Kaufmann and R. J. Hollingdale (New York: Vintage, 1968), pp. 545, 340. See also pp. 13, 377 and 378.

78. Gilles Deleuze and Clare Parnet, *Dialogues*, trans. Hugh Tomlinson and Barbara Habberjam (New York: Columbia University Press, 1987), p. 2.

79. Deleuze and Guattari, *Thousand Plateaus*, p. 293.

80. Ibid., p. 238.

81. See Gill Kirkup, Linda Janes, and Kathryn Woodward (eds.), *The Gendered Cyborg: A Reader* (London and New York: Routledge, 2000); *Technologies of the Gendered Body: Reading Cyborg Women*, (Durham, NC, and London: Duke University Press, 1996); and Judith Halberstam and Ira Livingston (eds.), *Posthuman Bodies* (Bloomington and Indianapolis, IN: Indiana University Press, 1995).

82. Donna J. Haraway, *Simians, Cyborgs, and Women: The Reinvention of Nature* (London: Free Association, 1991), pp. 150–3.

83. Ibid., p. 177.

84. Ibid., pp. 153, 150.

85. Ibid., p. 180.

86. See Kate Soper, "Future Culture: Realism, Humanism and the Politics of Nature," *Radical Philosophy* 102 (July/August 2000), pp. 23–4.

87. Paul Virilio, *Open Sky*, trans. Julie Rose (London and New York: Verso, 1997), p. 59.

88. Ibid., p. 118.

89. It also appears in Virilio's more recent works, *Politics of the Very Worst: An Interview By Philippe Petit*, trans. Michael Cavaliere (New York: Semiotext(e), 1999), and *The Information Bomb*, trans. Chris Turner (London: Verso, 2000).

90. Virilio, *Open Sky*, pp. 69–71.

91. Paul Virilio, *Polar Inertia*, trans. Patrick Camiller (London: Sage, 2000), p. 86. Originally published in 1990.

2

CATHERINE CONSTABLE

Postmodernism and film

This chapter will demonstrate the ways in which Jean Baudrillard's and Fredric Jameson's accounts of the postmodern have had a significant impact on the field of film studies, affecting both film theory and history. The most influential aspects of each theorist's work are outlined in the first two sections. The first section focuses on two key texts by Baudrillard: *Simulations* and *America*, while the second addresses Jameson's famous article "Postmodernism and Consumer Society." I shall indicate the ways in which their ideas have been taken up and/or challenged at the end of each section. The critical debates surrounding these conceptions of the postmodern have impacted upon film history due to cinema's dual status as both an icon of modernity and a symbol of the postmodern. The third section explores the many different definitions of the relation between the modern and the postmodern and traces the ways in which this distinction intersects with other key oppositions in film theory and history, such as classical/postclassical and narrative/spectacle. The final section will use current theoretical conceptions of affirmative postmodernisms in order to provide a reading of *Face/Off* that challenges its status as the ultimate in meaningless spectacle.

Baudrillard

One of Baudrillard's key theses is contained within the title of the first work in his compilation volume, *Simulations*. "The Precession of Simulacra" reverses the traditional mimetic relation between art forms and reality, in which the image is said to be a copy of the real. The title asserts that the simulacrum or image has ontological priority and thus *precedes* the real. Baudrillard explains this reversal with reference to Hollywood disaster movies. "It is pointless to laboriously interpret these films by their relationship with an 'objective' social crisis... It is in the other direction that we must say it is *the social itself which*, in contemporary discourse, *is organized according to a script for a disaster film.*"[1] The effect of granting precedence to the disaster movie, and other images, is that the real itself becomes film-like. Baudrillard's analysis of America demonstrates this point in that he views the country through the lens provided by Hollywood cinema. "It is not the least of America's charms that even outside the movie theatres the whole country is cinematic. The desert you pass through is like the set of a Western, the city a screen of signs and formulas."[2] It is this sense of a reality that has been completely pervaded by cinema, resulting in the apprehension of the real as film, which is one of the key metaphors for the postmodern.

Baudrillard offers an apocalyptic characterization of the postmodern in that the construction of the real as film is said to mark the destruction of reality. His famous account of the four successive phases of the image lays out the trajectory of his own disaster movie scenario. In the first, the image performs its traditional mimetic function and operates as "the reflection of a basic reality." The second phase references a Marxist conception of mass culture as that which covers over the material conditions of production. This image has an ideological function in that "it masks and perverts the basic reality." Baudrillard argues that the decisive break occurs at the third phase, in which the image is said to mask "the *absence* of a basic reality." The annihilation of the real is laid bare in the fourth phase, where the image "bears no relation to any reality whatever: it is its own pure simulacrum."[3]

Baudrillard uses Disneyland as an example of the logic of the third phase. Its status as a fantastical, infantile world serves to make us believe that we inhabit the opposite: a real, objective, adult world. This attempt to cover over the absence of the real is then unmasked and Baudrillard's analysis serves to propel us into the fourth phase. "Disneyland is presented as imaginary in order to make us believe that the rest is real, when in fact all of Los Angeles and the America surrounding it are no longer real, but of the order of the hyperreal and of simulation" (p. 25). The abolition of any qualitative distinction between Disneyland and the real world serves to turn America itself into Disneyland. The example is a good instance of Baudrillard's later intellectual style that Steven Connor aptly characterizes as "playful, but chilling camp."[4] The elements of mockery and exaggeration are clear in this presentation of the hyperreal as the transformation of reality into a cartoon. Moreover, the hyperreal is consistently characterized as both apocalyptic and comic. In a world become film, reality is a series of clips with the result that "a non-intentional parody hovers over everything" (p. 150).

The annihilation of reality is said to be the result of capitalism. "For, finally, it was capital which was the first to feed throughout its history on the destruction of every referential, of every human goal, which shattered every ideal distinction between true and false, good and evil, in order to establish a radical law of equivalence and exchange, the iron law of its power" (p. 43). The destructive power of capital is demonstrated in its undermining of the concept of "use-value," in which an object would be purchased because it fulfilled a particular function. Capitalism introduces a system of exchange in which the value of any object is determined by the others for which it can be substituted. Moreover, the overproduction of goods has resulted in the rise of advertizing in order to distinguish between them, ensuring that objects are no longer purchased for their use-value but rather for the lifestyles that they represent.[5] In this way, the capitalist dismissal of the criterion of functionality is seen to destroy objective reality. Baudrillard describes this logic as a "catastrophic spiral" because the circular dynamic of intersubstitutionality shatters a series of key oppositions including real/imaginary, true/false, and good/evil (p. 43).

The loss of the real and the consequent undermining of the logic of opposition are demonstrated by attempts to interpret the meaning of political events. Watergate can be seen as both a left-wing conspiracy against Nixon and a right-wing conspiracy in which a Republican mastermind, "Deep Throat," manipulated the left-wing press. It might be said that the latter interpretation has gained popularity thanks to its wider dissemination as a sub-plot of *The X Files*; however, both readings are equal as interpretations and are thus presented as intersubstitutional. "All the hypotheses of manipulation are reversible in an endless whirligig" (p. 30). This implosion of the logic of opposition also signals the end of structuralist models of language and meaning. Saussurian models privilege difference in that each sign is said to take on meaning through a relation to that which it is not, so that, in this instance, understanding the meaning of "right-wing" requires a conception of what it is not, namely "left-wing." Baudrillard's reading of Watergate demonstrates that oppositional terms do not form stable anchoring points within language. Furthermore, his reading draws attention to the potentially infinite proliferation of interpretations of any political event provided by the global media and cultural theorists. This excessive quantity of readings is said to result in "an improvisation of meaning, of nonsense, or of several simultaneous senses which cancel each other out" (p. 75, n. 4). The exponential proliferation of interpretations can be seen to display the catastrophic logic of the spiral because it ultimately results in the destruction of meaning itself.

Baudrillard continues his gleeful presentation of the dynamic of circularity as a form of nihilistic excess in his book *America*. He links the circulation of liquid assets in global capitalism to the electrical circuits that construct Las Vegas as a blaze of neon in the middle of the desert. The subject is constructed as an electronic image on a nightclub video screen, producing "an effect of frantic self-referentiality, a short circuit which immediately hooks up like with like, and, in so doing, emphasizes their surface intensity and deeper meaninglessness."[6] In contrast to the Lacanian paradigm of misrecognition in which the child's attempt to approximate to the perfect mirror image forms the kernel of a subjectivity that is forever divided against itself, the Baudrillardian subject is at one with the image. This progression beyond the mirror stage to "the video phase" is therefore said to mark the anni-hilation of interiority, constructing the subject as pure surface (p. 37). The circuit also signals the destruction of sexual, social, and cultural differences in favor of a series of looks that can be adopted according to the dictates of fashion: "mores, customs, the body, and language free themselves in the ever quickening round of fashion. The liberated man is not the one who is freed in his ideal reality, his inner truth . . . he is the man who changes spaces, who circulates, who changes sex, clothes, and habits according to fashion, *rather than morality*" (p. 96). The play of gender roles offered by pop idols such as Michael Jackson and David Bowie is seen to obey the postmodern imperative of continual change (p. 47).

Baudrillard's vision of an "orgy of liberation" (p. 96) has provoked nu-merous critical responses. The imagery of circulation appears to offer a kind of spurious egalitarianism in that the conflation of different circuits suggests that each subject has equal access to the capital required to enter into this particular round of fashion. Furthermore, the reference to Michael Jackson suggests that ethnicity is also available as a fashion statement. The white press's reading of Jackson's deteriorating body and face as indicative of the extremes to which he will go to become white, however, demonstrates that circulation across ethnic divides does not always serve to render the signs of different ethnic groups equal as signs.[7] Some feminist and postcolonial critics have been justifiably suspicious of the postmodern dissolution of the categories of subjectivity and truth at a time when women and people of color were just beginning to take up the status of subjects and to create new bodies of knowledge.[8] Other theorists have taken issue with Baudrillard's characterization of the postmodern as an "orgy of indifference" (p. 96). Vivian Sobchack argues that the postmodern dispersal of the category of Otherness results in a fluid construction of ethnicities as multiple plays of differences, which are not merely cosmetic.[9]

While Baudrillard's nihilistic presentation of the postmodern continues to provoke considerable critical debate within academia,[10] his account of a world become image, pervaded by its own superficiality and thus rendered meaningless, has been widely disseminated by the western media. The relish with which Baudrillard presents his apocalypse, and the continual use of par-ody that pervades his announcements of the end of reality, truth, knowledge, subjectivity, power, and politics, make it hard to judge the status of his assertions. Norman Denzin treats Baudrillard as a writer of science fiction rather than of cultural theory, concluding that the "visual effects are terrific but the narrative doesn't work."[11] The refusal to treat Baudrillard's work as theoretical is a common critical response and serves to draw attention to particular problems created by his style. In this account of *Simulations* and *America* I have focused on the formative role played by metaphors of circulation in order to emphasize the ways in which these images function as key moves in the overall argument. Thus, I would argue that reading Baudrillard's texts as symptomatic of a postmodern valorization of style over substance (however tempting) is ultimately inappropriate because the style *is* the substance. In taking up this mode of writing philosophy, Baudrillard presents himself as one of Nietzsche's successors. Both philosophers offer critiques of the concept of objective truth and both can be seen to adopt an overtly rhetorical style in order to draw attention to the metaphorical and interpretative status of their own theoretical writing. Baudrillard's apocalyptic pronouncements have a further function in that they serve to provoke a response, forcing the reader to rise to the challenge that he presents. In this way, Baudrillard's gleeful acting out of the role of *agent provocateur* can be seen to add an enjoyable vitality to the theoretical debates concerning the postmodern, as well as constructing him as the self-styled bad boy of the postmodern theorists.

Jameson

In "Postmodernism and Consumer Society" Jameson provides a three-stage analysis of the development of capitalism, correlating each new economic order with "the emergence of a new type of social life" and "the emergence of new formal features in culture."[12] The first stage, market capitalism, is characterized by industrial growth that creates goods for national markets. This classic era of capitalism marks "the heyday of the nuclear family" and the rise of the bourgeoisie, both of which are reflected in the dominant aesthetic form of realism (p. 115). The second stage, monopoly capitalism, conforms to the age of imperialism and is characterized by the creation of world markets, organized around nation states. In this stage the "cultural dominant" is modernism. The third and final stage is that of multinational capitalism, which is marked by the development of global markets and the undermining of national boundaries. This current era of multinational capitalism is characterized by the rise of bureaucracy, signaling the demise of the bourgeois individual subject of the classic era. The cultural dominant is postmodernism, which is seen as a reaction against modernist art forms (pp. 115, 112).

Alex Callinicos argues that this attempt to locate a decisive break between the second and third stages of capitalism is highly problematic.[13] For Jameson, however, the transition from monopoly capitalism to multinational capitalism is also reflected in the different functions allocated to the image. Following Baudrillard's conception of the decisive break between the second and third phases of the image, Jameson links the rise of the postmodern to a rejection of traditional Marxist conceptions of the ideological function of mass culture. The postmodern image does not cover over the means of production; it is the key product of multinational capitalism. Connor argues that the similarities between Jameson's and Baudrillard's accounts are the result of their take-up of the Situationists' work on the "society of the spectacle," which predicted that the image would come to take on a decisive economic role.[14]

Jameson's work is highly influential because he defines some of the key aesthetic features of the postmodern, such as the erosion of the distinction between high and low culture, the incorporation of material from other texts, and the breaking down of boundaries between different genres of writing (p. 112). The demise of the bourgeois individualist subject also impacts on the field of aesthetics because it constitutes the death of the traditional conception of the artist as genius. As a result, art can no longer be the expression of a "unique private world and style." Postmodern artists cannot invent new perspectives and new modes of expression; instead, they operate as *bricoleurs*, recycling previous works and styles. Thus, postmodern art takes the form of pastiche: "in a world in which stylistic innovation is no longer possible, all that is left is to imitate dead styles, to speak through the masks and with the voices of the styles in the imaginary museum" (p. 115).

Margaret Rose argues that Jameson's account of art as pastiche reworks Baudrillard's conception of the unintentional parody encapsulated in the postmodern era.[15] For Baudrillard, the parodic aspect of the hyperreal is the result of the total reconstruction of reality as aesthetic spectacle. Such parody constitutes a kind of empty mockery because it marks the impossibility of returning to the real. Jameson's definition of pastiche as "blank parody" draws on Baudrillard's key features of emptiness and loss. For Jameson, parody is a comic imitation, a send-up, of an original text or artistic style. The exaggeration of aspects of the original provokes laughter by emphasizing those textual features that diverge from the linguistic norm. In contrast, pastiche is "parody that has lost its sense of humor" (p. 114). It does not provoke laughter because the imitation can no longer be held in relation to any linguistic norms. The loss of the norm also marks the end of originality because the unique nature of the artist's perspective is measured by its distance from conformity.

Postmodern pastiche is ultimately seen to result in the loss of history. This is partly because of the continual promulgation of a diversity of linguistic and aesthetic styles that are taken out of their historical context and presented as currently available. Jameson gives the example of *Body Heat*, which draws on the classic *film noir* plot of *The Postman Always Rings Twice* as well as replicating its small-town *mise-en-scène*. He argues that the setting serves to detract from the contemporary references within the film, such as the cars, constructing it as "a narrative set in some indefinable nostalgic past, an eternal '30s, say, beyond history" (p. 117). The nostalgia film is also said to gratify the audience's desire to return to their own pasts. In this way, *Star Wars* appeals to adults because it recalls the Saturday afternoon serial and thus evokes a sense of the past through "the feel and shape of characteristic art objects of an older period" (p. 116). The attempt to gain access to the past through the promulgation of "pop images and stereotypes about that past" paradoxically ensures that it becomes unattainable (p. 118).

If Baudrillardian parody marks the annihilation of reality, Jameson's pastiche marks the annihilation of temporality. It is the pervasive quality of the image that systematically destroys the possibility of reaching the real and the past. Jameson builds on this sense of atemporality in his comparison of postmodernity with the state of schizophrenia. Drawing on Lacan, he argues that the experience of chronological time is "an effect of language" (p. 119). Thus, constructing time is linked to the creation of meaning in that both are based on an understanding of the interrelations between signifiers and the ways in which these create the concept of the signified, or the "meaning-effect." Jameson defines schizophrenia as "an experience of isolated, disconnected, discontinuous material signifiers which fail to link up into a coherent sequence" (p. 119). As a result, the schizophrenic does not have a chronological sense of past, present, and future, and consequently lacks any sense of the self as a coherent identity that persists across time. It is this sense of being condemned to the perpetual present that Jameson takes to be emblematic of the postmodern condition.

Giuliana Bruno's excellent reading of *Blade Runner* utilizes both Baudrillard's and Jameson's conceptions of the postmodern. She reads Rachel as a perfect simulacrum because she does not imitate human emotions but rather simulates them, undoing the distinction between a real human being and a bad copy. This complete undermining of the opposition between true and false is summed up by Rachel's inability to say whether she is a replicant or not. Bruno argues that the sets in *Blade Runner* conform to Jameson's definition of postmodern pastiche because the architecture combines elements of Greek, Roman, and Egyptian styles. She also reads the replicants' attempts to access the past through photographs as symptomatic of the loss of history. "We, like the replicants, are put in the position of reclaiming a history by means of its reproduction."[16] Within *Blade Runner*, the replicants' photographs are revealed to be fakes, dismantling their past, while their preset termination dates deny them a future. Thus, Bruno reads the replicants as examples of postmodern schizophrenia because they are condemned to the intensity of the perpetual present.

While Jameson's definition of the postmodern has been taken up to form film readings, some theorists have also been critical of his conceptual categories. Barbara Creed takes issue with Jameson's category of the nostalgia film, arguing that he fails to analyze the precise nature of the audience's longing for the past. She suggests that the longing for the dead form of the adventure serial "with its true heroes and distressed heroines" might well represent "a desire to relive a 'time' when gender roles were more clearly defined, stable [and] predictable."[17] Moreover, she argues that the account of nostalgia needs to be related to feminist work on gender and desire. Linda Hutcheon argues that Jameson's announcement of the end of history is premature and that the current interrelation of history and textuality needs to be constructed in a more positive way.[18] Indeed, Jameson does revisit his work on the presentation of history within the nostalgia film, analyzing *Something Wild* and *Blue Velvet* as examples of a more "properly allegorical processing of the past."[19] The later category of "post-nostalgia" films, however, replicates many of the problems of the earlier account.

Jameson's accounts of parody and pastiche have also been criticized. Hutcheon argues that his construction of parody serves to trivialize the concept. She argues in favor of recognizing a variety of different modes, thus opening up the possibility of political forms of parody.[20] Rose criticizes both Baudrillard and Jameson for defining parody and pastiche in entirely negative ways.[21] I would argue that this criticism foregrounds the logic of negation that underpins both these versions of the postmodern. By announcing the annihilation of reality and temporality respectively, Baudrillard and Jameson simply define the postmodern in terms of the wholesale destruction of key concepts that have preceded it. This is problematic because their work can be seen to rest on the repetition of one highly questionable argument, namely: if reality, truth, knowledge, history, etc., are not entirely objective and unchanging, then there is no such thing as reality, truth, knowledge, history, etc. Hutcheon's intervention into the debates on history and parody can be seen to refute this argument by insisting on a broader range of possibilities. It is this move beyond the logic of negation that I shall explore more fully in the final section, "Affirmative postmodernisms."

Modernism/postmodernism

While both Baudrillard's and Jameson's accounts of the postmodern serve to dissolve the distinction between the aesthetic and the socioeconomic, Mariam Bratu Hansen utilizes the distinction in order to draw attention to the problematic positioning of Hollywood cinema. She argues that debates on modernism within film theory have focused exclusively on the aesthetic category of high modernism, positioning Hollywood cinema of the studio era as the epitome of a contrasting classical style. In this way film theory can be seen to replicate the opposition of modernist/classical, which has been developed in philosophy, literature, and fine art.[22] Thus, classical Hollywood cinema is said to utilize a traditional model of linear narrative made up of causal links, which are largely character-centered. The artificiality of the represented world is said to be concealed by the use of continuity editing, and the textual elements of style and performance are typically subordinated to the overarching narration.[23] The dominance of the narrative leads to the later conflation of the classical with the uncritical dissemination of ideology in contrast to the self-reflexive and progressive aesthetic forms of modernist cinema, which are said to deconstruct ideology.[24]

Hansen argues that the subsumption of Hollywood cinema of the studio era within the aesthetic category of the classical overlooks its relationship to modernity. She argues that Hollywood cinema was "the incarnation of *the modern*, an aesthetic medium up-to-date with Fordist-Taylorist methods of industrial production and mass consumption, with drastic changes in social, sexual, and gender relations, in the material fabric of everyday life, in the organization of sensory perception and experience."[25] Moreover, the film texts are said to play out the complexities inherent in the cultural experience of negotiating with modernity and modernization. Hansen can therefore be seen to offer another interlinking of the economic, the social, and the aesthetic in her construction of Hollywood cinema as a new form of "vernacular modernism." She argues that the recognition of a range of *modernisms* is vital for dismantling a number of the overly simplistic oppositions that have dominated film theory and history.[26]

Hansen's reworking of film history can be seen in her analysis of Soviet cinema. She argues that the traditional designation of Soviet montage as a form of modernism focuses on its relation to Soviet avant-garde aesthetics while overlooking the role played by Hollywood cinema.[27] Her rejection of the modernist/classical opposition can therefore be seen as providing a means of mapping the interrelations between two different national cinemas. Hansen's recognition of a range of modernisms is particularly useful in Film Studies, given the number of different candidates nominated for the title of modernist cinema. Jameson provides some nominations of his own, arguing in favor of two modernist movements.[28] The first is located in the silent era and encompasses the work of Eisenstein, Stroheim, and Chaplin, while the second takes place in the 1950s and is manifested in the work of auteurs such as Hitchcock, Bergman, Kurosawa, and Fellini. Jameson's use of the category of the auteur is consistent with his definition of modernist art as the expression of a unique private world.

Jameson's nomination of a 1950s generation of modernist auteurs has been complicated by the advent of the postmodern. Some theorists have responded by nominating a new generation of postmodern auteurs, including Nora Ephron, David Lynch, Quentin Tarantino, and Kathryn Bigelow.[29] The use of the category of the auteur in this context is clearly problematic, however, given Jameson's and others' accounts of the death of the Author. Other theorists have contested the status of Jameson's nominees. Denzin reads Hitchcock as a modernist whose works serve to usher in the postmodern. Analyzing the representation of voyeurism in *Rear Window*, he argues that it enacts the onset of the hyperreal because the voyeur's gaze is seen to eradicate objective reality.[30] Linda Williams also presents Hitchcock as a pivotal figure but she focuses on *Psycho*. The murder of the chief protagonist, Marion Crane, breaks the conventions of classical narrative, shattering the audience's expectations. The audience is left to wonder about the next attack and simply "to register the rhythms of its anticipation, shock, and release."[31] It is this development of a "'roller-coaster' sensibility" celebrating the visceral qualities of the image rather than focusing on narrative and characterization that Williams argues is central to postmodern culture.

Williams's interlinking of the postclassical with the postmodern also focuses on economic changes in the film industry. She argues that the change from the steady continuous output of the studios to a "package unit system relying on the enormous profits of occasional blockbusters to drive economic expansion into related acquisitions in the leisure field" constitutes a significant shift.[32] The rise of the blockbuster has been marked by an increasing reliance on multimedia tie-ins: from theme-park rides to computer games, soundtrack CDs, and music videos, which serve to generate further profits. Theorists have argued that the global marketing of the blockbuster has resulted in the development of its aesthetic form. The attempt to transcend linguistic and cultural boundaries in order to exploit international markets has led to an emphasis on spectacle and special effects.[33] This interlinking of capitalist globalization with the emergence of a new aesthetic form clearly constitutes another version of Jameson's third stage. Moreover, the construction of the blockbuster as formative of a "New Hollywood" that is synonymous with the rise of spectacle and the demise of narrative and characterization has gained popular currency.[34]

The issue of whether or not New Hollywood does constitute a new aesthetic form is a key area of academic debate. While theorists agree that the rise of the blockbuster has corresponded with a new economic structure, some have argued that the products of New Hollywood simply conform to the model of classical narrative.[35] The status of the classical paradigm within Film Studies has been called into question, however, because it is thought to privilege the role of narrative at the expense of other aesthetic forms, such as spectacle. Geoff King argues that the opposition narrative/spectacle has resulted in the widespread definition of the latter as meaningless textual excess. In contrast, he positions spectacle as an intrinsic aspect of Hollywood cinema, which constitutes one of several textual norms. Moreover, he argues that spectacle can have a narratorial function, setting up key themes and contributing to the plot development.[36] King's work therefore seems to erase the division between the classical and the postclassical/postmodern in that he argues in favor of a series of coexistent continua.

While I would agree with King that spectacle has always played a significant role in Hollywood cinema, its current designation as *the* defining feature of the blockbuster may give it a different status at the present moment. In addition, both the mass media and academia draw on a Baudrillardian conception of the postmodern in their construction of spectacle as a nihilistic, empty, aesthetic form. The widespread conception of spectacle as the demarcation of the end of humanist aesthetics is another example of the logic of negation in action. As a result, blockbusters are frequently criticized for providing characters that lack psychological depth, and narrative structures that do not conform to moral frameworks. Although King's conception of the narratorial function of spectacle does challenge the negative view of the blockbuster, his emphasis on the functionality of spectacle *per se* means that he cannot address the ways in which postmodern films might offer something new. The issue at stake here is the possibility that the utilization of spectacle in the blockbuster could change previous conceptions of characterization and narration.

Affirmative postmodernisms

I have chosen to analyze *Face/Off* because it seems to epitomize the aesthetics of spectacle that is a key aspect of the all-action blockbuster. *Face/Off* was John Woo's third Hollywood film and his presence in America can be seen as a part of the economic strategy of globalization. This film was judged to be a success, taking over $100 million in box-office receipts by its sixth play week.[37] Woo is famous for his glossy visual style and his presentation of highly choreographed, excessive screen violence. Indeed, Brooker and Brooker argue that the "amoral, superficial and self-referential portrayal of violence" has become a key feature of postmodern aesthetics.[38] While they focus on the work of Quentin Tarantino, the rhetoric of empty "ultra-violence" is frequently used to describe Woo's films. I shall argue that it is necessary to move beyond the popular conception of Woo's work as super-ficial and excessive in order to begin to appreciate the aesthetic strategies presented by *Face/Off*. The analysis will also indicate the ways in which the film achieves its distinctive sense of fun; an important consideration that Linda Williams argues has been absent from academic analyses of film texts for too long.[39]

This section will therefore map out a different way of approaching the postmodern, one that neither defines it as the end of modernism nor sim-ply assimilates it to tradition. This involves moving beyond the rhetoric of nihilism, while accepting that the postmodern does involve changes that re-quire a (re)working of previous aesthetic categories. The attempt to think through alternative, positive constructions of the postmodern is also ad-dressed by Brooker and Brooker. "We have ... to think with more discrimina-tion and subtlety about the aesthetic forms and accents of postmodernism – so famously 'all about style' but not by that token always and only about 'merely' style."[40] They focus on the ways in which Tarantino's highly styl-ized presentation of stock characters in *Pulp Fiction* serves to reinvent and expand generic conventions. The story of the flirtatious boss's wife draws on established elements from the gangster genre, while her overdose provides an unexpected Gothic reference. Furthermore, the hypodermic needle that is stabbed through Mia's heart can be seen as effecting her resurrection from the dead, simultaneously recalling and undermining the Gothic convention of the vampire's stake. On this model, the referencing of previous aesthetic forms and styles moves beyond Jameson's conception of empty pastiche, sustaining an "inventive and affirmative mode" of postmodernism.[41]

Face/Off begins with a botched assassination attempt in which Castor Troy aims to kill FBI agent Sean Archer, only to kill Archer's son. Archer succeeds in capturing Castor and his brother, Pollux, to discover that they have planted a bomb, the whereabouts of which is unknown. In order to get the information from Pollux, Archer agrees to undergo radical surgery in which he is reconstructed as Castor, and is subsequently sent to jail. The plan goes wrong when Castor assumes Archer's identity, infiltrating the police force. Archer then breaks out of jail and integrates himself with Castor's friends. The transformation allows each protagonist to make amends for the actions committed by his *doppelgänger*. Thus, Castor offers "parental" advice, teaching Archer's daughter, Jamie, to fend off unwanted advances from teenage boys by using a switchblade; and Archer saves Castor's son, Adam, from being killed in a raid. Archer finally kills Castor at the end of a series of "final" denouements. He is restored to his previous appearance and united with his family, which includes his new adoptive son, Adam.

Face/Off is instantly recognizable as a postmodern film. The pre-credit scene in which Archer's son is shot while sitting on a merry-go-round horse with his father clearly draws on the denouement of *Strangers on a Train*, in which the wooden horses are presented as similarly grotesque. Focusing on the staging of the murder, Robin Dougherty argues that the "breathtaking sepia-and-slow-motion style" renders the scene "so over-the-top trite it makes a statement."[42] While he does not enlarge on this comment, I would suggest that it appears trite because the audience is well aware of having seen it before. The overt foregrounding of the visual style also has two functions: it draws attention to the scene's status as one of Archer's memories, as well as signaling the Hitchcock homage through the approximation of black and white. The credit sequence of *Face/Off* crosscuts between numerous locations, including the church in which Castor sets up the bomb and the airport where Pollux is waiting for him. The use of music ranges from the diegetic presentation of the "Hallelujah Chorus" from Handel's *Messiah* to the extra-diegetic rock music that accompanies Castor's arrival at the airport, resulting in a mixture of high and low cultural references.

The staging of Castor's belated appearance at the airport provides one of the best adverts for Donna Karan menswear ever filmed![43] As Castor steps out of the car the breeze catches the fluid folds of his long, black coat, sending it up into the air behind him. Shot in slow motion, he strides towards the plane in time to the throbbing accompaniment of the rock music. His henchmen remove his coat, revealing a shimmering burgundy shirt and darker trousers. They then help him into the matching jacket, thus providing the means to show off the Karan suit in its entirety. This opening draws attention to the marketing tie-ins for the film. *Face/Off* was originally advertised in American style magazines for young men, and the film caused an unprecedented rise in sales for Donna Karan menswear because it served to reach previously untapped markets. Capitalizing on this success, *Face/Off* had two separate launches on its release in the United Kingdom, including a style premiere for magazines such as *GQ* and *Arena*.[44]

The use of Nicholas Cage to model for Donna Karan draws attention to the considerable differences between his and John Travolta's physiques. While this serves to make the central premise of the plot preposterous, the film focuses on the external details of characterization, such as gesture, in order to sustain the identity swap. Each of the key protagonists is associated with a specific vocabulary of movement and vocal intonation. Archer is demarcated by a shared familial gesture in which the tips of the fingers pass across another person's face, as well as by sudden, explosive physical movements and rapid crescendo in vocal delivery, both of which serve to convey anger and trauma. In contrast, Castor is associated with fluid, graceful movements, frequently breaking into dance and occasionally into song. His catchphrase to Archer is the line, "You're not having any fun, are you?" The opposition between the villainous Castor and the law-abiding Archer is thus encapsulated by a series of dichotomies including solidity/fluidity, pain/laughter, trauma/fun.

The identity swap means that Archer is played by John Travolta, then by Nicolas Cage, and finally by Travolta again. Castor is played by Cage and then by Travolta. One of the key pleasures offered by *Face/Off* is the way in which the diegetic motif of swapping over utilizes each star's performance style. Thus, Cage's transformation from Castor to Archer is marked by the change from a monotonal performance of exuberant excess, encapsulated by his cavorting to Handel, to a markedly discontinuous emotional display in which the trauma of becoming his own worst enemy is clearly indicated. While both performances demonstrate the star's trademark bravura style, the role of Archer is reinforced by Cage's other appearances as a trauma victim, notably in *Moonstruck* and *Con Air*. Travolta's transformation into Castor enables him to take up his customary repertoire of fluid, dancing movements encapsulated by his famous performances in *Grease, Saturday Night Fever* and *Pulp Fiction*.

At the level of the diegesis, the characters of Archer and Castor conform to well-worn stereotypes: the lawman who is haunted by the murder of his son, and the psychotic villain. This, coupled with the explicit use of performance style, could be seen as conforming to the cardboard characterization that so offends the critics of the blockbuster. Such a negative reading, however, would simply fail to get to grips with the diverse ways in which star performance and persona are mobilized in order to effect the characterization and narration. Cage's appearance as Archer utilizes his performance style to create an illusion of depth. The scene in which he acts out the process of becoming Castor through a violent assault on a fellow prisoner pivots on the moment at which he is unable to kill him. His imitation of Castor's excessive macho posturing is literally halted in a moment of stasis and horrified reflection, creating a sense of discontinuity and thereby a return to an inner self. This sense of depth is reinforced by the congruence of the character of Archer with Cage's other roles. Importantly, the combination of a specific performance style and particular intertextual references serves to create depth, thus challenging the assumption that psychological realism is the only way to construct character interiority. My reading of the film also has implications for Baudrillard's analysis of the construction of the postmodern subject as image. In his account, the short-circuiting of interior depth is syn-onymous with the subject's circulation as a series of images, all of which are equally superficial. Cage's performance as Archer clearly demonstrates the ways in which patterns of repetition set up interconnections between images that serve to privilege some appearances over others.

The patterns of repetition set up by Travolta's performance do not work in quite the same way. While his appearances as Castor clearly utilize his trademark performance style, the scene in which he visits Archer's home for the first time mobilizes his star persona in a way that detracts from his diegetic role. The song "Poppa's got a brand new bag" forms a sound bridge to the exchange in Jamie's room in which "Archer's" designs on his new daughter are clearly indicated by a cut from his appreciative expression to a point-of-view shot that travels up the length of her body. The disquieting implications of this scene are immediately undercut, however, by the manner in which "Archer" takes his exit. Lighting a cigarette and blowing a smoke ring, he dances out of the doorway, singing along to the retro music. This emphatic assertion of Travolta's star persona through a direct reference to his roles in musicals provides an intertextual context that does not reinforce Castor's status as a dangerous sexual predator, thus propelling the scene into comedy. (The change of tone created by this use of intertextuality becomes very clear if one thinks about the very different implications of having Cage play the same scene.) Travolta's star persona is used to suspend aspects of his character, allowing the film to sidestep the issue of Castor's psychosis. The result is a fluid construction of characterization, which serves to present the villain as appealing rather than as completely monstrous.

It is only by moving beyond the negative construction of the postmodern as lacking acceptable forms of characterization and narration that we can begin to appreciate the aesthetic strategies of *Face/Off*. This also involves abandoning the conception of Woo as the purveyor of empty ultra-violence. Critics tend to divide into two camps: those who find Woo's "highly stylized blood-letting" morally problematic because it aestheticizes mutilation and death,[45] and those who favor such aestheticization, reading it as excessive and amusing. Both camps ultimately share a conception of "ultra-violence" as an empty aesthetic. The critical reaction to the scene in which the pol-ice raid Dietrich's house demonstrates this point. The presentation of the highly stylized gun battle to the diegetic music of "Somewhere over the rainbow," playing on Adam's personal stereo, was read either as a sick jux-taposition of music and image or as an enjoyable example of the film's "outré nonsensicalness."[46] What is noticeable is that neither set of critics bothers to pay attention to the textual detail of this particular scene.

Adam is shown in an overhead shot, wandering over to stand on some glass insets in the floor. His blond hair and the use of underlighting construct him as an idealized vision of innocence in contrast to the darker images of the violence that surrounds him. The key moment of the battle occurs when Archer observes him standing alone and dives across the floor, pulling him out of the line of fire. Woo's use of slow motion draws out the movement of the high forward rolls. Archer seems to fly to Adam's rescue and his movement symbolizes the moment at which he is freed from the weight of guilt felt at his son's death. The lyrics of the song accompany Archer's unbelievable second chance to save an innocent and redeem himself. Thus, the music is initially disconcerting but it clearly underscores the narrative function of the scene in a traditional way. What is important is that the assumption that Woo's presentation of violence is simply style without substance actually prevented critics from engaging with the symbolism in the scene. Moreover, the suggestion that such aestheticization is necessarily immoral ignores the way in which the act of saving the child forms the ethical trajectory of the protagonist.

The ethical trajectory played out during the first part of the raid on Dietrich's house can be contrasted with the parodic presentation of the oppositional moral framework that structures Archer's and Castor's many confrontations. The first of the "final" denouements takes place in a church and utilizes an excess of christological imagery, including doves, candles, and a crucifix, in order to present Archer as the ordained knight-errant. The confrontation between Archer and Castor conforms to a well-worn scenario, which is sent up by Castor during the scene. After mimicking the position of Christ on the cross, Castor comments: "the eternal battle between good and evil, saint and sinner, but you're still not having any fun!" The commentary, coupled with Castor's gleeful response to the five-way Mexican stand-off, suggests that the stylistic flourishes provide the essential fun that a straight depiction of the moral categories would lack. His comments are clearly addressed to a knowing audience, inviting us to enjoy the visual excesses of the serial denouements, including the James Bond homage of the boat chase that culminates in a vast wall of fire.

The stylized presentation of the violence in *Face/Off* is not an empty mockery that serves to display the impossibility of securing any ground of value. Such a Baudrillardian reading is too extreme given that the battles stage the redemption narrative as well as the conflict between good and bad. While it is true that the triumph of the good is presented as formulaic and that the role of textual commentator vindicates the bad, the displacement of moral categories in favor of reflexive entertainment does not constitute the abolition of all ethical value. Indeed, the logic of the redemption narrative can be seen to require the move beyond the opposition of good and bad. Thus, Castor's advice on self-defense has surprisingly good effects, enabling Jamie to defend herself against him using his own switchblade. Archer's redemption also involves taking on some of Castor's characteristics, particularly his ability to live in the present.

The exuberant reflexivity of *Face/Off* that is demonstrated in its fore-grounding of performance and textual play does not constitute an emptying out of signification. On the contrary, the focus on performance mobilizes intertextual references in order to sustain different forms of characterization and to effect changes of tone. Thus, postmodern reflexivity can be seen to offer the audience the enjoyment of tracing textual references in ways that serve to augment and/or detract from the characterization and the narrative structure. The considerable pleasure derived from tracing the references does not constitute a form of modernist distanciation but is rather a gentler movement in and out of the diegetic world, in response to cues offered by the film text. Intertextuality can be seen as the key means of sustaining differential readings of postmodern film texts because the cues will be constructed according to the specific references known to individual viewers. The range of possible readings is not unlimited, however, given that *Face/Off* is reliant upon knowledge of a limited set of films featuring Cage and Travolta. The use of parody in the film is typical of the blockbuster. The representation of masculinity as the self-conscious acting out of gender roles does not really have a subversive effect, given that both Archer and Castor conform to traditional models of machismo. The willingness to foreground gender as play, however, can have subversive potential. Creed reads *Aliens* as exemplary in its comic deconstruction of gender roles.[47] Importantly, understanding the potential of these films is reliant upon the development of theoretical models of affirmative postmodernisms. It is only by moving beyond negative conceptions of the postmodern as a nihilistic form of capitalist excess that we can possibly begin to appreciate the value of having fun.

NOTES

1. Jean Baudrillard, *Simulations*, trans. Paul Foss, Paul Patton, and Philip Beitchman (New York: Semiotext(e), 1983), pp. 75–6, n. 5.
2. Jean Baudrillard, *America*, trans. Chris Turner (London: Verso, 1988), p. 56.
3. Baudrillard, *Simulations*, pp. 11–12. References hereafter in the text.
4. Steven Connor, *Postmodernist Culture: An Introduction to Theories of the Contemporary*, 2nd edn. (Oxford: Blackwell, 1997), p. 56.
5. Callinicos suggests that the disintegration of use-value is typically said to mark the transition between Fordism and post-Fordism. See Alex Callinicos, *Against Postmodernism: A Marxist Critique* (Cambridge: Polity, 1989), p. 134.

6. Baudrillard, *America*, p. 37. References hereafter in the text.

7. Richard Dyer, *White* (London: Routledge, 1997), p. 50.

8. Robert Stam and E. H. Shohat, "Film Theory and Spectatorship in the Age of the 'Posts,'" in Christine Gledhill and Linda Williams (eds.), *Reinventing Film Studies* (London: Arnold, 2000), pp. 386–8.

9. Vivian Sobchack, "Postmodern Modes of Ethnicity," in Peter Brooker and Will Brooker (eds.), *Postmodern After-Images: A Reader in Film, Television and Video* (London: Arnold, 1997), pp. 120–6.

10. Chris Rojek and Bryan S. Turner (eds.), *Forget Baudrillard* (London: Routledge, 1993).

11. Norman Denzin, *Images of Postmodern Society: Social Theory and Contemporary Cinema* (London: Sage, 1991), p. 34.

12. Fredric Jameson, "Postmodernism and Consumer Society," in Hal Foster (ed.), *Postmodern Culture* (London: Pluto, 1985), p. 113. References hereafter in the text.

13. Callinicos, *Against Postmodernism*, pp. 132–44.

14. Connor, *Postmodernist Culture*, pp. 51–2.

15. Margaret Rose, *Parody: Ancient, Modern, and Post-modern* (Cambridge: Cambridge University Press, 1993), pp. 217–19.

16. Giuliana Bruno, "Ramble City: Postmodernism and *Blade Runner*," in Annette Kuhn (ed.), *Alien Zone: Cultural Theory and Contemporary Science Fiction Cinema* (London: Verso, 1990), p. 193.

17. Barbara Creed, "From Here to Modernity," in Brooker and Brooker (eds.), *Postmodern After-Images*, p. 45.

18. Linda Hutcheon, "Postmodern Film?," in Brooker and Brooker (eds.), *Postmodern After-Images*, p. 39.

19. Fredric Jameson, "The Nostalgia Mode and Nostalgia for the Present," in Brooker and Brooker (eds.), *Postmodern After-Images*, p. 27.

20. Hutcheon, "Postmodern Film?," pp. 39–40.

21. Rose, *Parody*, pp. 227–8.

22. Mariam Bratu Hansen, "The Mass Production of the Senses: Classical Cinema as Vernacular Modernism," in Gledhill and Williams (eds.), *Reinventing Film Studies*, pp. 332–5.

23. David Bordwell, Janet Staiger, and Kristin Thompson, *The Classical Hollywood Cinema: Film Style and Mode of Production to 1960* (London: Routledge, 1988), pp. 3–24.

24. Hansen, "Mass Production," pp. 335, 337.

25. Ibid., p. 337.

26. Ibid., pp. 337–8.

27. Ibid., pp. 333–4.

28. Peter Brooker and Will Brooker, "Introduction," in Brooker and Brooker (eds.), *Postmodern After-Images*, pp. 6–7.

29. Ibid., p. 6.

30. Norman Denzin, *The Cinematic Society: The Voyeur's Gaze* (London: Sage, 1995), pp. 119, 128.

31. Linda Williams, "Discipline and Fun: *Psycho* and Postmodern Cinema," in Gledhill and Williams (eds.), *Reinventing Film Studies*, pp. 355–6.

32. Ibid., p. 373 n. 1.

33. Geoff King, *Spectacular Narratives: Hollywood in the Age of the Blockbuster* (London: I. B. Taurus, 2000), p. 2.
34. Ibid., p. 193 n. 3.
35. Bordwell, Staiger and Thompson, *Classical Hollywood Cinema*, pp. 360–77.
36. King, *Spectacular Narratives*, pp. 3–5.
37. Manohla Dargis, "Do you like John Woo?," in José Arroyo (ed.), *Action/Spectacle Cinema: A Sight and Sound Reader* (London: BFI, 2000), p. 68.
38. Peter Brooker and Will Brooker, "Pulpmodernism: Tarantino's Affirmative Action," in Brooker and Brooker (eds.), *Postmodern After-Images*, p. 91.
39. Williams, "Discipline and Fun," pp. 252–3.
40. Brooker and Brooker, "Pulpmodernism," p. 91.
41. Ibid., p. 97.
42. Robin Dougherty, "Review of *Face/Off*," in Arroyo (ed.), *Action/Spectacle Cinema*, p. 80.
43. This observation was made by Pamela Church-Gibson in her conference paper "Of Men, Movies and Musculature: Mass Culture, Masculinity and the New Millennium," Newcastle Conference on Masculinity, 2001.
44. Ibid.
45. Dargis, "Do You Like John Woo?," p. 69.
46. Dougherty, "Review of *Face/Off*," p. 79.
47. Creed, "From Here to Modernity," p. 51.

3

STEVEN CONNOR

Postmodernism and literature

Against poetics

Postmodernism was not the invention of literary critics, but literature can certainly claim to be one of the most important laboratories of postmodernism. Perhaps because of the sheer weight of numbers in literary studies during the 1970s and 1980s, as compared with the numbers of scholars writing or students reading in architecture, film studies, or the embryonic disciplines of women's studies or cultural studies, ideas of postmodernism tended in these formative decades to be framed by reference to literary examples.

Literary postmodernism has tended to be focused on one kind of writing, namely, narrative fiction. The most influential books on literary postmodernism, such as Linda Hutcheon's *A Poetics of Postmodernism* and Brian McHale's *Postmodernist Fiction*, are devoted to postmodern fiction.[1] It seems oddly fitting that what Hutcheon calls the "poetics of postmodernism" should turn out to be most in evidence in its fiction. One might almost say that the move from modernism to postmodernism involves a move from poetry to fiction. Whether in the puckered vortex of the imagist poem or in the dynamic anthologies of allusions, meanings, and voices characteristic of long poems like Eliot's *The Waste Land*, Pound's *Cantos*, David Jones's *In Parenthesis* and William Carlos Williams's *Paterson*, the effort of the modernist poem was to condense the complexity of time and history, to make them apprehensible in a single frame. When Joseph Frank announced influentially that modern literature was characterized by its striving to achieve a "spatial form," which allowed and required the work to be seen all at once in a single cohering perspective, he was helping to form the acceptance that the representative modernist work ought to be some kind of poem, even if it at actually looked to all intents and purposes like a novel, or a play.[2] Poetry meant the scaling of time into space, of succession to simultaneity. The closely focused, highly technical form of literary analysis characteristic of the New Criticism, determined to find wherever it could structures held in taut, ironic tension, seemed to have arisen in order to respond specifically to modernist poetry. In the 1950s and 1960s, the practice of close reading and practical criticism spread these New Critical understandings of the nature and the value of literary analysis. The point of a literary training was not only to render one able to construe poems with great facility, but also to discover poems to construe – complex, dynamic, but internally balanced and self-sufficient verbal structures – wherever one looked, and to turn whatever one looked at analytically into a kind of poem.

One can name as "postmodernist" the dissatisfaction with this atemporal temper, along with the disposition to attend to that which registers the passage of and exposure to time rather than its gathering up. Where modernist literature worked on time, literary postmodernism would work in time. If modernism means the assumption that literature approaches to the condition of poetry, postmodernism means the tendency to assume that literature is intrinsically narrative. Indeed, the study of literary modernism itself seems subsequently to have been affected by this shift, as a version of modernism that had previously been focused on its representative poets – Yeats, Eliot, Pound, and Stevens – has been retrofitted by the taste of scholars and students alike to shift the focus markedly to its novelists: James, Conrad, Lawrence, Richardson, Joyce, and Woolf.

Modernism had also been characterized by efforts to establish the dignity and seriousness of the novel by developing for it a kind of poetics, centered on principles of structure. This poetics operated according to the principles of a scenography. That the question of perspective, of who "sees" and how, should bulk so large both for modernist writers of fiction and for theorists of it, such as Henry James and, following him, Percy Lubbock and Wayne C. Booth, is an indication of the strong cooperation between the emerging "poetics" of the novel and a visual conception of its form. The purpose of writing is to make its reader "see," said Conrad, in his preface to *The Nigger of the "Narcissus"*, the effect of this being to suggest the naturalness and desirability of seeing novels and stories as pictures – and, what is more, as portraits (of a lady, of the artist as a young man) and snapshots rather than as moving pictures. To be sure, many modernist novels are also much concerned with the multiplication of voices and perspectives and the concomitant difficulty of orchestrating those voices and perspectives. But one of the ways in which this orchestration takes place is by displacing questions of voice into questions of point of view. Rendering the question "Who speaks?" in the form of the question "Who sees?" makes it a question of a position rather than of an event. What is an orchestra, after all, but a spatial diagram of the means of music-making, a visible reservoir of the musical possibilities that can be unfolded in time?

Some postmodernist narratives appear, by contrast, to depend on the voice rather than on the eye, or, more precisely, to make the voice hard to encode either as a way of seeing or as itself something seen. We hear rather than see the narrators in Beckett's trilogy of novels, and the last of the sequence, *The Unnamable* (1958), gives us an unaccommodated voice, panting, ranting, and wrangling on, in a space and time that it seems to be making up as it goes along, so that whatever we seem to see of the scenes it evokes is an emanation of this voice and liable at any moment to revocation. Salman Rushdie's *Midnight's Children* (1981) is a written testimony that is similarly scored by the garrulous ragtime of the voice.

The emergence of a temporal postmodernism required more than the enhanced prominence and prestige of narrative, however; it required also a different attitude towards or theory of narrative. In fact, there was a considerable time-lag between the growth in the privilege accorded to narrative over poetry and the development of a nonpoetic understanding of narrative. During the 1960s and 1970s, the rise of structuralism generated the new science of "narratology," which set itself to the job of sifting and sorting the recurrent elements of which narratives were formed. The principal techniques of narratology were derived from the analysis of folk tales and myths with large numbers of variants, in which the purpose was to reduce the apparently arbitrary play of variation to a number of recurrent structures or patterns. There was always something a little contradictory about mapping the open and unfolding processes of narrative on to static or circulating structures. Structuralist analysis of narrative was a little like trying to account for a game of solitaire by demonstrating that the pack was organized into four suits of thirteen different values. Such an explanation accounts for the game only in the sense of showing the elements of which it is made up. It does not explain what is intrinsic to the game, which is to say the particular path taken from an unsorted to a sorted condition and the patterns formed in the process of playing it out: the slow building of possibilities, the retardings, and rushes towards the goal. What escapes this analysis is precisely the playing of the game, which is to say, the game itself.

These strains came to the surface in certain examples of poststructuralist analysis of narrative. One example would be Roland Barthes's *S/Z*, a reading of Balzac's story *Sarrasine*, which attempted to apply the categorial and permutative techniques of structural analysis in such a way as to leave the act of reading open and infinite.[3] Even a narratologist such as Gérard Genette, whose work consists for the most part of careful discrimination and ordering of the constituents of narrative, is nevertheless drawn to moments or examples where narrative appears to exceed or perturb categories.[4]

It was not until the mid 1990s that these internal strains within the understanding and analysis of narrative produced the first significant secession in the name of postmodernism. Andrew Gibson's *Towards a Postmodern Theory of Narrative* draws on the work of Lyotard, Deleuze, and Derrida to argue for an analysis attuned to the mobile force of narrative rather than to its arrested or abstracted form.[5] Of course there are different forms of narrative – the epistolary novel, Bildungsroman, romance, western – but it is not identical with them. The "narrative" part of narrative seems always to be pushing at or beyond those containing frames. For Gibson, the force of narrative is that in it that overflows limits. An analysis that is attuned to this movement allows the thought of becoming to flourish alongside the desire for being. This involves more than just changing the axis of analysis, so that, instead of attending to what is simultaneous in narrative, one would attend instead to what is successive. For linearity is itself a way of making time cohere, being the syntax of time's passage rather than the passage itself. Instead, Gibson is drawn to narrative forms and forces that disrupt this linearity, proceeding by darts and flashes and syncopations, yielding a conception of time as irregular and random. This has sometimes created difficulties for those for whom the only movement of time is a line and for whom the nonlinear is always processed as circular, or static.

To say that literary postmodernism has been focused on narrative is obviously not to say that all narrative is henceforth by that simple and sufficient token postmodernist, or postmodernist in the same way. As in the other arts one can usefully distinguish what may be called a reactive from an intensive postmodernism. The hegemony of narrative in the cultures of the North, in evidence in advertising and computer games as well as in the vast and unabashed craving for story evidenced by the fiction bestseller lists and in the film industry that feeds and magnifies them, represents a general intolerance of other modes of the literary, and a numbed or nauseated aversion to the powers previously possessed by poetry, the sermon, the letter, the essay, the meditation, and other, less story-shaped literary modes. This is part of a reaction against the allergy to narrative characteristic of modernism, and thus is in a general sense a symptom of the waning of modernism's authority.

But the increased interest in the powers of narrative by postmodern critics such as Jameson, Hutcheon, and McHale represents an attempt not simply to thaw out the absolutisms of modernism, but to push modernism further, in order that it renew itself in its very self-contradictions. Brian McHale's influential suggestion is that where modernist fiction is epistemological – that is, concerned with problems of knowledge and understanding, postmodernist fiction is ontological – that is, concerned with the creation and interrelation of worlds of being. This distinction has been troublesome for those who have failed to see that the latter is an intensification of the former, rather than a clean break with it. To move from epistemology to ontology, from world-witnessing to world-making and world-navigation, is to recognize that the problems of knowing are both intensified and transformed when the very acts of seeing and understanding are themselves taken to generate new worlds or states of being.

Nor should the particular salience of narrative in postmodernism mean that there is no significant postmodernist poetry or postmodernist drama, or that criticism has been silent about them. But it does seem to explain the fact that, even here, the tendency has been to focus on work that in various ways illustrates emergent force rather than completed form, working out rather than completed work. Marjorie Perloff's *Poetics of Indeterminacy* argues, for instance, that postmodernist poetry is characterized by a decompression of the ego-centered modernist lyric, in favor of looser, more accretive and improvised and contingent structures, which build their form through time, rather than imposing a form on it: the poem as pigtail or patchwork rather than ontological lassoo.[6]

Postmodernist work in the theatre has come to mean work that no longer conforms to assumed definitions of what should happen in a poem or a play. Some of this work failed to conform because it deliberately fell short or failed to meet the minimum requirements of a genre. Peter Handke's *Offending the Audience* is a telling example of this. It is a play in which all that happens is that four speakers explain at great length and in great detail that they are not going to act, that there will be no scenery, no act of representation – in sum, no theatre.[7] Other examples of postmodernist theatre refused to allow themselves to be recognized as theatre by going in the other direction, the direction of excess, for instance the marathon productions of Robert Wilson, such as the opera *Einstein on the Beach* of 1976, which he co-wrote with Philip Glass, or the even more budget-bursting *the CIVIL warS: a tree is best measured when it is down*, a production planned for the 1984 Olympic Arts Festival in Los Angeles, which involved sections developed and performed by 500 performers in thirteen languages. Such theatrical events explode the frame supplied by the expectations of theatre. The experience of watching works like this seems designed to be unencompassable, to stretch and defeat the capacity to summarize it, or to gather it together into an "experience." It is a theatre that depends at once upon the traditional privilege and necessity of presence and the impossibility of being fully present at it. Postmodern theatre is theatre in which you have to be there in order to undergo this non-epiphany, to recognize that – to borrow a phrase from William Gibson, "there is no *there* there."[8]

Lying behind all these instances of exorbitance may be Jean-François Lyotard's formulation in *The Postmodern Condition* of the difference between modernist and postmodernist art. Both modernist and postmodernist art, writes Lyotard, attempt to bear witness to the sense of exposure to what romantic theorists called the "sublime," that which is unmanageably large or unmasterably complex. Both modernist and postmodernist art willingly attempt to conceive the inconceivable, express the sense of the inexpressible, and take the measure of the immeasurable. But when modernist art does this, says Lyotard, it does so in a way that nevertheless holds the experience together or reduces it to some recognizable form. The postmodernist work, by contrast, is said to be that which "puts forward the unpresentable in presentation itself; that which denies itself the solace of good forms."[9]

Postmodernist art (and postmodernist writing in particular) is therefore thought to know that it cannot match up to what goes beyond comprehension in contemporary experience. It aims to pit what Lyotard calls its "little expertise" to the task of falling short in such a way as to bear witness notwithstanding to what it must fail to encompass. Lyotard frequently describes this relation of nonrelation between the postmodernist work and the postmodern world as a relation of "incommensurability," meaning, literally, a relation of nonmeasurability. Things that are incommensurable cannot be measured against each other because no common scale or measure is available for the purpose.

But it is not often noticed that to call this lack of relation "incommensurability" is inevitably to make the idea of measurement itself, or relation in terms of size, extension, or quantity, the principal concern. One is measuring incomparability in terms of the failure of measure, in particular. It is indeed striking how often discussions of kind or genre in postmodernism resolve into questions of quantity, ratio, or proportion. So the claim about the affinity between postmodernism and narrative with which this essay began may reduce to, or at least be renderable as, a question of scale. Time means excess; the nonfinality of time means its infinity, means there is always more than you can bargain for. The work that signifies without attempting to capture the eventfulness and becoming of things is a work that either falls short of its object in order precisely to dramatize its shortfall, or engorges itself, in order to seem to approach to the infinite (but still, in the end, must acknowledge that it falls short). It is the possibility that postmodernism may have something essentially to do with disturbances of scale and proportion that the remainder of this essay will attempt to enlarge.

Orders of magnitude

Modernism is a curious mixture of abstraction and excess. The principle of abstraction is to be seen in modernism's various eschewals and denials, for example in the turn away from referential objects in modernist painting and the withholding in modernist fiction of the traditional satisfactions of rounded characters, absorbing plot, and happy endings. The principle of excess works, in contradiction to the subtractive principle, to increase art's scope, for example by allowing many more kinds of subject into literature and art – madness, sexuality, boredom, fantasy, randomness – and demanding many more ways of rendering those subjects. It is often said that, for modernism, less is more. Many a modernist work contrived to be less and more at once: less than the world in its concentration and condensation (the events of a single day in Joyce's *Ulysses* and Woolf's *Mrs Dalloway*) and yet containing more than the world in its accumulation of allusion and interconnection.

Perhaps no modernist narrative has been subject to such a variety of readings as Joyce's *Ulysses* (1922), making it exemplary both of modernism and of postmodernism. Early readers saw *Ulysses* as an aleatory wallow in the filth of circumstance, its stylistic incontinence exactly parallel to its refusal to leave out details of human life such as defecation, masturbation, and perverse sexual fantasy. But a modernist reading of the novel's relation to modern life was also available from the moment of its appearance. This reading takes its lead from T. S. Eliot, who famously represented the "mythical method" of *Ulysses* as a way of giving an order and a meaning to the otherwise futile disorder of the world. This was extended into a full-blown modernist account of the novel in the elaborate and semi-authorized explication offered by Stuart Gilbert.[10] It now became clear that the novel was no simple surrender to the chaotic phenomena of modern urban life, but was rather an elaborately crafted deterrence of them. In the parallel it constructed between the wanderings of Homer's Ulysses in the *Odyssey* and the movements of Leopold Bloom around the streets of Dublin on a single day in 1904, *Ulysses* relies upon a structure which necessarily abstracts and simplifies the manifoldness of the world. Modernist readings of the novel, such as Gilbert's, and the many subsequent explications he encouraged, spelled out this logic. Once one understood the nature of Joyce's project, the seemingly unmasterable complexity of the work could be cancelled down like the orders of magnitude on either side of an equation. Modernism contains the promise that, once one grasps its algebra, even a work like *Ulysses* adds up to reassuringly less than the sum of its parts.

But, after this balancing of the books, a third kind of reading of the novel started to become possible during the 1970s and 1980s. Where modernism saw a work heroically making sense of flux and chaos, and guaranteeing the powers of art as a last outpost of order in a world in which religion was expiring, science had thrown in its lot with war and commerce, and politics was being taken over by the mob, postmodernism began to think that the very flux that modernists saw as a threat might actually be an energizing force. Twenty years ago, examination papers in English literature routinely demanded that students show how modern literature coped with the problem of disorder, as though that condition were a given. But the word "disorder" is rarely met with now in examination and essay questions, having been replaced by words like "multiplicity," "proliferation," "openness," and "hybridity," words that suggest that the unordered is an exhilarating provocation rather than a traumatizing ordeal. Rather than representing a threat to be tamed, the multiple becomes a promise or horizon to which art must try to live up. Few things evidence the naturalization of postmodernism more emphatically than the fact that what used to look like disorder now looks like brimming plenitude.

This does not represent a simple giving up of the kind of aesthetic privilege claimed by the modernist work, for postmodernism had up its sleeve another form of privilege for literary art. The early years of postmodernism in literary studies saw a strong and pervasive "linguistic turn." The plenitude which postmodernist fiction would set out to match was represented not as a plenitude of things, but as a plenitude of words. It is in this sense that a work such as *Ulysses* can begin to be construed as a postmodernist work. The structure of the novel is an abstraction or reduction of the world; but the way in which this structure is elaborated enables the novel to claim to include, or at least to imply its inclusion, of something like the whole world. If abstraction in literature means that the world must give way to the word, then the sheer proliferation of verbal and stylistic forms in *Ulysses* can allow the multiplicity of the world back in the form of the multiplicity of the word.

By the 1980s, only the oldest of old fogeys was still asserting that the greatness of *Ulysses* consisted in the way in which it reduced the world to rule, or transfigured it into form. Everywhere one looked, *Ulysses* was being discovered and proclaimed as the great precursor of postmodernist novels in letting in, or letting itself out into, the multiplicity of things. The fact that this multiplicity was taken to be a condition of language and an effect of the power of language in the world meant that the legislative function of the novel remained intact, if shakily so. Rather than retreating from worldliness into the Word, postmodernism could continue to embrace the world, though on the condition that this world was known and shown to be made up of words. Where modernist literary texts acknowledged their linguistic constitution in a blushing or grudging manner, postmodernist texts candidly embraced and celebrated their wordedness in the form of wordiness. Postmodernist texts turned modernist worries about the limits of language into a chattering polyglossary. Where a writer like Beckett enacted the kind of shrivelling away of language under the pressure of doubt, postmodernist texts were excited by the prospect of the illegitimate, the unspeakable, and the unknowable. They became exorbitant, exuberant. Above all, they grew *big*.

Mention of the work of Beckett must signal a pause in this argument about the defining incontinence of postmodernist fiction. Beckett is reported to have contrasted his work with that of Joyce in terms of their relative capacity. In Joyce, words are made to do "the absolute maximum of work," said Beckett: "The more Joyce knew the more he could. He's tending towards omniscience and omnipotence." Beckett saw his own work as tending to the other extreme, of ignorance and impotence.[11] Thus, where Joyce's works reach towards maxima of allusive inclusiveness, first of all seeking to encapsulate an epic history of Europe in the account of a single day provided in *Ulysses*, then in *Finnegans Wake* seeking to recapitulate all the stories that have ever been written in all languages, Beckett's works stage a series of defeats, retreats and dwindlings. His stark prose text *Worstward Ho* (1983) is conjured out of the very desire to get on with the business of going back, alternating between the reach for accretion signified in the word "on" and the glum thumbs-down of its palindromic retraction, "no": hence, "nohow on." Borrowing a fine old schoolgirl snigger, we could say that where Joyce's modernism conjugates like a verb, Beckett's postmodernism, like the cases of a noun, declines.

In one sense, Beckett's refusal of the arts of success might be said to mark the inauguration of postmodernism, in that it involves a refusal of modernist potency. Beckett's "minimalism," his systematic noncompliance with the labour of accumulation and display of largesse, and his embrace of the art of impotence set a considerable precedent for artists of every known denomination looking for ways of letting things be, or taught to see the excitement of such an enterprise. In another sense, the austerity of Beckett's work, especially his later work, such as *Company* and *Ill Seen Ill Said*, seems like the last reassertion of a modernist impulse to master the world in the word, though not by bulimic absorption of reality, but rather by anorexic abstention from it. The work will define and maintain its integrity by an ascesis rather than an excess. Beckett's work can be said to be postmodernist in its powerful remission of the power of the artist, and its suspicion of the idea of the integrity of the work, but modernist in its continuing sense of the fragile, residual vocation of the condition of "being an artist," even if one is condemned to failure.

But there is another way in which, for all their apparent slim pickings, Beckett's works have nevertheless proved a richly suggestive resource for writers of the sort of fiction that gets called postmodernist. For Beckett's art of retraction always seems countermanded by the drive to resumption, repetition, and reproduction. Rather than simply disappearing from view, Beckett's work disappears *into itself*, endlessly recycling characters, ideas, and word-fragments. The mysterious *perpetuum immobile* of Beckett's writing, in all its persistence and resilience, along with his own restless travels between genres, media, and even languages (writing most of his works twice, in English and in French, and taking a close, proprietorial interest in the German and Italian versions of his work), makes it seem to exemplify a curious, self-consuming kind of obesity.

It is this principle of self-aggrandizement that makes the link between Beckett and the less ambiguously big fiction of postmodernism intelligible. Among the heavyweight works associated with postmodernism we might mention the novels of Thomas Pynchon, Gabriel García Márquez, Carlos Fuentes, John Fowles, John Barth, Salman Rushdie, and A. S. Byatt. Even shorter works of postmodernist fiction seem designed to suggest amplitude and spread: the novels of Angela Carter might be an example here. Critical writing about postmodernism has evolved its own larger-than-life style to register this outsize quality. One can expect to be told by reviewers and critics of postmodernist novels that they are "teeming," "tumultuous," "many-stranded," "multicolored," "compendious," "heteroglossic," "encyclopedic," etc.

Realist fiction was forced into dropsical distension because it felt it had to measure up to the world. When modernist fiction grew big (Proust, Mann, Musil, Joyce), it was in an effort to consume the world. Postmodernist fiction became big in an effort to outdo the world. In saying this, it must also be recognized that there is little in this postmodernist rivalry between word and world of the sense of obscurity or obstacle to be overcome. Both Woolf and Joyce resorted to earthworking metaphors to describe the work of writing their novels, Woolf speaking of "digging out" caves of memory and of the past behind the present appearance of her characters in *Mrs Dalloway*, and Joyce describing the writing of *Ulysses* as like boring into opposite sides of a mountain in the hope of meeting somewhere in the middle. The postmodernist work of fiction borrows its energy from a world it conceives of as accomplice rather than as antagonist. Rather than pitting its resources against a resistant world, postmodernist fiction attempts to outdo the world in the way the surfer does, staying audaciously just ahead of the wave from which all his impetus derives.

One of the apparent exceptions to this aspiration to the outsize in postmodernist fiction is Don DeLillo, even though he has often been represented, alongside Salman Rushdie, as the most representative of contemporary postmodernist novelists. Indeed, one of the very best summary accounts of postmodernism uses DeLillo's novel *White Noise* as a kind of syllabus of postmodern motifs, interspersing its own commentary with illustrative reports on and extracts from the novel.[12] In their exploration of the instability of identity, the enigmatic omnipresence of information, the cryptic excesses of consumption, the global power of spectacle, and the ironic sense of the interweaving of disaster and triviality, DeLillo's works form a seemingly perfect fit with postmodern theory. Just as John Frow uses *White Noise* as a reservoir of postmodern themes, so *White Noise*, like other DeLillo novels, seems equivalently to draw on postmodern theory for its material. But this may be precisely the point at which the thesis about DeLillo's postmodernism may start to fray. For if DeLillo's work and the postmodern condition that it seems to document go so hand-in-glove together, then what has happened to the principle of unrepresentability or incommensurability? How does the fittingness of DeLillo's postmodernism fit with the failure of fit that is supposed to be a postmodern principle?

It is perhaps partly in awareness of this overcongruence between his work and the theory that it bears out that DeLillo undertook to produce his own big novel. *Underworld* (1997) is big in the way that "condition of America" novels traditionally are, namely because of its internal diversity. From its beginning, the novel establishes a rhythm of gathering and dispersal. The opening chapter evokes the famous last game of the baseball World Series of 3 October 1951, won by the New York Giants against the Yankees with a home-run hit by Bobby Thomson. Present in the crowd are Jackie Gleason, Frank Sinatra, and J. Edgar Hoover, along with a young black kid called Cotter, who has literally gatecrashed the game. The focusing effect of the game is intensified by the fact that the news has just broken of the Russian detonation of an atom bomb. The first chapter ends with Cotter running off clutching the ball that has been hit out of the field of play and, so to speak, into the novel. Thereafter, the book reads like a slow-motion explosion from the cosmological big bang of this moment. It is held together not so much by the characters or their intersections as by the continuing itinerary from hand to hand of the ball used in the game – or what is alleged to be it – in a version of the school composition theme of "The Travels of a Sixpence."

The novel is excessive not just because of the number of characters and storylines it contains, but because it also seems to generate so many mirrorings or models of its own construction. One of these models establishes a paradoxical ratio between life and time:

> There is a balance, a kind of standoff between the time continuum and the human entity, our frail bundle of soma and psyche. We eventually succumb to time, it's true, but time depends on us. We carry it in our muscles and genes, pass it on to the next set of time-factoring creatures, our brown-eyed daughters and jug-eared sons, or how would the world keep going. Never mind the time theorists, the cesium devices that measure the life and death of the smallest silvery trillionth of a second . . . We [are] the only crucial clocks, our minds and bodies, way stations for the distribution of time.[13]

The idea is that a life paradoxically contains, as a kind of advance fund or store, the lifetime to which it will seem to be subject. Just as a life may be both a clock that measures the passing of time and a battery that, so to speak, gives time out, so may a book seem both to contain time concentrated between its covers, and to be exposed to the passing of time. Any book both takes place in time and itself, as we say, takes time. In asking whether a lifetime belongs to the individual or not, the book seems simultaneously to be asking whether the time of its reading is inside or outside it.

The notion that time might be stored, dispensed, and depleted as well as merely lived, as though it were a substance rather than a condition, connects with the book's concern with waste. Nick Shay, one of the most important characters in the novel, is an expert in waste management. Just as what matters in the novel is what moves in the space between individual characters – the baseball, for example – so waste is a kind of peripheral or in-between substance. In a sort of homage to Pynchon's *The Crying of Lot 49*, another postmodernist novel that uses the idea that the world may be held together by the secret, spiralling interconnectedness of things, *Underworld* offers a vision of a world in which waste, or the principle of nonconnection and insignificance, has itself become an organizing principle.

> Cities rose on garbage, inch by inch, gaining elevation through the decades as buried debris increased. Garbage always got layered over or pushed to the edges, in a room or a landscape. But it had its own momentum. It pushed back. It pushed into every space available, dictating construction patterns and altering systems of ritual. And it produced rats and paranoia. People were compelled to develop an organized response. This meant they had to come up with a resourceful means of disposal and build a social structure to carry it out – workers, managers, haulers, scavengers. Civilization is built, history is driven.[14]

The noise has become the signal, the surplus has become the essence. In thematizing this question, in offering its own vision of a history centered around detritus, the novel both acknowledges its own wasteful excessiveness and partially redeems that condition by making excess its privileged theme or meaning. Is the sheer breadth and bulk of the novel intended to signify a Lyotardian unrepresentability, a sublime of waste, or does the novel's own systematizing of waste add up to a scheme, a principle, a work, an economy? Perhaps the postmodern has come to consist in the very disturbance of scale – what Paul Virilio has gloomily called the "pollution of life-size that reduces to nothing earth's scale and size"[15] – which makes it difficult to determine this kind of ratio.

But perhaps another reason for the success of outsize postmodernism such as DeLillo's is that the value of incontinence has become so generalized. In our all-you-can-eat advertizing culture, enough is nowhere near as good as a feast, and to be any good at all a feast must be inedibly large. We might suggest that the sublime, which Lyotard defined as the apprehension of something too large or too complex to be apprehended by a conceptual understanding, now is more likely to provoke not awe, but a kind of voracity and the reassurance it gives. The sense of not being able to master the hugeness and complexity of things can become a consolation, a way of being at home within one's limits, while also being allowed a thrilling peek into immensity.

The difference between modernist and postmodernist conceptions of scale is brought out not just by the differing values of length, but also by a transformation in the value of brevity. The modernist short story represents narrative bending or folding inwards on itself, to mimic the concentration of the imagist poem, with its vortical chimney of energies. The short story bulks large in the fiction of many modernist writers: James, Conrad, Joyce, Lawrence, Woolf, Mansfield, Nabokov; its point often being to distil and inhabit a "moment of being." It is not that there is no temporal extension in these stories; but they tend to focus on the moments of revelation, realization, or transformation, at which suddenly everything is made clear, and time is therefore drawn to an epiphanic point. The modernist short story gathers time up. Modernist novels like Virginia Woolf's *To The Lighthouse* may similarly focus around isolated moments that are charged with significance.

Postmodernist writers have also been drawn to the short story: Jorge Luis Borges, Donald Barthelme, Robert Coover, and Italo Calvino being notable examples. But the postmodernist short story is characterized not by insulation and concentration, but by eccentricity and interference. Where the modernist short story aims at a completion through subtraction, postmodernist writers use the short story in order to display connectedness without completion. This interest in the interference patterns set up across short narratives leads to the distinctively postmodern phenomenon of the book formed from suites or complex ensembles of separate fictions. One of the first of such works was Robert Coover's *A Night At the Movies* (1987), a collection of fictions unconnected in their plot but forming a linked sequence in terms of their shared project of reworking a series of cinema genres.[16] Another example is Julian Barnes's *A History of the World in 10½ Chapters* (1989). The book opens with an account of the biblical flood told by a woodworm lodged in the timbers of Noah's Ark, and runs through a series of historical episodes linked by the idea of voyages and arks. One tells the story of the terrorist hijacking of a pleasure cruiser; another recalls the story of the shipwreck of the French frigate the *Medusa* in 1816 and the painting of its disastrous aftermath by Géricault. Another story tells of the expedition to Mount Ararat of an astronaut who has got religion. The book's title teases its reader with the ludicrous failure of fit between the largeness of world history and the crass smallness of the ten and a half chapters in which it is to be condensed. It is suggested that, within this arbitrary, partial, and abridged account of the history of the world, it is the half-chapter, a parenthesis on the unassimilable, disordering powers of love, that is at the heart of things.[17] Iain Sinclair's *Downriver* (1991) also demonstrates the possibilities of the (non)cohering collection. It consists of a series of narrative "postcards," segments of narrative or fantasy involving an even larger and more disparate collection of characters from a century or so of London's East End.[18] The stories can live neither with nor without one another. David Mitchell's rather more friendly collection, *Ghostwritten* (1999), consists of nine separate stories, all involving different characters in different parts of the world, but held together by threads of coincidence and parallelism. In one story, we learn of a Hong Kong solicitor living what turns out to be his last day of life, who has despatched a chair to the wife from whom he has separated. In a later story, the chair arrives, as though it had been posted from one part of the book to another.[19]

All of these works may be said to be structured according to a logic not of development, or of the unfolding of a preexisting form, but of compilation, a word that is often taken to mean a piling or heaping together, but may in fact derive from Latin *compilare*, meaning "to plunder."

The disorderly short-story sequence is matched by the implicated sequences of novels written by Samuel Beckett, Paul Auster, and John Banville. Rather than giving us a series of events in an order that either follows a "natural" chronological sequence or is available to be reconstituted as such by the reader, Paul Auster's *New York Trilogy* constructs a labyrinth of inconclusive whodunnits that have little connection with one another in terms of plot but seem nevertheless to form a tissue of mutually enclosing narratives in which relations of succession are neither dispensable nor easily decidable.[20]

In this it anticipates John Banville's *Frames* trilogy (though both are anticipated by the mysterious recurrences of characters and events in Beckett's trilogy).[21] The first novel in Banville's sequence, *The Book of Evidence*, is a confession by the tricksily self-inventing Freddie Montgomery, which narrates the sequence of events leading up to his imprisonment for the murder of a young servant girl during the course of an art robbery. The second novel, *Ghosts*, tells of a group of seven characters stranded on an island, perhaps somewhere off the coast of Ireland. The narrator of the novel, Montgomery, has evidently been released from prison and has come here to act as the amanuensis of an art connoisseur, Professor Kreutznaer. It is as though we were presented with *The Tempest* as told by a kind of posthumous, spectral Caliban. In the third novel, *Athena*, Montgomery, now with his name changed to Morrow, is inveigled into working for a small-time gangster, authenticating a series of paintings that he recognizes as coming from the house where his murder was committed. In the process, he meets and has an intense affair with a woman he names only A. She seems to be an attempt on the part of the narrative to bring to life Josie, the murder victim of *The Book of Evidence*, who has already reappeared as the remote and mysterious Flora in *Ghosts*. The sequence can be read as the attempt, by imagining a world that will escape the inventions of artifice, to give back through literary artifice a life casually taken in the pursuit of art. By returning on itself and undoing the work of time, the sequence attempts to liberate itself from fantasy and artifice, and therefore open itself up to succession, newness. But, as the title of the sequence indicates, each novel frames and is itself framed by the others, and every new birth, or movement forwards into the unprecedented, is haunted by the shadow of recurrence. The fact that the novels never quite add up – as instanced, for example, in the fact that all the paintings (by painters whose names are near-anagrams of "John Banville") playfully evoked in *Athena* turn out to be forgeries, apart from one called *The Birth of Athena* – may represent the possibility of an art that can be atoned for with what lies beyond art only through its acknowledgment of what it cannot include, or be at one with.

Paradoxically, this sense of the ungraspability of the world has resulted in some areas in a fiction consciously organized not in temporal ways but according to flatter, more arbitrary models. Literary fiction began to adopt as its model the encyclopedia, the guidebook, the dictionary, the game. Examples here might be Italo Calvino's *The Castle of Crossed Destinies*, which generates its narratives from a tarot pack; Primo Levi's evocation of the Holocaust in terms of the chemical elements in *The Periodic Table*; Georges Perec's *Life: A User's Manual*, a jigsaw puzzle of intersecting stories centering on the inhabitants of an apartment block, which is provided with an index, a chronology and checklist; and Milorad Pavic's *Dictionary of the Khazars*, a half-fanciful account of a vanished seventh-century empire rendered in the form of interlocking dictionary entries, which was issued in "male" and "female" editions, differing from each other only in one crucial section.[22] A notable recent example is Richard Flanagan's *Gould's Book of Fish*, which tells its story of Australia's colonial past through a taxonomy of fish.[23] If narrative may be defined roughly as that form of reading that is constitutively exposed to interruption because of the demands of life and work and therefore made up of linked resumptions (the novel read at one sitting being the counter-factual ideal towards which the modernist novel perhaps strives), system-fiction of this kind both makes possible and enjoins a reading time made up, so to speak, of interruptions rather than resumptions. One is encouraged to make dips and forays into the text in the way in which one consults a dictionary, rather than being carried along on the temporal line of the fiction. Such fictions reveal an antagonism between the broken time of reading and the regularized time represented both by the idealized all-in-one-go of the temporal instant and by the idealized all-at-one-sitting of the narrative line.

Fiction has always subsisted upon the larger ideological fiction of the reader's continuous and uninterrupted attention, or the synchronization of the narrative time of the novel and the reader's actual reading time. In a postmodern epoch, this normative link between reading time and the individual subject begins to dissolve, as technological resources are developed that will perform acts of reading vicariously or at a distance, recording, sorting, and storing information for acts of reading at different times, which no longer have an obvious or regular relationship with the reading times (or even perhaps the lifetimes) of individual readers.

Under these conditions, it is a matter for the novel no longer of keeping its reader in step with it, or of protecting itself against interruption, but of synchronizing with what can be called a "culture of interruptions." In such a culture, in which time is out of step with itself, the past and future being made present to us in simulation, and the present deferred and distributed into other times, a general condition prevails of what I once called "contretemps" – "counter-time."[24] Two features in particular characterize this culture. One is the massively increased frequency of cultural impingements of all kinds, as different cultural forms and media encounter one another and exchange their characteristic cadences, tempi, and durations. To take only one example: on the one hand, while the discontinuous attention encouraged and required by contemporary television may seem antagonistic to novel-reading, television can also borrow the temporality of the novel on occasion, for example in the solemnity and slow, accretive release of the classic serial. Novels, on the other hand, can also borrow the total flow and flickering of attention of television and visual media generally – examples here would be Angela Carter's *Wise Children* (1992), Salman Rushdie's *The Satanic Verses* (1987), and Michael Westlake's *Imaginary Women* (1987). The mimicries and miscegenations of such a culture offer themselves as so many breakings in by one form on another.

The second feature of the culture of interruptions is the development of new forms of analog and digital reproduction, especially in audio and video-tape and associated technological forms, for the storage, retrieval, and manipulation of information of all kinds. Such technologies generalize the habits of unpredictable and discontinuous readership that had been characteristic of the novel in earlier periods, for they expose every real-time performance or event to the possibility of under-reading and over-reading, threatening their capacity to control interpretation and response in the audience, and contaminating the primal scene of their live performance with the possibility of other scenes, styles, and speeds of readerly consumption.

Postmodernist fiction responds with narrative structures and processes that seek to ramify rather than to resist this general interruptiveness. Examples here would be the recursive collisions of worlds in Joyce's *Finnegans Wake* (1939); the proliferating, imbricated times of Gabriel García Márquez's *One Hundred Years of Solitude* (1970); the shifting time-frames of Rushdie's *The Satanic Verses*; the temporal compendia contained in John Barth's fiction, especially *Chimera* (1972) and *The Tidewater Tales* (1987); the structured interferences of Christine Brooke-Rose's *Amalgamemnon* (1984); and the interceptive procedures of Italo Calvino's *If On a Winter's Night a Traveller* (1979), made up as it is of a series of part-novels that keep cutting across one another.[25]

More recently, and following in a fairly direct line from the experiments in cut-up and do-it-yourself fiction represented by B. S. Johnson's *The Unfortunates* (1969), a novel supplied in twenty-seven separate sections that may be assembled and read in any order,[26] there has been the appearance of hypertext computer novels. Among the best-established of these are Michael Joyce's *Afternoon: A Story* (1987), which offers different readers (or individual readers at different times) multiple options for following through different aspects of plot and character; and Shelley Jackson's *Patchwork Girl* (1995), which is a kind of electronic improvization upon Mary Shelley's *Frankenstein* that offers to make good the promise, contained in the novel, of a female monster. It makes available to the reader a kit of text fragments that can be stitched together in many different configurations, each building a different, textual body for the monster. If these texts still remain in the grasp of the author, who has devised the pathways and digressions, the possibility of configuring such works in networks of association would make available wholly unplanned forms of reading, as readers move not just from level to level within a single hypertextual environment, but also between different hypertext environments. Writers such as George Landow have seen the development of hypertext as a literalization of the dreams of infinitely open readings proposed by poststructuralist theorists of the 1970s.[27]

But perhaps even hypertext is an attempt to ride the wave of something that is in fact much bigger. Since relatively early in the computer revolution, communities of users have been building fictional worlds out of collective acts of fabulation. The MUDs or "multi-user domains" of the 1980s have grown in size enormously. Indeed, the sheer scale of the MUD seems to be part of its point. A website announcing a recently developed game/narrative environment, *TriadCity*, promises that

> the sheer scope of possible player experience is much larger than most imaginary environments. Where a large adventure-style MUD might have 3,000 rooms, TriadCity will have more than 30,000 when complete, with tens of thousands of automated and non-automated characters interacting. And this includes just the world inside the city walls; a potentially infinite world awaits outside.[28]

One could never read even a fraction of the stories accumulated in such an environment without giving over one's whole life to the enterprise. But, of course, this has been true in a sense since at least the beginning of the nineteenth century, by which time the amount of published fiction had outstripped the capacity of any one individual to read it in a lifetime. But, in previous eras, the literary text, and especially the work of fiction, represented an alternative to the world: in order to read, one retreated from the world, or suspended it. Now, fiction and world seem absolutely to interpenetrate, seeming more and more to be woven from the same fabric. How are we meant, as we say, to take in this condition? How do you measure the world and the world-making act of story up against each other, how do you fit story into the world and the world into story, when each so thoroughly includes and is made up of the other? In continuing to make orders of magnitude unignorable, postmodernist fiction seems to show that we cannot entirely do without the old systems of weights and measures, as we attempt to take readings of a world that has gone off the scale.

NOTES

1. Linda Hutcheon, *A Poetics of Postmodernism: History, Theory, Fiction* (London and New York: Routledge, 1988); Brian McHale, *Postmodernist Fiction* (London: Methuen, 1987).

2. Joseph Frank, "Spatial Form in Modern Literature," in *The Widening Gyre: Crisis and Mastery in Modern Literature* (New Brunswick: Rutgers University Press, 1963), pp. 3–25, 49–62.

3. Roland Barthes, *S/Z*, trans. Richard Miller (New York: Hill and Wang, 1974).

4. Gérard Genette, *Narrative Discourse*, trans. Jane E. Lewin (Oxford: Blackwell, 1980).

5. Andrew Gibson, *Towards a Postmodern Theory of Narrative* (Edinburgh: Edinburgh University Press, 1996).

6. Marjorie Perloff, *The Poetics of Indeterminacy: Rimbaud to Cage* (Evanston, IL: Northwestern University Press, 1981).

7. Peter Handke, *Offending the Audience and Self-Accusation*, trans. Michael Roloff (London: Methuen, 1971).

8. William Gibson, *Mona Lisa Overdrive* (London: HarperCollins, 1995), p. 55.

9. Jean-François Lyotard, *The Postmodern Condition: A Report on Knowledge*, trans. Brian Massumi (Manchester: Manchester University Press, 1984), p. 81.

10. Stuart Gilbert, *James Joyce's "Ulysses": A Study* (London: Faber, 1930).

11. "Moody Man of Letters," interview with Israel Schenker, *New York Times*, Sunday 6 May 1956; section 2, p. 3.

12. John Frow, "What Was Postmodernism?," *Time and Commodity Culture: Essays in Cultural Theory and Postmodernity* (Oxford: Clarendon, 1997), pp. 13–63.

13. Don DeLillo, *Underworld* (London: Picador, 1997), p. 235.

14. Ibid., p. 287.

15. Paul Virilio, *Open Sky*, trans. Julie Rose (London and New York: Verso, 1997), p. 58.

16. Robert Coover, *A Night at the Movies, or, You Must Remember This* (London: Heinemann, 1987).

17. Julian Barnes, *A History of the World in 10½ Chapters* (London: Cape, 1989).

18. Iain Sinclair, *Downriver (or, The Vessels of Wrath): A Narrative in Twelve Tales* (London: Paladin, 1991).

19. David Mitchell, *Ghostwritten: A Novel In Nine Parts* (London: Sceptre, 1999).

20. Paul Auster, *New York Trilogy* (Los Angeles, CA: Sun and Moon Press, 1986).

21. John Banville, *The Frames Trilogy* (London: Picador, 2001). The trilogy first appeared as *The Book of Evidence* (London: Picador, 1988), *Ghosts* (London: Secker and Warburg, 1993), and *Athena* (London: Secker and Warburg, 1995).

22. Italo Calvino, *The Castle of Crossed Destinies*, trans. William Weaver (London: Secker and Warburg, 1976); Primo Levi, *The Periodic Table*, trans. Raymond Rosenthal (London: Joseph, 1985); Georges Perec, *Life: A User's Manual*, trans. David Bellos (Boston, MA: D. R. Godine, 1987); Milorad Pavic, *Dictionary of the Khazars: A Lexicon Novel in 100,000 Words*, trans. Christina Pribicevic-Zoric (London: Hamilton, 1988).

23. Richard Flanagan, *Gould's Book of Fish: A Novel in Twelve Fish* (Sydney: Picador, 2002).

24. Steven Connor, "Reading: The *Contretemps*," *Yearbook of English Studies* 26 (1996), pp. 232–48.

25. Italo Calvino, *If On a Winter's Night a Traveller*, trans. William Weaver (London: Secker and Warburg, 1981).

26. B. S. Johnson, *The Unfortunates* (first published London: Panther, 1969; reissued, London: Picador, 1999).

27. George P. Landow, *Hypertext 2.0* (Baltimore, MD, and London: Johns Hopkins University Press, 1997).

28. "What Is TriadCity?" <http://www.smartmonsters.com/TriadCity/Differ/big. jsp>, accessed 25 April 2003.

4

STEPHEN MELVILLE

Postmodernism and art: postmodernism now and again

Perhaps a failure, certainly a problem

Writing on "postmodernism" at the beginning of the twenty-first century is an uneasy business, and perhaps particularly so in relation to the visual arts. The term has undoubtedly gained a certain cultural currency, but its meaning (or meanings) and value seem in many ways more obscure than ever. The most secure usages – in dance and in architecture – seem to pick out a moment of something like style in ways that make it little more than one further moment within the general artistic logic of modernism, while the attempts to use it in ways that pick out some presumably deeper challenge to modernism over all do not seem to have succeeded in doing so. The phrase "postmodern art" seems for the most part to have run aground somewhere between these two possibilities, having secured no particularly strong style or period usage but also having failed to secure any broader or deeper generalization of postmodernism. At times it can seem that all that is actually left is a sort of gesture toward some general social or cultural fact that is taken to be peculiarly resistant to, or evasive of, the kinds of fuller parsing that accompany our usage of terms such as "modern" or "modernist." This may sometimes function more or less successfully as a password of sorts, but it also feels like a word or phrase whose grammar has more or less mysteriously failed it. One might, of course, hope that what appears as its failure is in fact, but unrecognizably, its actual grammar.

It does seem to be a distinctive feature of the term "postmodern" as it is currently employed that it can serve, in a way that neither "modern" nor "modernist" can, as a qualifier of the word "theory," and this is clearly related to the role "theory" is often said to play in relation to the arts or practices we are tempted to call "postmodern." It is as if "postmodernity" were to be recognized by its affinity for "theory," or as if it were the presence of "theory" internal to those practices that signalled their postmodernity. Of course, that might also mean that postmodernism was itself first of all a "theoretical" development – a transformation in the status or condition of "theory," its coming to have claims and consequences very different from what we have expected of theory or theories.

These are distant observations, the noticings of a non-native speaker or someone pretending to be a non-native speaker, and they cannot gain expression apart from the liberal use of quotation marks that mark off the distance between the language the observer speaks and the language he or she observes and remarks. But one of the things this observer of postmodern usages will be unable to avoid noticing is that a closely related practice of quotation marks seems to be integral to the formation called "postmodern theory," and that this finds, here and there, some kind of echo in many of the arts or practices also qualified as "postmodern." It becomes tempting to think that the figure of the non-native speaker or the one who pretends to be a non-native speaker has some kind of intimacy with "the postmodern," and so perhaps also with its fugitive grammar and its peculiar grip on or by "theory."

The general thought to which the observer may now be inclined is that postmodernity – and the observer now imagines that he or she is somehow part of it and so does not know any longer whether it can be hedged off in quotation marks or not – is somehow deeply about something like our (his or her) non-nativity, about a presence or a present that never quite happens. The term "postmodernism" would have as its main job to remark our incapacity to address our present from within it. This would be its radicalism with respect to all things modern and modernist, as it would be also the ground of its own elusive and peculiar grammar.

One might then find oneself – observer, observed, postmodern – saying something like: The problem with modernism – thing and term alike – lay precisely in the assumption of universality and presence that accompanied its claims to some kind of purity or absoluteness. The postmodern difference lies precisely in its refusal of such universality; and it is this refusal that underlies both its radical critique of the modern and its inability to establish itself with the kind of authority and centrality that characterize claims to modernism. What looked at first like an uneasiness in or real trouble with the term is in fact a direct consequence of its actual strength and value. Postmodernism just is the collapse of universals, and so it can only ever be local and strategic, announcing itself only in order to disqualify all those terms that would let it mean and matter the way "modern" and "modernist" have. Once spoken, "postmodernism" gives way to a dispersion of terms that no longer play the games of history and universality and presence that have been the warp and weft of our imaginations of art, culture, society, and so on. "Postmodern theory" would be something like the set of propositions expounding or justifying this situation; but it would also be essentially exposed to these same conditions and would thus be itself local, strategic, and dispersed.

There are undeniable satisfactions in coming round to such a formulation: it has a certain pleasing symmetry, a gratifying reflexivity, and a seeming ability to account for itself wholly and without remainder, an appropriate philosophic and implicitly social or political weight; and perhaps above all it holds the promise of a kind of release into ourselves, a real freedom from burdens (of the past, of communality, of imagining larger futures) we no longer have the strength or desire to bear. But these very satisfactions can also seem to be exactly those once promised by the modern, and, contemplating them, one may feel one's self tumbling into a kind of black hole in which postmodernism suddenly appears as modernism collapsed on and through itself, a universe turned inside out to no greater profit than that we have managed to render ourselves definitively strangers to one another, equipped with nothing more than a language we do not believe to be our own and can no longer imagine as shared or sharable – as if a certain solipsism were suddenly revealed at the heart of the modern.

Pulled up short by this thought, we might well find ourselves returning once again to the opening question: is this the postmodern or its failure? If we take it as its failure, we should need to know enough about what the postmodern was or might have been to show what it means for it to fail. We should want also to be able to say something about why it should have failed in the way it evidently has. And we should presumably want our account to be sufficiently fine-grained and specific that we could get a satisfyingly sharp sense both of what is at stake and of how the concrete forms through which those stakes are or have been registered might matter to them.

Some visual claims

If there is a single point of purchase for discussions of postmodernism in the visual arts, it is Douglas Crimp's 1979 exhibition "Pictures" and the texts that quickly came to surround it, most notably Craig Owens's "The Allegorical Impulse."[1] Among the other artists included in this exhibition and playing a central role in Crimp's and Owens's theses on postmodernism, one might want to particularly mention Laurie Anderson and Cindy Sherman. But I shall start from the work of one of the (now) less well-known artists in the "Pictures" group, Robert Longo.

Among the works by Longo that were shown are a number of drawings, largely made by studio assistants after photographs made by him. The drawings are very large – 8 ft × 5 ft – making the single figure represented in each somewhat larger than life. The figures are clearly caught in a moment of some kind of extremity – twisting, turning, bending, the placement of their limbs more nearly an index of that action than a matter of separately willed activity. Their clothing is hard to place – somewhat formal, office wear perhaps, but also slightly "retro," possibly closer to "costume" than to "clothing"; and it too is caught up in whatever the action rendered is – ties whirling away from the body, straps slipping off a shoulder. Modeling within the rendered figure frequently vanishes into the sustained black of pants, suit, or skirt, giving the figure the feeling almost of a silhouette cut out against the blank white ground, which remains almost wholly unreadable except where the figure's feet seem more or less clearly to demand some unrepresented surface on which they press. Although the figures feel "theatrical" in some way, it is less clear that they can be described as "dramatic," because it is not at all clear whether the action one sees is to be grasped as a salient moment within some larger narrative possessed of something like a plot – this is, say, the moment at which the figure is struck by a bullet – or if one is simply witnessing one not particularly privileged moment within a continuing sequence of movements – the figure is dancing and this is just the moment the camera and drawing caught, not fundamentally different from any of the others it might equally have caught. By the same token, one is unsure whether one is witness to an action (dancing, jumping, playing air guitar) or to a reaction (recoiling, falling backward) to something being done or something being imposed. The clinging theatricality of the images is similarly ambiguous as between action and something closer to reenactment or performance. One does not know what sense might be discovered in the image were the background so apparently cut away to be restored, just as one does not know what difference it might make to have this particular image bracketed by its immediate "before" and "after." One is simply left before the image with its striking salience and with its opposed and undecidable readings. These various features are all closely related in the account Crimp and Owens offer of this and the other work in the "Pictures" show; for starters, it is probably enough just to say that they all seem to reflect a certain foregrounding of mediation in the work.[2]

The most embracing claim made for the work of Longo and the others associated with Metro Pictures was that it was, in a special sense, allegorical. Before turning to that special sense, it is useful to take some note of the rough historical scope of this claim. The rejection of allegory as a way of making or receiving visual art appears to be one of the foundations of the practices we call "modernist." To claim that the work of the postmodern artist is allegorical is to suggest that visually it appears or behaves more like the work of, say, Poussin than like that of Jackson Pollock. Our ordinary understanding of allegory already suggests at least some of the significant differences here. On one side, allegory is a way a work means, and that seems to be at some odds with the strong tendency within modernism to refuse meaning in favor of something like the pure experience or sheer being of the work. On another side, allegory assumes a real sharing of compositional means across diverse media, whereas modernist art, especially visual art, has insisted upon the separation and distinction of mediums. Both of these modernist tendencies are particularly prominent in the criticism of Clement Greenberg and Michael Fried. The highest praise either has to offer takes the deceptively simple form of asserting that this work – by Pollock, or by Morris Louis, or by Frank Stella, to name a few of the artists one or both of these critics have been most closely associated with – just is a painting (and in each case this claim will be understood to have the force of a kind of revelation or discovery of what painting has been all along; painting is historically understood to move toward ever more explicit showing of its self, so the "is" in "This just is a painting" is peculiarly emphatic, almost an active verb rather than a mere copula).

Having gone this far, it is clear that one cannot get a great deal further by looking to work of Poussin's kind. While this new work does evidently share in some way in the kind of artifice – the explicit posing, let us say, of meaningful tableaux – that we find in more traditional allegorical painting, it does not appear to lend itself to the decoding we take to be central to allegory. Longo's photographic drawings, like Cindy Sherman's early film stills, suspend us before something that appears to mean or to show something, but the clues that would let us extract that meaning from the work – something we are certainly entitled and expected to do before the Poussin – are unavailable. We seem to have the interval between surface and depth that is constitutive of allegory without actually having the depth that anchors or justifies – underlies and supports – that surface.

For the traditional allegorist, allegory is a practice of continued metaphor: "the ship of state" is, by itself, a metaphor, but if we continue that metaphor across the entire surface of the canvas or the whole length of a poem so that the waves and storms, the lands and people, safe arrivals and shipwrecks all count in making out the fate of the state, we shall have an allegory – a pictorial or poetic whole that everywhere and consistently means something other than its surface literally shows. The artists associated with Metro Pictures appear to be working with a different understanding of allegory's duplicity, one that is ultimately rooted in a different vision of how signification works. One can get some feel for this by imagining allegory as something that might equally be driven not by metaphor but by a kind of continuous punning, each word or image opening explosively away from itself. Such allegory is wholly an effect of signification – the working of words or images in relation to one another and apart from anything one might want to imagine as an underlying ground of meaning. Our description of this work is thus tugged back toward elements of our description of modernism: this work, too, does not go beyond itself; it shows itself as what it is and does not hand itself over to a meaning that exists prior to and outside of it, as we may be tempted to say Poussin's painting does.

This is perhaps enough to let one see that the claim to a certain postmodernism advanced here has some real historical bite: this work is seen to be renewing a capacity for or engagement with signification that modernism had refused, and in doing so it is also opening the apparent self-enclosure of the modernist medium, if not exactly to the world, then at least to the full range of discourses through which it appears. And it is doing so not by returning to premodern practices and imaginations of meaning but by rediscovering their ground as properly internal to the material dimensions of the modernist medium itself (allegory is a possibility not of meaning but of visual or linguistic signification and so leads not beyond them but only further into their play). The notion of a medium remains as central here as it was for modernist art and criticism, but the notion itself has shifted away from something more or less like material presence and toward an emphasis on what is inevitably mediated in it – in, for example, the ways in which painting, however abstract, brute, gestural, and so on it may be, does not escape the play of signification everywhere at work in and as our seeing of the world. Whatever the Pollock is, it is also an image, and works that way too; and what may bother us in it is the desperation of its attempt to pretend otherwise, to imagine itself as beyond or exempt from such circulation, from reproduction, signification, historicity. The purest works of postmodern allegory are perhaps Sherrie Levine's photographic reappropriations of prior photography in their naked assertion of the absolute priority of repetition and mediation over originality and presence.

The positions taken by Crimp and Owens find their most immediate informing context within the particular history of postwar American art and criticism and most specifically in relation to the perceived dominance of the formalist criticism of Clement Greenberg and Michael Fried. As this work is most commonly presented, it involves an image of artistic modernism as a process of purification in which each of the arts finds itself driven back ever more forcefully and narrowly on to the resources that are its and its alone. The motor force for this movement is variously understood in Marxist and Kantian terms, but both references insist on the necessity of art's finding for itself a position from which to withstand the demystifying and leveling force of modern culture and society. This critical position is widely understood to have come to crisis in the 1960s with the radical challenges of both

Pop Art and Minimalism, and Michael Fried's 1967 essay "Art and Object-hood" has been equally widely understood as a crucially explicit statement of this crisis.[3]

Both Crimp's and Owens's essays first appeared in the pages of *October*, a journal whose theoretical and critical interests, from its founding in 1976 through the present, have been responsive above all to the complexities of artistic work that is most directly described as postminimalist and have been notably less responsive to the tendencies associated with Pop.[4] While it risks still further schematizing an already highly schematic account, it seems right to say that what Pop most evidently contributes to in the work of Anderson, Levine, Longo, Sherman, and the others may be a certain alertness to matters of quotation, reproduction, and image. But this taken by itself need lead no further than painting practices of the kind currently associated with, for example, David Reed or Fabian Marcaccio. While it is an important fact that such current practices can appear importantly to follow from the work that initially drew Crimp's and Owens's attention, it is also important that in strong senses they do not in fact do so, or do so only partially and weakly. (In general, such work participates in and contributes to a collapse of the postmodern into something one might call merely "posthistorical.")

Pop Art appeared in many ways as a simple break with modernism, a refusal or parody of its central terms. Minimalism, by contrast, appeared as something closer to an intolerable consequence of those terms: the movement that was understood to lead painting ever closer to its pure, central self suddenly appeared to pass right through that self (thus revealed in that passage as empty) into something else. Painting turned out, at its core, not to be painting at all but merely the deployment of an object in space (and because this was discovered as a fate or fact of painting, the relation of these objects to the kinds of work one recognizes as sculpture was, and remains, obscure). For Greenberg and Fried, this was self-evidently a failure of art; the heart of Fried's attack on Minimalism is a powerful attempt to show how Tony Smith's own account of the experience informing his art falsifies both. For Rosalind Krauss and other strong champions of minimalist work, it functioned more nearly as a revelation of the embodied subject as a limit to the claims for pure optical presence apparently urged by Greenberg and Fried, and in Krauss's later work this was further extended by the recognition that the subject, in its embodiment, was itself always also an effect of structure, of its installation in and appropriation to language. One can imagine this latter proposition as the basis on which Minimalism gains a certain access to the *donnés* of Pop – but it will then be important that the quotation and appropriation should appear in this context not as ways in which a subject refers to itself but as the very stuff out of which it is constituted. One might then try out the difference between reading one of Cindy Sherman's early *Untitled Film Stills* in the lineage purely of Pop, where it will seem to engage the circulation of certain images of women in American culture by referring to them (that is, one will understand Sherman's images first of all as "references"), and by taking them as postminimalist self-portraits that have the division of the subject as both their object and their condition. In the first case, Sherman "herself" will either be outside her images, merely posing them for critical reflection, or she will be imagined to slide unknowably beneath or behind the imposed images. In the second there will be nothing behind the image to know, since Sherman insists in it (it is, multiply, her image, of her). It is important to notice that the first reading does not need its object to be a photograph – all that really counts for it is the visible reference to film, and its being a photograph is, at best, a matter of something like decorum; for the second reading, its being a photograph is part and parcel of what it means to say that the image is *of* Sherman. The goal of this exercise would be to make clear the ways in which the work itself has become relational: the structure we have called allegorical cuts into the work itself and is not simply a matter of what or how the work means: it structures how it is, what it is as a work.

The more one explores the immediate art-historical and critical context of the work in question, the more one sees how specific and precise the claims for it are, and so also how easily they can become blurred or lost; one sees in particular how easily the structural reading can fall back into one that is merely thematic. So perhaps the claims for the preeminence of "medium" so central to Greenberg's and Fried's accounts of modernism may not so much have gone away as become radically more specific, internal to the work as such; one might go so far as to say that, where the earlier account imagined a process of ongoing self-criticism participating in a progressive revelation of the medium, this newer work pushes that self-criticism all the way through to the medium, blurring the distinction between work and medium in such a way as to make each work or body of work responsible for showing the medium whose internal division makes it possible.

This account clearly touches on a number of elements that enter into the general sense of "postmodernism" outlined in the first part of this essay: practices of quotation or appropriation are clearly central to much of the work; there is a certain placing of the subject, both authorial and represented, in question; there is a studied distance from such terms as "originality" and "genius" in favor of a practice oriented to mediation and repetition; there is a marked interest in rhetorical or signifying excess, and an equally marked engagement with discursive structures that function not simply in art but in visual culture more broadly (in rather different ways, Sherman and Anderson are perhaps the most salient instances); and one may well feel – Anderson and Longo might be particularly apt examples – a certain haunting of this work by the figure of the "non-native speaker" that so oddly emerged in that first part. But it should also be clear that there is more than one way to gather these elements up, to understand how they fit together, what they are supported by, and what their consequences might be.

The relevant differences here can be put in a couple of discrete but inter-related ways. The contrast that is already at work in the account offered of the work has been between gathering it up more or less purely in the lineage of Pop Art or granting a more crucial role to Minimalism. A closely related theoretical contrast that became more visible as the 1980s unfolded and the term "postmodernism" became more general and more generally discussed would be between gathering it up more or less on the side of Fredric Jameson's account of "postmodernism" as the cultural reflex of late capitalism (this is roughly the vector of Owens's own subsequent work) or on the side of Jean-François Lyotard's understanding of "postmodernism" as modernism's rewriting and thus less a "period" in the historical sense than a kind of re-punctuation within a discourse with which it cannot be said to break. (One might try out the related thought that the postmodern would be a break with the modern only insofar as it repeats modernism's own impulse toward rupture, which it thus reinscribes or revises in a particularly complex manner.)[5] One way to explore the relatively good fit between the art-historical and theoretical contrasts would be to note how far both the Pop and Jamesonian alternatives go towards opening the thought of the postmodern as distinctively post-historical, the thought that a certain historical motor is for one reason or another unavailable or in abeyance, leaving the resources of the past as little more than a kind of image bank available for whatever recycling the present appears to call for; and how far, by contrast, the more deconstructive account goes toward opening or reopening an account of the complexity of our inhabitation of history, asking about the ways in which such things as revision and interpretation, forgetting and repression, may be less stances toward history than dimensions of it.

These contrasts, and their linking, can claim no more than rough justice and do so in part by offering still rougher conceptual shortcuts through terrain that has its proper historical and sociological thickness. Such roughness, in its justice and its injustice, is only extended by the further claim that, in relation to the visual arts, what was almost twenty years ago a discussion or debate about "postmodernism" has now almost wholly vanished into the academic contrast between an emergent study of "visual culture" and a more or less resistant practice of what continues to be interested in calling itself "art history." Visual Culture is clear enough that its chosen domain is that of the image; art history, its substantially deeper institutional root-edness notwithstanding, is perhaps only beginning to take up the question of its object at the level implicitly demanded by contemporary art and criticism.

An interlude

In the summer of 1996 Rosalind Krauss, certainly a strong supporter of much of the work discussed in this essay, was centrally involved in two events that offer a measure of the distance traversed and that are distinguished in this context above all by their lack of interest in the term "postmodern."

The first was an exhibition at the Pompidou Center in Paris entitled *L'informe: Mode d'emploi.* The extended argument in support of the exhibition can be fairly said to continue on the line marked out by Owens's "Allegorical Impulse" (with its deep debt to Krauss's own earlier and continuing work) by pushing its terms through to the fuller sense she finds for them in the work of Georges Bataille. The exhibition did not, however, present itself in any relation to anything called "the postmodern" – it was, one might say, an attempt to make visible what modernism is when one recognizes it as everywhere structurally opened beyond itself, having "formlessness" as, if not exactly its truth, at least its condition. Krauss and her co-author, Yve-Alain Bois, are at some pains to distinguish their appeal to Georges Bataille's notion of the *informe* from apparently similar appeals underpinning several other more or less contemporary exhibitions centered on "the abject." That she makes the difference out largely in terms of highly contrasted readings of the work of Cindy Sherman should not be surprising, nor that she does so in terms of a contrast between "operational" and "semantic" readings that is for all practical purposes equivalent to the contrast between "structural" and "thematic" readings this essay has drawn upon.

The summer of 1996 also saw a special issue of *October*, assembled by Krauss and Hal Foster, devoted to the question of Visual Culture and especially its orientation to the image. For many of *October*'s readers, accustomed to thinking of it as a journal distinguished by its openness to "theory," its willingness to take such a polemic stance toward what was widely taken as "theory's" natural outcome came as something of a surprise. There are good reasons why it ought not to have done so, reasons this essay has hoped to recall to visibility.

Can we say that these two events stand for the two vanishing points of "postmodernism" – its disappearance into the rewriting of modernism and its disappearance into the theoretical field understood to subtend the appeal to Visual Culture? If we are willing to say that, are we willing also to say that such vanishing points are proper to it, a consequence of what it is and how it happens? Do we count one as its success and the other as its failure, or are the two more closely twinned than that?

Who do we think we are?

Closing an essay with questions finally won through to is a fine old practice, and in many ways I am content if I have indeed managed to bring out something of the force and scope of questions that at the moment appear more in need of asking well than of any pretense to resolution. But you have good reason to remain unsatisfied insofar as the largest questions raised in the introduction – questions about the stakes involved in claims to postmodernism, about prospects of solipsism, about whether or how far we stand as strangers to one another – are left untouched.

The narrative I have sketched around the appropriation artists of the early 1980s is driven by concerns about painting. The history in question is one in which painting is or has been clearly dominant – has been the privileged form in which modernism has seemed to cast and claimed to find itself. This would appear to be at least reflected in the strongly pictorial orientation of most of the work of these appropriation artists, and one can perhaps imagine even arguing that this work ought to be considered, in some extended but justifiable sense, as belonging to – taking its sense from, making its difference in – painting. There would be reasons for this. One would be following Hegel in saying that within the plastic arts painting is the medium that most fully reflects and engages our finitude (in confining itself to two dimensions, in implying a content or meaning that escapes it and that it can only represent, and in making an issue of its boundedness). That finitude is the modern fact *par excellence*, the fact that modernity has most difficulty in, and so also most need of, acknowledging. That acknowledgment is what is needed would itself be a further registration of that finitude; any attempt to sort out the grammar of this word leads back to the priority it assigns to the other and the prior.

For Hegel, the dominance of painting is also always partial (another dimension of its orientation to finitude) and shared with the other distinctively modern arts, music and poetry. In all these respects, painting is strongly opposed to sculpture with its compelling claim to make present both itself and the people that gathers around it, that finds or founds itself as a people there, in that shared presence (the model for this, hardly surprisingly, being classical Greece). As a moment in the history of art, modernity is marked by the impossibility of sculpture in this strong sense; it may continue to be made, but no people can find itself there any longer and its means and possibilities are deeply determined not by its own resources, which are in a certain sense closed to it, but by those of painting, poetry, and music.

While the standard descriptions of Clement Greenberg see him, with considerable justice, uneasily stranded between Marx, in his early writings, and Kant later, these Hegelian motifs are interestingly at work throughout his writings, as they are also in the sculpture he (and subsequently Fried) most care about, particularly the work of David Smith and Anthony Caro. This is work that is with some justice described as pictorial, as assemblages of outer aspects apart from any inner core,[6] and one can imagine it as doing the work Hegel assigns to sculpture – a work that would in this instance be balanced between imagining and realizing a community – under the conditions of modernity or under the conditions of painting. It presents itself to its beholders without claiming to find any more substantial ground of the gathering it nevertheless accomplishes; there is no deeper or more inward core that gathering can claim to prolong and express.

Minimalism was as fully a crisis for this line of work as it was for painting, and Fried's implied critique of it as sculpture turns on the way it both lays claim to a center, positing an interior of which it would be the expression, and simultaneously empties that center, withdrawing it from the beholder, who is left in his or her isolation, able to establish a relation neither to its presented surface nor to its pretended depth and so also finds himself or herself in no coherent relation to those other viewers with whom his or her experience might be shared. The tendency of minimalist artists to refuse the status of sculpture for their work, either generating narratives that bind it to painting or claiming the neutral status of object, would, of course, be part and parcel of this.

Richard Serra is the sculptor – there is no evading the term here; he insists upon it himself – who most clearly and firmly grasps the changed situation of sculpture in the late 1960s, creating a powerful body of work that can be seen as testing over and over again the capacity of minimalist procedures to have fully sculptural outcomes. The result can be described as minimal in a special and somewhat different sense: what Serra produces is work that is undeniably sculptural and nothing more, as if its largest ambition were simply to assert the blunt fact of sculpture over against its modern impossibility. At best, the achievement remains uneasy and suspect. For some it comes too heavily encumbered with a rhetoric of (distinctively masculine) genius and too many images of artistic heroism, for others it banks too much on the otherwise unearned power of its materials and scale, and it seems rarely if ever able to break with what Fried had picked out as minimalism's distancing and even threatening of its isolated beholder. This last charge would be the most serious – a way of saying that at its best it manages no more than to assert the possibility of sculpture while still remaining enclosed in the minimalist space and condition of Objecthood. This may, of course, just be what it means – what it is – to make sculpture in its impossibility, and so it is also a way of saying Serra's achievement.

That the work means to be something more, or other, than this is abundantly clear. From early on Serra aims at some kind of compelling intervention into what is called "public space," but for an extended period his efforts in this direction (the most dramatic example would be *Tilted Arc*) only end up reasserting isolation and privacy as the effective truth of such spaces: such community as one might imagine forming around this work has no shape beyond its isolated individualities, and that is no community at all.

Gravity, Serra's 1993 piece for the Holocaust Memorial Museum in Washington, DC, does not at first appear much different from anything that has gone before – the materials and their working are pretty much the same and it appears to figure within its site in much the way Serra's public work usually does, by dividing it. On the facing wall one reads a text from Isaiah that one might imagine spoken also in front of *Tilted Arc* – "You are my witnesses." This text belongs, of course, not to the sculpture but to the museum and more crucially still to the event the museum exists to have witnessed. But *Gravity*'s way of speaking for – or being spoken by – its context is new in Serra's work. *Tilted Arc*'s "witnesses" are locked into their individuality and so the truth they presumably are witness to has to do with the falsity of the presumed publicness that is the work's context. Serra puts the underlying thought well in an interview: "Site-specific works emphasize the comparison between two separate languages, their own and that of their surroundings, unlike modernist works which give the illusion of being autonomous from their surroundings, functioning critically only in relation to their own tradition."[7] *Gravity*'s witnesses witness in their plurality rather than in their isolated individuality, and, in finding themselves before or around the sculpture, find also a place where two languages or two voices merge, each speaking for or through the other.

That *Gravity* does this is evidently a matter of its details: of, for example, its scale and the particular orientation that lets it both divide and in some measure disrupt the rather ceremonial stairway while not setting itself exactly against it. It is a matter also of its verticality, which is less a matter of its actual height or proportion than of the slight angle the steel block makes with the steps, so that it feels, as Serra has put it, impaled on the landing, as if fallen into that position rather than built up or based there (and so it has also the contingency of that event). It is that action just here that gives the piece the force the title puns into explicitness. *Gravity* no longer simply testifies to the impossibility of sculpture, although it is important that it continues to do that, but also stands irreducibly as an achievement of it (of sculpture, of its impossibility).

Gravity, I suggest, occupies a special place within what is now visible as a rather large body of distinctively later work by Serra. Much of this is built out of doublings and repetitions, either of earlier work or within the pieces themselves. Perhaps particularly prominent within this body of work are the *Torqued Ellipses*, made from 1996 on. As a geometrical form the ellipse is defined by its double divided focii, and the *Torqued Ellipses* are made by, in effect, further doubling that eccentricity, the pieces stretched between one ellipse on the floor and that same ellipse rotated away from that initial orientation and describing the upper limit of the work. The structural logic here is close to that found in such earlier works as *TWU*, where an externally visible geometric ground plan is resolved into a different geometrical opening on to the sky, visible only from the interior. The *Torqued Ellipses* are also allied to another series of works, roughly contemporary with them, in which the pieces – for example, *Snake* at the Guggenheim's new museum in Bilbao – are built out of a linear doubling of enchained and variously inverted sections, reminiscent of *Tilted Arc* except that they are as if peeled off a conical surface rather than a cylinder. It is hardly surprising that all of this rapidly generates a further series of *Doubled Torqued Ellipses*. The fluid passages between the more linear instances and those that draw on the ellipse suggests strongly that these interlocking logics of eccentricity, doubling, and repetition are ways of realizing the containment or self-containment of a work equally defined by its capacity to pass beyond itself.

You are no doubt owed more by way of description both of individual works and of how this body of recent work can be said to hang together, but instead I shall simply offer what I hope will be a usable characterization of the specific difference underlying it, and a remark or two about why I think it matters.

What happens here is a passage from a notion and practice of site-specificity imagined in terms of establishing a relation between two separate languages or discourses to a practice in which the relation to the site is bound up with the terms of the work's self-relation, as if what has to be shown, made palpable and visible, is the priority of difference over the languages or discourses to which it gives rise. Or, alternatively, it is as if what has to be shown is the way in which art's discontinuities are exactly the terms of its continuity with the world. If this is not exactly a return to the image of autonomy Serra has always contested, as well as to the kind of Hegelian image of sculptural presence that accompanies it (and it is neither), it is nevertheless a turn against the image of radical and resistant separateness his early work fostered. At least under this description, Serra's recent work picks up in a rich and deeply interesting way on the sculptural problematics of David Smith and Anthony Caro. If, about that earlier work, it seemed right to speak of a community gathering itself across its dispersion, perhaps with these pieces of Serra's it is more accurate to speak of a dispersion open to encounters, to the forming and reforming of transient communities, finding their terms of mutual acknowledgment only as they happen or fail to happen. Something like that is what seems to happen as one moves within and among the *Torqued Ellipses* – something like this seems to be their difficult and interesting social fact.

And should we call this work "postmodern?" Or do we more nearly feel it as offering us a kind of peace with a question oddly both insistent and empty? I do not really know how to choose here. But I would hope that if one does choose to call it postmodern, that calling can only be for a time and in a time, the calling also a certain hearing or reading of modernism. And this would be a form of the difficult peace it offers – a peace that has less to do with settling or affirming boundaries and grammars than with admitting their contingency and exposure to interruption as conditions of their always uneasy inhabitation.

NOTES

1. See Douglas Crimp, "Pictures," *October* 8 (1979), and Craig Owens, "The Allegorical Impulse", parts 1 and 2, in *Beyond Recognition: Representation, Power, and Culture* (Berkeley, CA: University of California Press, 1992).
2. For a broader view and fuller account of Longo's work, see Howard N. Fox, *Robert Longo* (Los Angeles, CA: Los Angeles Museum of Art, 1989).
3. See Michael Fried, "Art and Objecthood," in *Art and Objecthood: Essays and Reviews* (Chicago, IL: University of Chicago Press, 1998).
4. But it is notable that Owens finds an important precursor for the allegories of the Metro Pictures group in the work of Robert Rauschenberg, particularly as that work is discussed by Krauss in her essay "Rauschenberg and the Materialized Image," *Artforum* 13 (1974).
5. See Fredric Jameson, *Postmodernism, or, The Cultural Logic of Late Capitalism* (Durham, NC: Duke University Press; London: Verso, 1991) and Jean-François Lyotard, *The Inhuman: Reflections on Time*, trans. Geoffrey Bennington and Rachel Bowlby (Cambridge: Polity, 1991), especially the essay "Rewriting Modernity."
6. See Rosalind Krauss, *Terminal Iron Works* (Cambridge, MA: MIT Press, 1971).
7. "Dialogue with J. C. Schlaun," in Richard Serra, *Writings, Interviews* (Chicago, IL: University of Chicago Press, 1994), p. 171.

5

PHILIP AUSLANDER

Postmodernism and performance

At first glance, the phrase "postmodernism and performance" seems straightforward: a critical rubric that designates the postmodernist practices within a specific cluster of cultural categories. Yet even when touched upon lightly, this rubric shatters into a multitude of related yet distinct shards, each a different facet of the relationship it describes. I shall attempt in this chapter to outline some of those facets. I shall not survey the field; rather, I shall discuss selected works and figures that exemplify particular issues and practices. I shall also focus on the performance scene in the United States, simply because it is the one I know best. Although I shall discuss several types of performance, I shall focus largely on questions concerning postmodernism and theatre because the particularly problematic relationship between those terms raises provocative questions. The complexities and difficulties of thinking through the conjuncture of theatre and postmodernism are worth discussing for the ways they point to issues involved in locating postmodernism within the history and practices of particular art forms.

In large part, the conceptual complications of the relationship between postmodernism and performance derive from the instability of both terms, neither of which has a single, universally agreed-upon meaning. I shall not survey definitions of postmodernism here – suffice it to say that those who have made connections between postmodernism and performance have worked from a range of different definitions of postmodernism. I shall say something about the term "performance," however, because each of its meanings suggests a different connection to postmodernism. We most commonly associate the concept of performance with events whose appeal is primarily aesthetic, whether the traditional performing arts (theatre, dance, music, and opera), popular entertainments (e.g. circus, stand-up comedy, Las Vegas floor shows), or newer art forms (e.g. performance art). I shall leave music (and, for the most part, opera) aside, and observe that theatre, dance, and stand-up comedy have all been discussed in relation to postmodernism.

The concept of postmodernism functions in at least three different (but not mutually exclusive) ways in relation to aesthetic performance, depending on the type of criticism involved. (I speak primarily of criticism because, with the signal exception of some early postmodern dancers, performing artists generally have not used the word to describe their own work; it is a term used mostly by critics and scholars.) Relative to aesthetic performance, postmodernism has been used as: (1) a periodizing concept, (2) a way of describing the contemporary culture in which performances occur, and (3) a stylistic descriptor. Uses of the term "postmodern" to describe a moment in history (1) are somewhat difficult to distinguish from uses of the term to describe contemporary culture (2). Nevertheless, some commentators attempt to define a postmodern era by addressing such questions as when it began and how it differs from earlier historical moments, while others are content to describe contemporary culture as postmodern without delimiting its historical boundaries. Some critics use "postmodern" in still another way, as a stylistic term to identify new developments in aesthetic genres with well-established conventions (3). All three uses intersect, of course, since most critics ultimately wish to discuss how the distinctive characteristics of particular performances relate them to postmodernism in its historical and cultural senses.

One important manifestation of the differences between the historical and cultural conceptions of postmodernism is evident in the different uses of the adjectives "postmodern" and "postmodern*ist*." The term "postmodern" is often used to identify a particular historical period usually thought to have begun after World War II, though careful attention to the dates of most of the performances I discuss here will suggest that postmodernism in performance is largely a phenomenon of the 1970s and 1980s. "Postmodernist" often refers to cultural works that possess stylistic features that align them with postmodernism as a structure of feeling, an episteme, rather than a chronologically defined moment. Some performances that are clearly postmodern in the historical sense (that is, later than and different from their modern counterparts) are not necessarily stylistically postmodernist. (Some varieties of postmodern dance and most performance art monologues are examples.) I shall use the difference between "postmodern" and "postmodernist" as an heuristic to demonstrate throughout this essay the complexities of thinking about performance in terms of postmodernism.

The three uses of the term "postmodern" that I have described occur in discussions of theatre, dance, and the other performing arts. Another genre of aesthetic performance central to discussions of postmodernism is performance art (also called performance, art performance, and, especially in the United Kingdom, live art). The relationship of performance art to postmodernism is different from the traditional performing arts in that performance art, which developed after World War II (though it has antecedents in the performance experiments of the early twentieth century avant-garde movements) is often taken to be an intrinsically postmodern art form, both historically and stylistically, rather than an art form with postmodern manifestations. One does not hear about "postmodern performance art" in the way one hears about "postmodern dance" and "postmodern theatre" because it is assumed that there is no other kind of performance art.

The final, and perhaps trickiest, definitional issue I shall mention is the way the concept of performance has become a trope in theories of postmodernism itself. Much of the discourse on postmodernism and aesthetic performance uses theories of postmodernism as grounds for analyzing trends in performance, thus suggesting that postmodernism and postmodern culture conceptually precede performance and that certain performances may be seen as symptomatic of postmodernism. But one of the earliest points at which the ideas of postmodernism and performance intersected was a collection of essays called *Performance in Postmodern Culture* (1977) (not *Postmodernism in Performance*, for instance). Michel Benamou, one of the editors of *Performance in Postmodern Culture*, adopts the opposite of the usual position in the introduction to this collection, where he identifies performance as "the unifying mode of the postmodern."[1] The dominant characteristic of postmodern culture, as he describes it, is that everything performs: technologies perform; art is no longer content to stay on the museum wall; literary critics see their writings as performances; political and social developments are performed in the public arena – the media, in particular, make political and social developments performative.

It is ironic that, whereas critical discussions of specific performance practices usually draw on ideas of postmodernism and its characteristics from other disciplines (especially architecture and literary theory), other disciplines have appropriated the idea of performance. As an interpretive paradigm, the idea of performance has been used to describe everything from static art forms to everyday behavior, to political demonstrations and terrorism, to large-scale social conflicts. The "postmodern turn" in a variety of humanistic and social scientific disciplines amounts mainly to viewing those disciplines and their objects of study in performance terms. Scholars in history, sociology, anthropology, and many other fields have come to see their respective discourses as contingent rather than absolute; as engaged with specific audiences rather than autonomous; as existing primarily in a specific, time-bound context; and as characterized by particular processes rather than by the products they generate. It is significant that one of the new, arguably postmodern disciplines to emerge from this intellectual ferment is performance studies, which takes performance in the expanded sense that subsumes aesthetic performances, ritual and religious observance, secular ceremonies, carnival, games, play, sports, and many other cultural forms as its object of inquiry and unites the tradition of theatre studies with techniques and approaches from anthropology, sociology, critical theory, cultural studies, art history, and other disciplines.

In this brief overview, we have already arrived at a disorienting postmodern juncture. When thinking about aesthetic performances in relation to postmodernism, the basic critical question is usually: in what sense is a given performance or kind of performance postmodern(ist)? Benamou turns that question around to suggest that the critical question central to discussions of postmodernism and performance is: in what ways is postmodern culture performative? Postmodernism, which seemed initially to be the privileged term in the rubric "postmodernism and performance," is now the subordinate term. What should we be looking for – the postmodernism in performance or the performance in postmodernism? Wherever we begin, we shall inevitably end up talking about both, though the emphasis here will be on the former.

Periodizing postmodernism in theatre and dance

As dance historian, critic, and theorist Sally Banes points out in *Terpsichore in Sneakers*, her crucial work on post-modern dance, "the term post-modern means something different in every art form."[2] (Banes and some other commentators hyphenate the term "post-modern"; I have retained this orthography when discussing their work.) For one thing, what counts as postmodern for any particular art form is relative to what counts as modern for the same form; the unevenness of the concept of postmodernism across the arts is partially a function of a similar unevenness in definitions of modernism. Banes defines the historical transition from modern dance to post-modern dance quite clearly, both chronologically and stylistically. "By the late 1950s, modern dance had refined its styles and its theories and had emerged as a recognizable dance genre. It used stylized movements and energy levels in legible structures . . . to convey feeling tones and social messages" (p. xiii). Feeling that "the bodily configurations modern dance drew on had ossified into various stylized vocabularies, dances had become bloated with dramatic, literary, and emotional significance, dance companies were often structured as hierarchies" (p. xvi), the first wave of post-modern choreographers (1960–73) sought to create dances that would be nonliterary in content, created from accessible movement vocabularies (sometimes based on everyday movement and using untrained dancers), and more democratic. As Banes develops her account, she does not reduce the multiple styles of dance after modern dance to a single type but still is able to offer a persuasive narrative of post-modern dance as a reaction against modern dance that occurred at an identifiable historical moment.

When we turn from dance to theatre, however, it is not possible to paint such a clear picture. For one thing, it is difficult to establish what postmodern theatre may have reacted against because a coherent description of modern theatre is hard to construct. Normally, the expression "modern theatre" refers to the realistic (as opposed to Romantic) plays and performance practices that began to develop around the mid-nineteenth century in England and culminated initially in the late nineteenth-century European realist plays of Ibsen and Chekhov, then in the realist drama that flourished in the United States and United Kingdom after World War II. To identify modern theatre with realism, however, is to imply that the postmodern impulse in theatre would be antirealistic. The problem there is that antirealist theatre developed alongside realist theatre in the nineteenth century (with the Symbolists, for instance) and really constitutes an alternative strain of modern theatre. This confusion has made it very difficult to place certain figures. For example, are Bertolt Brecht and Samuel Beckett, playwrights who challenged realism equally radically though from very different directions, to be considered modernists or postmodernists or transitional figures?

The analysis of postmodernism in theatre is further complicated by the relationship between text and performance that characterizes the form. There is a disjuncture between the performance and the text being performed in theatre that does not exist in dance. In dance, performance style and genre are encoded in the choreography. It is no more possible to perform a classical ballet in a postmodern dance style than it is to perform it in a tango style. (It might be possible to do a postmodern dance based on the underlying narrative or theme of a classical ballet – a postmodern *Swan Lake*, for instance – but that would require new choreography in a style associated with postmodern dance. It would be impossible to perform Balanchine choreography, say, in a postmodern style.) In the contemporary theatre, however, it is assumed that style is not written into dramatic texts; it is therefore perfectly possible to imagine Shakespeare or Greek tragedy performed in a postmodern style. In fact, some important examples of postmodernist theatre – such as the work of the director Peter Sellars, whom I discuss later – are precisely those in which a nonpostmodern play was presented using a postmodernist production style. Opera is an interesting case in this context in that the musical aspect is similar to dance, while the staging is similar to theatre. If one plays the score as written, one cannot perform a nineteenth-century opera in a postmodern musical style. But the same nineteenth-century opera could be staged in a postmodernist style.

We cannot explore the idea of postmodern theatre, then, without exploring the questions of postmodern drama and of postmodern production styles. For the reasons I have already suggested, very few suggestions have been offered as to what may constitute postmodern drama, but I shall risk some speculations. One simple but important point is that pluralism is historically a postmodern phenomenon in the theatre (though not necessarily a postmodernist one). The vast majority of the playwrights produced on the modern, Anglo-American and European stages well into the 1960s were white males whose sexuality generally was not discussed openly if it was not known to be hetero. As a result of the influence of theatrical movements directly informed by the identity politics of social movements in the late 1960s and 1970s, women playwrights, playwrights of color, and queer playwrights are now much better represented both in the theatre and in the monologue performances that have become the most popular style of performance art.

Though still debated, nontraditional casting in which actors whose race (and sometimes gender) does not match those of the characters they play is another form of pluralism characteristic of the postmodern stage. Intercultural performance, in which elements of performance traditions originating in different national and cultural settings are intermixed to form the theatrical equivalent of world music, is also a postmodern theatrical practice. It, too, has been highly controversial, prompting questions concerning the degree to which artists from western societies appropriate from performance traditions they do not really understand and the cultural imperialism that may be implicit in their use of such traditions. British director Peter Brook's production based on the ancient Indian *Mahabarata* (produced in 1989) was a flashpoint for these debates.

Performance art monologues

This postmodern plurality of voices is particularly evident in the monologue performances that proliferated in the 1980s and 1990s. This genre probably originated with Spalding Gray, a veteran of the New York experimental theatre scene who had worked with both the Performance Group, one of the most famous of the Vietnam War era radical theatres, and its descendant, the Wooster Group (I shall have more to say about this theatre later). Beginning in 1975, Gray became interested in working on intensely autobiographical performances that were acts of self-scrutiny for him. Initially, he worked with the Wooster Group on the series of highly abstract, collectively created

performance pieces known as The Rhode Island Trilogy. Around 1979, however, he began narrating his own life directly in a deadpan style somewhat
reminiscent of stand-up comedy. His first performance in this vein was *India
and After (America)*; he has gone on to make the autobiographical monologue his primary form of performance and continues to chronicle his life to
the present. He recounts both his professional life as a fringe performer who
flirts continuously with mainstream success and the neuroses and narcissism
that color his personal life.

Although Gray himself is a white, heterosexual, Anglo-Saxon, Protestant,
American male of upper-middle-class origins (albeit one inclined toward
lifestyle experimentation and bohemianism), he helped to open the door to
performers who self-consciously represent a range of very different identity
positions and social experiences. The performers who have availed themselves of the monologue form include Karen Finley, who has performed
intense, hypnotic rants with a feminist slant; Tim Miller, who describes
his experiences as a gay man; Charlayne Woodard, who has performed
monologues about her experiences as an African-American woman; Josh
Kornbluth, whose autobiographical account includes the experience of growing up in a Jewish Communist household; and many others. Some of these
performers, like Gray, were trained as actors, while others, such as Finley,
come from a visual arts background. Still others, like Margaret Cho, are
stand-up comics who emphasize autobiographical narrative in their performances. While some performers who employ this form remain close to its
origins in experimental theatre and performance art, others exploit its entertainment potential. The ubiquity of the autobiographical monologue was
so pronounced in the art world of the late twentieth century that one wag
described it as the screenplay of the 1990s (in the sense that everyone seemed
to have written one).

The death of character: postmodern/ist drama

Although the performance-art monologue is historically a postmodern form,
it is not postmodernist and is formally quite different from postmodernist
theatre. In an essay of 1983 pointedly titled "The Death of Character,"
theatre critic and scholar Elinor Fuchs discussed a development in theatre
that she considered to be the harbinger of postmodernism in theatre: a de-
emphasis of the modern concept of psychologically consistent dramatic characters in favor of fragmented, flowing, and uncertain identities whose exact
locations and boundaries cannot be pinpointed.[3] Insofar as most performance art monologues posit stable and locatable identities assumed to define
the performer, they are not postmodernist though they do represent part of

the postmodern trend of pluralism in performance. Taking Fuchs's observation as a starting point, I shall briefly discuss two plays: Sam Shepard's *Angel City* (first produced in 1976) and Jeffrey M. Jones's *Der Inka Von Peru* (first produced in 1984). I have chosen these examples because they provide insight into the status of character in postmodern dramaturgy. I include Shepard's play as an example of proto-postmodernist drama and also to provide a contrasting example that will help to foreground the postmodernist aspects of Jones's play.

Shepard is known as one of the most radically experimental writers associated with the New York Off-Off Broadway movement of the 1960s. Compared with some of his earlier plays, *Angel City* is relatively conventional; it has a fairly clear plot that develops in a more or less linear fashion. But when the second act begins, most of the characters are very different than they were at the end of the first act: the stereotypically sexy Hollywood secretary becomes a floor-scrubbing nun who speaks in an Irish accent, for instance. It is never quite clear whether these characters have been transformed somehow or whether they are enacting their own ideas or fantasies of themselves. In his preface to the play, Shepard states: "The term 'character' could be thought of in a different way when working on this play. Instead of the idea of a 'whole character' with logical motives behind his behavior which the actor submerges himself into, he should consider instead a fractured whole with bits and pieces of character flying off the central theme."[4]

Shepard's concept of character here certainly seems to evoke the idea of the fractured, postmodern self (though he does retain the notion of a "central theme"); in that respect, the play may be said to touch on the nature of postmodern subjectivity, a major question in postmodern culture and theory. In other respects, however, one would have to say that the play is not postmodernist at all. Shepard's decentered, fragmentary characters serve a play that is essentially satirical: Shepard bitterly attacks the film industry and indicts Hollywood for living by false, corrupting values, which it imparts to its customers. It is very possible that the characters' transformations are a result of the entertainment industry's colonization of their psyches. In its celebration of traditional values (represented by the protagonist's use of Native American ritual) that are rapidly being corrupted by the contemporary culture industry, *Angel City* is actually quite conservative.

From the point of view of one of the most influential theories of postmodernism, Shepard's overtly critical and satirical tone disqualifies *Angel City* as postmodernist despite the way Shepard points to a new, antimodern understanding of dramatic character. Fredric Jameson's discussion of how pastiche has replaced parody under postmodernism is useful to understand this dimension of theatrical postmodernism because he links it to "the disappear-ance of the individual subject," a phenomenon that has direct implications for the concept of dramatic character. According to Jameson, "Pastiche is, like parody, the imitation of a peculiar, unique, idiosyncratic style, the wear-ing of a linguistic mask, speech in a dead language. But it is a neutral practice of such mimicry, without any of parody's ulterior motives . . . Pastiche is thus blank parody, a statue with blind eyeballs."[5] Although *Angel City* is a satire, not a parody (though it contains parodies of movie genres), it is clear that Shepard had critical ulterior motives for writing it – its perspective cannot be described as neutral.

My other example, Jeffrey M. Jones's *Der Inka Von Peru*, is a play made up entirely of modified texts the author appropriated from existing sources, including a history of Peru, a romance novel, and other plays, Shakespeare's *Romeo and Juliet* and Oscar Wilde's *The Importance of Being Earnest* among them.[6] The combination of these sources produces five discrete but overlap-ping plots, most of which are melodramatic in nature. Lines of dialogue recur verbatim in shifting contexts and different versions of the same action (such as romantic intrigues) appear. While an audience may see the various plots as commenting on one another, there is no clear purpose behind this formal experiment, no direct thematic statement (as there is in *Angel City*). In Jameson's terms, the play is a pastiche of melodrama that evokes and incorporates a variety of texts and genres in a way that is often humorous but that does not provide the critical perspective of parody or satire.

Because the characters in *Der Inka Von Peru* are delineated through lines of dialogue drawn from different historical eras and genres of writing (some of the dialogue is in verse, some in prose) no character's use of language provides a consistent sense of that character's identity. Far from being individual subjects, the characters are patchworks of second-hand language who use words that clearly belong to others, not to themselves, not even to the author who created them. In his notes to the play, Jones delineates an approach to acting in which the actor breaks the text down into multiple fragments and figures out how to perform each fragment as if it were an autonomous action. The various fragments are then assembled. This way of thinking treats characters as textual entities rather than psychological ones, as collections of individual performed moments rather than products of a consistent, overall interpretation. Although Jones's description of the acting process displays a kinship with Shepard's ideas of the fragmentary character, Shepard retains the idea of a main theme – understood more in a musical sense than in a psychological one – from which the character's behavior departs, even when that behavior is wildly inconsistent. Jones's characters, who are pastiches drawn from numerous sources, have no such center.

Shepard and Jones both suggest that a postmodernist approach to acting is one in which characters are understood to be made up of fragments: words and actions that cannot be expected to add up to a psychologically consistent entity. In both the plays I have discussed here, the characters' fragmented state is the result of having absorbed their cultural environment. In Shepard's play, this is the case at a thematic level – the characters' behavior is influenced by their consumption of movies. In *Der Inka Von Peru*, however, the characters' relationship to their cultural environment is ontological, not just thematic. The characters do not represent human beings who have seen too many movies but are themselves literally collages of texts drawn from a variety of cultural contexts.

A postmodernist approach to directing

My discussion of postmodernism in dramatic literature has also been a discussion of what postmodernist acting might be. Turning from what we see on stage to the theatrical processes that created it, I shall look briefly at postmodernist directing. Modern approaches to directing might generally be characterized as emphasizing the discovery of a central action and theme in a play and expressing them through an appropriate and consistent production style. By contrast, Don Shewey describes the work of US-based director Peter Sellars as reflecting "the post-modern impulse toward cultural collage."[7] Sellars has brought the songs of George Gershwin into a play by the turn-of-the-century Russian author Maxim Gorky and modified the text of *The Count of Monte Cristo* (a play selected for the fledgling American National Theatre at least in part for its historical reference, since Eugene O'Neill's father, the actor James O'Neill, performed it throughout his career) by interpolating passages from the New Testament and Lord Byron, and music by Beethoven, among other materials. He is well known for nontraditional casting and also cast actors in his 1985 production of *Monte Cristo* who are associated with different cultural strata, including the New York avant-garde and the television industry. Rather than seeking a play's intrinsic focal points, he works associatively, juxtaposing texts and performance elements in various styles and connecting the play with other cultural texts to produce a hybrid.

As Shewey points out, Sellars's career as a director has been quite different from that of his predecessors in theatrical experimentation in that he has not had to define himself strictly as an avant-gardist but has worked in a variety of seemingly mutually exclusive cultural contexts, ranging from the Boston Shakespeare Company to Broadway to an abortive attempt to establish an American National Theatre in Washington, DC, to the world's opera houses, and to the Sydney Olympics, among many others. This is an important point: since at least the late nineteenth century, the world of performance has been stratified by distinctions between high and low culture (e.g. theatre and opera versus night-club floor shows and rock concerts) and between mainstream and avant-garde (e.g. Broadway versus Off-Off Broadway). These distinctions persist into the postmodern era, though some makers of performance have managed to transcend them. Sellars is one example; the actor Willem Dafoe, who has parallel careers as a performer with the Wooster Group and as a Hollywood film star, is another. Still another is performance artist Laurie Anderson, whose work straddles the line between avant-garde performance art and pop music and is popular with both audiences.

Postmodernism and stand-up comedy

Some popular cultural performance genres responded to the same issues confronted by the theatre in a postmodern cultural environment. Like theatre and performance art, stand-up comedy became a more diverse enterprise under postmodernism. In the United States, there is a long-standing tradition of male comics, many of them of Jewish heritage, who were joined from the 1960s onwards by African-American comics. The postmodern 1980s saw a much larger number of women than ever before doing stand-up, and both Asian-Americans and Hispanic-Americans became visible in that field as never before. Two of the postmodern developments I mentioned in connection with theatre had parallels in stand-up. As the eclipse of parody by pastiche indicated by Jameson shows, the very notion of comedy itself had become problematic under postmodernism. Comedy by definition requires stable referents, norms against which behaviors may be deemed humorous. In the absence of such norms, it is impossible to define comedy. Some comics responded by becoming metacomedians whose performances took the impossibility of being a comedian in the postmodern world as their subject.

Steve Martin, in particular, exemplified this tendency in his stand-up of the mid-1970s. Martin adopted the gestures, tone, and manner of the traditional stand-up comic, of a simultaneously smug and desperate comedian who would resort to wearing rabbit ears or a fake arrow through his head to get a laugh. The rabbit ears and arrow, novelty items available at any joke shop, represented the dead-end to which comedy had come: the only thing left to do was to recycle highly conventional signs for that-which-is-supposed-to-be-funny rather than attempting fresh comedy. Martin's pastiche of stand-up comedy was void of content: his performance persona was blank and cynical, clearly only going through the motions and treating the conventions of stand-up comedy as a dead language, as if to suggest that there was nothing left to laugh at except the idea that someone actually might try to make others laugh.

The other problematic confronted by both theatre and stand-up was that of character. Traditionally, stand-up comedians present a consistent persona to represent the perspective from which they make their comic observations. But just as some postmodernist playwrights created dramatic characters as collections of fragmentary texts rather than psychologically consistent be-ings, some stand-ups also eschewed the presentation of clearly defined comic personae. One of the most radical of these was Andy Kaufman, who appeared at some of his early club dates as The Foreign Man (later the basis for the character of Latke that he played on the television program *Taxi*). As The Foreign Man, Kaufman spoke in an almost impenetrable Eastern European accent and portrayed a completely incompetent comic who would botch the punchlines of his unfunny "jokes," then insist on starting his entire act all over again each time he made an error until the audience could stand it no longer. Kaufman did not reveal that The Foreign Man was a fictional con-struct, but would unexpectedly launch into a skilled impersonation of Elvis Presley that seemed beyond The Foreign Man's abilities and then thank the audience once again as The Foreign Man. In a television special, Kaufman added another layer to this performance by seeming to drop the character of The Foreign Man and becoming "himself," a nasty and aggressive fig-ure who demanded that the audience return items of clothing he had tossed while impersonating Elvis. This persona, while seemingly closer to the "real" Kaufman, was yet another construct, no more real than The Foreign Man or Andy as Elvis. In place of a consistent comic persona, Kaufman created a hall of mirrors in which no persona ever turned out to be a dependable representation.

Re-presentation in postmodernist performance

Jeffrey M. Jones's appropriationist playwriting and Peter Sellars's genre-busting directing are examples of theatrical practices one can describe as both postmodern and postmodernist. Nevertheless, both retain the basic procedures of the modern theatre: they are text-based and follow the Play–Production–Performance model in which a script is interpreted by a director and performed by actors. Even if the constituent elements in this process reflect postmodern culture and postmodernist aesthetics, the process leaves the apparatus of modern theatre unchallenged. Let us embark, then, on a dif-ferent quest by looking at theatrical practices that do challenge the authority of the modern theatrical apparatus.

We shall begin that quest with the Living Theatre, founded by Julian Beck and Judith Malina in New York City in the 1950s but best known for its productions in Europe at the high point of the 1960s counterculture, of which it is a famous exemplar. Beck and Malina inaugurated the Living Theatre as a poets' theatre specializing in the production of rarified dramatic works, but ultimately became interested in working collectively with other performers to create work directly without starting from a play. Their work in this vein began with *Mysteries and Smaller Pieces* (1964) and culminated in *Paradise Now* (1968). A large part of their motivation was political: as committed left-wing anarchists, they wanted the performances they made to reflect the values according to which they lived.

Directly and indirectly, two (if not three) generations of experimental theatre artists have taken inspiration from Beck and Malina's approach to making theatre without necessarily embracing their politics. The Open Theatre, The Performance Group, and the Bread and Puppet Theatre, among many other radical theatres of the Vietnam War era, took up the idea of collective creation and the notion that theatre did not necessarily begin with a script but could depart from improvization, ideas, and images shared among the cast, and similar sources. These theatres, in turn, provided models for groups that emerged in the 1980s and 1990s, their approach now often called *devising*. (Devised performance is thus distinguished from scripted theatre.)

This kind of theatre was postmodernist not only in the way it redefined the procedures and hierarchies of the modern theatre but also in its radical approach to the question of theatrical representation. Whereas it is usually supposed that the function of actors is to represent fictional beings, the performers in the radical theatres of the 1960s were often present as themselves. When the performers in the Living Theatre's *Paradise Now* confronted the spectators, saying, "I am not allowed to travel without a passport" and "I don't know how to stop the wars," they were speaking for themselves, not playing characters who were making these declarations.[8] Even when the Performance Group did Shepard's play *The Tooth of Crime* in 1972, the presence of the actors trumped that of the characters they played. This was partly because the environmental staging in which actors and audience occupied the same space necessitated that the actors speak directly to the spectators and instruct them as to where to stand or where to look. Because the actors were constantly moving in and out of character, one saw them as people who were sometimes acting and sometimes not – their presence as real performers outweighed their presence as fictional characters.

In an essay of 1982, Canadian performance theorist Josette Féral identified this nonrepresentational approach as the key difference between traditional theatre and performance art: "since it tells of nothing and imitates no one, performance escapes all illusion and representation."[9] (This is another point at which to observe that an aesthetic strategy that is postmodernist in relation to one art form may be modernist in relation to another. Féral derives her account of performance art's antirepresentational stance from the work of the art historian and critic Michael Fried, for whom opposition to representation is a hallmark of modernist visual art.)

The antirepresentational stance of the radical theatre and much performance art does indeed distinguish both sharply from conventional theatre. The monologue performances I mentioned earlier are not postmodernist insofar as they present the performer as possessed of a defined and stable identity, but they are postmodernist in their implications concerning representation, since the performer appears in his or her own person and claims to eschew fictional character. This is also true of earlier and more extreme versions of performance art, such as body art. When Vito Acconci, for example, sets out in *Conversions* (a film of 1971) to turn his body into a woman's body by burning the hair away from his breasts, attempting to enlarge them, and performing various movements with his penis tucked between his legs, it is Acconci, not a character played by Acconci, who executes these actions (and he really does perform them – he does not simulate burning his chest hair).

Of course, in all these cases the overall performance situation is more complex than the label "antirepresentational" suggests. Even though the performers do not represent fictional characters, the way their actions are framed by the performance context means that the audience does not perceive them directly as real people, either. What the audience sees is a performance persona that may resemble the performer's "real self" but is not actually identical to that self. The resulting "undecideable argument between presentation and re-presentation" (also apparent in the work Andy Kaufman did in a popular cultural context) is itself a postmodernist phenomenon, as Benamou suggests.[10]

Postmodernist political theatre

Once we move beyond the authorial and representational strategies of the radical theatres of the 1960s, however, we encounter a familiar problem: while their approach to making theatre and to representation were postmodernist, their politics and their way of making political art was not. The antirepresentational strategies of postmodernist theatre and performance art, strategies that overtly questioned the truth-value of any and all representations, could not accommodate the radical theatre's desire to represent both the society they sought to change and the utopian community they hoped to bring into being. Additionally, the radical theatre positioned itself as part of a counterculture set apart from the dominant culture. Inasmuch as the postmodern world of global communications and capital appears not to have an "outside," it seems fruitless for political artists to claim to interrogate postmodern society from such a position.

Postmodernist political art in all forms, then, does not deal directly with topical political issues in the manner of earlier political art. Rather, it must find ways of interrogating the political and social configurations of postmodern culture without leaving its own representations unquestioned and without claiming to take up a position outside of postmodern culture from which to comment on it. One theatre that developed such an approach is the Wooster Group, a New York theatre collective that evolved in the early 1980s from the Performance Group. Because of its history, many observers expected the Wooster Group to purvey a more conventionally political brand of theatre than it did and were somewhat taken aback by the Wooster Group's more oblique strategies. I shall briefly discuss one of its performances, *LSD – Just the High Points* (1984–5), to provide a sense of one version of postmodernist political theatre.

LSD, devised by the Wooster Group and its director, Elizabeth LeCompte, incorporated materials from a wide variety of cultural texts, including parts of Arthur Miller's play *The Crucible*, writings by and about members of the Beat Generation in the 1950s and LSD advocate Timothy Leary's circle in the 1960s, a reenactment of a rehearsal for *LSD*, and much else. Some of these texts were factual, some fictional; some, like *The Crucible*, were fictional recreations of actual events. The members of the Wooster Group presented these multiple texts through a variety of types of performance that included conventional acting, reading with text in hand, re-creating their own behavior from videotape, and repeating words while listening to them on a sound recording. At times, the performers spoke words associated with fictional characters while, at other times, they were there "as themselves," but these various presentations were not sharply delineated and they blended into one another. These performance strategies themselves raised questions about the interplay of presentation and representation, fact and fiction, that seemed to reflect a postmodern world in which those kinds of distinctions are no longer clear-cut.

The thematic terrain of *LSD* was broad and far-reaching. The articulation of a number of kinds of historical documentation through the varieties of acting, reading, and performing already discussed raised questions about the nature of both the documentary materials themselves and their re-presentation. Some of the materials were "official" accounts of earlier historical periods while others were more personal; the Wooster Group did their own research, interviewing members of Leary's circle. The performance implied, but did not answer, such questions as: Is informal spoken testimony more dependable than "official" (for-the-public) writings? Are there meaningful differences between the performers' reading, acting, or repeating these materials? What the production ultimately demonstrated was the eradication of difference among these many types of messages and articulations – written and spoken, factual and fictional, literal and metaphoric, public and private – through the mediation of performance; it thus mimed the eradication of such differences in postmodern culture at large. The production made no attempt to assess the truth-value of any one documentation over any other, or of any mode of presentation over any other: it was presented as much as a symptom of information's self-consumption as an analysis of it. The Wooster Group thus did not claim to comment on this phenomenon from without, but created an analytical image of an information-glutted, postmodern society by positioning itself at the interior of such a society.

To explain how the Wooster Group's image of an information-saturated society is analytical, I shall conclude by contrasting it with theatre practices that are symptomatic of postmodern culture but do not enable audiences to adopt an analytical stance toward it. Jameson points to an aspect of postmodern culture that has proven crucially important for the theatre when he uses the word "mediatization" to describe "the process whereby the traditional fine arts . . . come to consciousness of themselves as various media within a mediatic system."[11] This has meant that the theatre can no longer be seen as occupying a fine-arts context that is culturally distinct from film, television, and the other media. The collapse of the distinction between fine arts and mass media has meant that the theatre now functions as a medium and has to compete for audiences directly with the other media.

One result has been that the theatre often does not seek to provide original expression – rather it draws on film, television, and popular music for its materials. In some cases, this has meant that plays are actually live productions of films or television programs – Walt Disney's *Beauty and the Beast* is a case in point. More recently, stage musicals have been developed from the film *The Sweet Smell of Success* and the music of the pop groups Abba (*Mama Mia*) and Queen (*We Will Rock You*). To a large extent, this kind of cultural production supposes that audiences are interested only in seeing things they have seen before; the market has generally validated this supposition. When the theatre repurposes existing materials, its productions are no longer autonomous works of art but take their places on chains of individual commodities that constitute large cultural texts – in many cases, these commodities include books, sound and video recordings, fast-food tie-ins, plush toys, and bed sheets. The way the commercial theatre absorbs and recycles existing texts from other media is formally similar to the appropriationist strategies of Jones, Sellars, and the Wooster Group. Unlike the latter's self-consciously postmodernist work, however, these productions are merely symptomatic of the postmodern cultural condition and provide no foothold for an analysis of that condition.

Conclusion

Although it is possible to present a coherent developmental narrative of postmodern dance as a self-conscious response to modern dance, such a narrative is much more difficult to construct for theatre and other forms of aesthetic performance. Nevertheless, I have identified certain postmodern trends that cut across performance genres and cultural categories.

One of the most significant trends in postmodern performance has been toward pluralism and diversity. This has meant that the theatre is no longer as dominated by ostensibly heterosexual white male playwrights as it once was: plays by authors clearly acknowledged to belong to a range of other identity positions are now much more visible than in the past. Pluralism is also manifest in the still controversial practices of nontraditional casting and intercultural performance. Dance, too, has a form of nontraditional casting: since the 1960s, postmodern dance has employed a range of body types never seen previously in dance, including untrained dancers, dancers with non-athletic bodies, and disabled dancers. Even such popular cultural forms of performance as stand-up comedy reflect the trend toward pluralism: since the 1980s, the range of identity positions represented on the stand-up comedy stage and in television programs and films derived from stand-up is much greater than at any earlier time. In a different vein, I have argued here that the growing trend in commercial theatre toward repurposing existing cultural texts into performances is likewise a postmodern development.

In addition to having manifestations in the traditional performing arts, postmodernism has seen the development of new art forms, performance art among them. The term "performance art" covers a vast array of practices. I have alluded here to only two, which are at opposite ends of the performance-art spectrum. The body art of the early 1970s was conceptually and physically demanding, even seemingly masochistic. Although there are performance artists who continue to work in updated versions of that genre, including the Montenegran artist Marina Abramovic and the French artist Orlan, much performance art today takes the more popular form of the autobiographical monologue. In some hands, such as Karen Finley's, the monologue can be a highly charged and aggressive form of performance that places substantial demands on its audience. In the majority of cases, however, the autobiographical monologue is an accessible and popular form through which performance art, once considered an experimental and avant-garde genre, has entered the cultural mainstream.

Comparing the features of historically postmodern performance with performance that articulates postmodernism as a new structure of feeling, we run into contradictions. Some performance practices that are unquestionably postmodern, such as those of most performance-art monologists and much of the theatre that reflects postmodern pluralism, are not postmodernist because they rest on the epistemological assumptions characteristic of the modern, including the idea of the unitary self. Postmodernist theatre has challenged that assumption by presenting characters whose fragmentary identity is constructed from bits of cultural texts. Even in stand-up comedy, some performers have undermined the idea of a consistent, distinctive comic persona.

A similar contradiction appears when we consider the radical theatres of the 1960s. These theatres deserve a place in an account of postmodern performance on account of the ways they destabilized the hierarchical apparatus of modern theatre through their frequent elimination of the playwright in favor of collectively devised performances. These theatres frequently eschewed traditional actorly representation in favor of performers who appeared in their own persons, as is often the case in performance art as well. (This shift led to a practical and theoretical distinction between traditional acting and a new category of performance, which includes acting alongside other ways in which people present themselves to others.)

Nevertheless, the political and social ideals that often motivated the radical theatres of the Vietnam War era cannot be reconciled with a postmodernist perspective on political art because the radical theatres remained committed to representing both the forces they opposed and the utopian society they hoped to bring into being. Postmodernist political art, by contrast, views all representations with suspicion – that suspicion is the actual subject of postmodernist political art, which tends to raise questions about the representations by which we are surrounded without positioning itself outside those representations or claiming to answer the questions it raises about them. The Wooster Group, which has been greatly influential on many experimental theatres arising during the 1980s and 1990s, may be the best example of postmodernist political performance.

NOTES

1. Michel Benamou, "Presence and Play," in Michel Benamou and Charles Caramello (eds.) *Performance in Postmodern Culture* (Madison, WI: Coda, 1977), p. 3.

2. Sally Banes, *Terpsichore in Sneakers: Post-Modern Dance* (Middletown, CT: Wesleyan University Press, 1987), p. xiv.

3. Elinor Fuchs, "The Death of Character," in Fuchs, *The Death of Character: Perspectives on Theater After Modernism* (Bloomington, IN: Indiana University Press, 1996), pp. 169–176.

4. Sam Shepard, *Angel City, Curse of the Starving Class and Other Plays* (New York: Urizen Books, 1976), p. 6.

5. Fredric Jameson, *Postmodernism, or, The Cultural Logic of Late Capitalism* (Durham, NC: Duke University Press; London: Verso, 1991), pp. 16–17.

6. Jeffrey M. Jones, *Der Inka Von Peru* in *7 Different Plays*, ed. M. Wellman (New York: Broadway Play Publishing, 1988), pp. 103–79; with "An Afterword" on pp. 437–40.

7. Don Shewey, "Not Either/Or But And: Fragmentation and Consolidation in the Post-Modern Theatre of Peter Sellars," in Bruce King (ed.), *Contemporary American Theatre* (New York: St. Martin's Press, 1991), p. 265.

8. Judith Malina and Julian Beck, *Paradise Now* (New York: Vintage, 1971), pp. 15–16.

9. Josette Féral, "Performance and Theatricality: The Subject Demystified," trans. Terese Lyons, *Modern Drama* 25 (1982), p. 177.

10. Benamou, "Presence and Play," p. 3.

11. Jameson, *Postmodernism*, p. 162.

6

JULIAN MURPHET

Postmodernism and space

The temporal line in the sand drawn between us and modernism by postmodernism's prefix is generally associated with a "crisis of historicity."[1] The withering away of the authority and certainty of our historical sense has another side, however: namely, the reaffirmation of our spatial imagination. This "spatial turn" has been variously avowed by many of our epoch's most illustrious intellectuals. Michel Foucault, for one example, insisted that "the anxiety of our era has to do fundamentally with space, no doubt a great deal more than with time. Time probably appears to us only as one of the various distributive operations that are possible for the elements that are spread out in space."[2] On the face of it, this statement looks willed and arbitrary, a mere inversion of Kantian categories for the purposes of polemic. We may do well to attend to John Frow's salutary suspicion that postmodernism designates "nothing more and nothing less than a genre of theoretical writing" in which the elaboration of strong oppositions is always the foundational gesture.[3] Yet it is at least conceivable that we postmoderns live "more spatially" than the moderns, who somehow had it in them to live "more temporally" than we. The insistence of contemporary theory on this score is, arguably, not fanciful, but a response at the level of the concept to shifts in the structure of our world. This chapter explores that possibility by way of an historical presentation of reemergence of spatial consciousness in an escalating scale of magnitude, from the body, through the textures of everyday life, our cities, and ultimately to the planetary stage we are calling "globalization"; all of which are in fact inextricable – "postmodern space" being, precisely, their compression into a single, complex plane of immanence, whose contours and elevations we are still in the process of mapping.

Surfaces

Beginning, then, with the intimate spaces of the body, it is remarkable how malleable, fungible, and marketable these have become in the last forty years.

From nose-jobs and liposuction to breast implants, the market in body parts and transsexualism, the body today is a space available as never before to transformation through technical intervention. At the same time, "the body" has been unleashed as an instrument of visual persuasion throughout the spaces of everyday life. The flip side of bodily mutability (whose canonical site remains Michael Jackson's face), and its appeal to the pleasure principle, is the excess of denuded body images in advertising, film, and television, whose appeal is ultimately to the wallet itself. Our bodies experience a crisis of identity, torn on the one hand by the importunings of transformability (Be thinner! bustier! stronger! different!), and on the other by serial incarnations of an airbrushed Ideal of the body no ordinary mortal can hope to match. The social fetishism of body surfaces has had a corrosive effect on the very meaning of sexuality, which tends to shed its connotations of guilt, repression, or unspoken desire, to become the leading visual edge of our commercial culture. As a result, with its Unconscious scooped out and plumped on to the visual, the Ego slackens and grows flabby, and subjectivity itself evaporates under the glare of media light. The subject raises itself out of the troubled depths of self-reflection into the sensitive surface of its epidermis. To this extent, the famous "death of the subject" is a spatial affair.

The philosopher Henri Lefebvre, whose thought more than anyone else's has helped to establish the "spatial turn," summarized the dynamic thus:

> Bodies are transported out of themselves, transferred and emptied out, as it were, via the eyes: every kind of appeal, incitement and seduction is mobilized to tempt them with doubles of themselves in prettified, smiling and happy poses; and this campaign to void them succeeds exactly to the degree that the images proposed correspond to "needs" that those same images have helped fashion. So it is that a massive influx of information, of messages, runs head on into an inverse flow constituted by the evacuation from the innermost body of all life and desire.[4]

It is a pessimistic portrait of the body, which nevertheless underscores the point that, today, bodies cannot be conceived apart from that "massive influx of information" that invests and shapes them. The visual Niagara with which our society deluges our bodies is now more vital to our apprehension of our own most intimate spaces than the blood and tissue of its organic being. "The body" for us has less to do with that brute biological substratum of pulsions and reflexes than with the cultural stream of messages that enters and fashions us through the eyes. Now that the human genome is being decoded, indeed, the distinction between biology and "information" is rapidly disappearing. Like the rebel characters in the Wachowskis's *The*

Matrix (USA, 1999), we are learning how to perceive bodies as so much mobile code.

The *milieux* into which our postmodern bodies are then inserted can best be described through the concept of superficiality. In buildings, commodities, the arts, and the very practice of everyday life, not depths but surfaces dominate; surfaces that, unlike the mass-bounding architecture of Mies and Le Corbusier, the solid chrome hulk of the Cadillac, the seductive dreamscapes of painterly Surrealism, the depth-portending style of the Joycean or Proustian sentence, or the fluvial immensity of the Parisian boulevard, have peeled free from their cumbersome depths. According to Jean Baudrillard, America (which he reads as the *sine qua non* of postmodernity) represents "the triumph of surface and of pure objectivization over the depth of desire."[5] Postmodern space flattens into two-dimensional, Keatonesque deadpan, and resolutely refuses the "seriousness" and redemptive vocation of modernist space. Looking out at the built environment of Los Angeles's downtown, Baudrillard characteristically mused: "All around, the tinted glass façades of the buildings are like faces: frosted surfaces. It is as though there were no one inside the buildings, as if there were no one behind the faces. And there *really* is no one. This is what the ideal city is like."[6] The "ideal city," voided (as we shall see) of real human content by the speculations of finance capital, glares back at the subject with insouciant blankness. Quite unlike the "unreal city" of modernism, which seduced even as it repelled, the postmodern city deploys its simulated, self-duplicating surfaces with the goal of repelling desire itself.

The triumph of surface over depth is best embodied in those peculiarly American theme parks, most famously Disneyland, where the very absence of desire frees up a delirious artifice, which is glorified as an escape from necessity. Space here is a simulacrum, perfectly realized and objective, alive with connotations, yet utterly divorced from any underlying reference to an original model or archetype; rather, it replays spatial stereotypes from a cartoon imaginary, "a sentimental compression of something that is itself already a lie."[7] And it is also a space whose delightful inanity masks, as E. L. Doctorow once had it, an extraordinary new experiment in the regulation and control of human bodies as consumers: "The ideal Disneyland patron may be said to be one who responds to a process of symbolic manipulation that offers him his culminating and quintessential sentiment at the moment of a purchase."[8] "'This is what the real Main Street should have been like,' one of Disneyland's planners or 'imagineers' says. 'What we create,' according to another, 'is a 'Disney realism,' sort of Utopian in nature, where we carefully program out all the negative, unwanted elements and program in the positive elements.'"[9] Such a sentimental "perfection" of space which abolishes the negative is the ideal of corporate postmodernism. It is designed to solicit nothing more than a satisfied smirk and a beeline to the cash register. The Disney corporation's living laboratory of total urban design, in the township of Celebration, Florida, only carries this tendency to its logical extreme, and offers a sobering image of the future as a *Truman Show* for each of us.[10]

The larger issue is one of the generalized diffusion of the "real fakes" of Disneyesque simulacra throughout urban space. Edward Soja comments that

> Over the past thirty years... these "real fakes" have escaped from their formerly circumscribed territories and manufactories to infiltrate more deeply than ever before into the intimate everyday life of postmodern urban society, economy, polity, and culture. In these new secular sites and situations, the hypersimulations of urban reality have been blurring... the older distinctions between our images of the real and the reality itself, inserting into the confusion a hyperreality that is increasingly affecting where we choose to live and work, what we wear and eat, how we relate to others, who we vote for, how we shape our built environment, how we fill our leisure time – in other words, all the activities that together constitute the social construction of urban life."[11]

The libidinization and plannification of urban life as a whole through the agency of the image is the result. When every new building or cityscape is itself but a simulacrum, a playful pastiche or quotation of some apocryphal and absent original, we who inhabit these spaces are ourselves "hyperrealized," and dimly become conscious of ourselves as walk-ons on the balsa-wood sound-stage of a blockbuster whose narrative eludes us. The blockbuster's logic, as David Harvey makes clear, is economic: "Imagining a city through the organization of spectacular urban spaces became a means to attract capital and people (of the right sort) in a period (since 1973) of intensified inter-urban competition and urban entrepreneurialism."[12]

Fredric Jameson's epochal essay on "The Cultural Logic of Late Capitalism" first proposed depthlessness as "perhaps the supreme formal feature of all the postmodernisms."[13] From Warhol's deadened canvasses to the freestanding wall of Wells Fargo Court in Los Angeles, Jameson presented spatial superficiality as an ineluctable property of all culture today. The absence of depth in the cultural object matches the absence of depth in the consuming subject: both are henceforth fashioned out of recycled bits and pieces from the bottomless image bank with which contemporary society dissimulates itself as transparent, informational, and pure. The great ruse of postmodern spatiality is that it hides nothing. Everything is now on show, individuals are "bodies" rather than "subjects," and acts of literature are "texts" rather than "works." Yet it is precisely in this sufficiency and unreservedness of postmodern space that it nonetheless hides consequences from us; which the ideologies of the past did by lying. By literally putting everything on show, on a multitude of screens and databases, what vanishes is any faculty of critical discrimination – any distance between "us" and "it." Color television is, according to Perry Anderson, the technological key to this whole process of flattening and intensified ideology. The "saturation of the imaginary" made possible by this medium (especially now that is is being integrated with the World Wide Web) is so exorbitant as to be prohibitive of any critical distance from which to assess the totality of its representations. What it allows for the first time is something like the perception of simultaneity itself, stretched to a limitless two-dimensionality by the compulsive habits of channel-surfing. But the "vicarious geography" of the present installed in each of us by this "Niagara of visual gabble" offers no foothold for the possibility of critique.[14]

Alternatively, the true substance of what Marc Augé has called "supermodernity" can be discerned in those spaces that are its conduits and transportational nodes: airports, hotels, motels, highways, resorts.[15] Appropriately called "non-places" in Augé's vocabulary, such spaces refuse any attachment to their environment. They are prepackaged abstractions, comfortably familiar the world over, allowing us to repress that minumum of difference which might disturb us out of the endless reveries of consumption, travel, and rest. A Holiday Inn in San Francisco is much the same as a Holiday Inn in Harare. Tourism is the industrial behemoth behind this process of spatial homogenization, and its logic of equivalence carries across to that remarkable sameness of consumer spaces everywhere, which dictates that every great capital city will now be festooned with the same clothes in the same shop windows, available for the same price with the same credit cards. Multinational boutique and fast-food outlets are as much about the experience of "non-place" as they are about consumption. Entering a Banana Republic in Amsterdam, you are in effect entering a transnational zone, not a local shop. The spatial experience of shopping there is as close as you are likely to get to the "essence" of space today: clean, abstract, bland, and monitored; and those you see languishing on the pavement outside are not welcome.

Postmodern urbanism

But here we have already stumbled over what is perhaps the most obvious spatial pivot in the transition from a modernist to a postmodernist space: the transformation of the function of the cities which conduct our social, economic, and cultural currents. This change affects both the intrinsic properties of the cities concerned (population, ethnic diversity, planning, zoning, architecture, "civil society," transportation, policing, shopping, etc.), as well as their mode of insertion into the now "globalized" economy (informational accumulation and circulation, monetary transfers, tourism, etc.). On both counts, what is first discernable is a freeing-up of practices and patterns to include more diversification and "mixed" strategies, within the overall consolidation of a regime of power based in the privileged centers of wealth.

During what we now think of as the high modernist period (1870–1929), it was the function of the metropolis to serve as the nerve center of the political, financial, and cultural life of its imperial nation state; and of the newer industrial cities to produce goods to increase the state's wealth by processing its colonial raw materials. They also sopped up the waves of migration from both the decline of the rural agricultural sector at home and the mobility from abroad stimulated by new transportational possibilities. Industrialization, new residential districts for the urban proletariat and bourgeoisie, transportation and sanitation infrastructures, the rationalization of old centers, the commercialization of the street fronts, and many other developments, completely reshaped urban life in Europe. In America, high-rise CBDs, industrial cores and satellites, rings of working-class residences, and an incipient suburbanization confirmed the shape of capitalist space in functional, instrumental ways. The "Chicago School" of urban theorists conceptualized this urban environment in somewhat "naturalist" or fatalist terms, while Lewis Mumford complained that the citizens of such cities "find themselves 'strangers and afraid,' in a world they never made: a world ever less responsive to direct human command, and ever more empty of human meaning."[16]

The accuracy of his prognosis was soon made apparent. State-led and boom-backed urbanism after World War II, especially in the USA, followed a Keynesian program of urban renewal and reinvestment, albeit within a context of wildfire suburbanization, highway construction, and residential segregation; a process that consolidated downtowns with monolithic high-rises, and dissipated critical urban mass (and political fermentation) in a breathtaking expansion of the peripheries. Meanwhile, with the Marshall Plan in Asia and the rapid entry of the rest of the decolonized world into the global economy, overnight urbanization there altered the very concept of the city, shifting its definition away from a "metropolitan" and elitist center of culture and towards a global rationalization of urban form. Architecture and city planning followed a highly technocratic logic of top-down instrumentality, degrading the pleasures of the urban field but enhancing its efficiency and productivity. Critically, this model applied willy-nilly across the First (capitalist), Second (Communist) and Third ("developing") Worlds, with urban development largely in the hands of state monopolies rather than of private enterprises.

What has come to be called "urban postmodernism" is what followed the failure of this "late modern" model of bureaucratic city planning in the capitalist world, after the late 1960s – after widescale working-class, Black and student protest, the emerging oil crisis, and recession. It has also, fittingly, been conceived as a relief from the stifling monotonies of state-monopoly control over urban form. It implies the relative decline of state investment in urban renewal, and the rise of international capital in the construction and control of urban space. In the First World, particularly the USA, this has first of all entailed the disinvestment of capital in the classical industrial sector: downsizing, outsourcing, disaggregating the Fordist plant – all spatial readjustments of an industrial economy now "globalized" (we shall return to this notion) and able to take full advantage of cheap labor pools, lax pollution laws, low taxation, parallel production, and other opportunities in the developing world. This restructuration of the urban economy in America has entailed a comprehensive adjustment of the uses and values of urban space. The ever-increasing importance of finance capital, services, entertainment, and programmed consumerism in the West has impacted profoundly on urban form: towering corporate headquarters, a glut of office space, cinema complexes, vast indoor malls, all encased in the sheen of a sexy new architecture no longer merely functional, but "aestheticized" for pleasurable consumption.

Yet this privatization of urban space carries with it less comfortable overtones, not the least of which has been an increasingly draconian approach to the control of bodies within it. High-tech surveillance, private security firms, indigent-repellant tactics, even strategies such as aromatic and auditory suggestion in consumer space now typify the experience of the urban. On the macro scale, this discipline of everyday life carries over into policing and incarceration, where more citizens (particularly young "ethnic" males) are harrassed, arrested, and imprisoned than at any time in history. Mike Davis's classic portrayal of "Fortress LA" makes much of this twin corporate-architectural and police "assault on public space" in Los Angeles. While the LAPD "hammers" gangs and ethnic others in a violent "war on drugs," the "designers of mall and pseudo-public space attack the crowd by homogenizing it" in a process which "produces a veritable commercial symphony of swarming, consuming monads moving from one cashpoint to another."[17] This takes place as part of a general project of sanitizing urban space by commercial fiat. Urban reconstruction that relies on private investment demands the excision of all those "unclean" spaces of the other: the homeless, the poor, the illegal, all of whom, like the very presence of the past itself, are pushed outward to the vanishing point of the urban perimeter. The forced clearing of the Bowery and Tompkins Square in New York City remains the emblematic moment in this history of spatial cleansing.

The privatization of public space by international capital has meant the erosion and, according to some critics, even the extinction of what used to be called "civil society" or the public sphere. "Postmodern space" also means the liquidation of those vestigial places where, for instance, the middle class of Europe once congregated to forge a collective identity under the shadow of the *ancien régime*: clubs, halls, cafés, gardens, boulevards. Nothing of any comparable spatial scope has taken the place of these precious arenas of public–private interlocution. Today, if you meet anybody at all, it is as a fellow consumer, commuter, or employee (or, at best, leisure-seeker or jogger), and not, surely, as a fellow citizen. The Starbucks phenomenon is, in this view, nothing but a cynical exploitation of the vacuum left by the lapse of civil society. In Mike Davis's estimation there has been a veritable "war on public space" in cities such as Los Angeles, where the design of the new citadel-like Downtown has worked deliberately to "'kill the crowd', to eliminate that democratic admixture on the pavements and in the parks that [Frederick Law] Olmsted believed was America's antidote to European class polarizations."[18] The work of Michel de Certeau may have focused critical attention on the vitality of those tactical practices and stories with which citizens appropriate urban space for their own ends. Yet most of his work on walking in the city and spatial storytelling was addressed to what is arguably a "modernist" or "late modernist" space. And he also indicated that the effects of an incipient "postmodernization" (where, in the absence of a public sphere, all the storytelling is done for you by television) are unsettling: "where stories are disappearing . . . there is a loss of space: deprived of narrations . . . the group or the individual regresses towards the disquieting, fatalistic experience of a formless, indistinct, and nocturnal totality."[19] The intrusion of electronic media and the internet into our daily habits of communication has only confirmed the mediation of personal intercourse by multinational capital, which stifles spontaneous or traditional "uses" of space in a virtual realm "formless, indistinct and nocturnal." This has led to what Steven Connor calls the "telematically-permeated sedentariness of contemporary life."[20]

Lest I be thought to be suggesting that this elimination of public and "dirty" space by corporate capital has somehow been entirely successful, it remains to be said that all of this is restricted to only the choicest "zones" of international investment, and has gone ahead cheek by jowl with perhaps the most destabilizing factor in the entire postmodern scene: namely, the mass movement of bodies across the globe, demographic shifts out of all proportion with historical precedent, which now invest the urban sphere with an incalculable diversity of "cultures." Most of the newer immigrants in the First World either fuel the informal industrial economy or occupy the relatively deserted "petty bourgeois" sector; but what is most important is that these various neo-ethnicities inscribe their differences into the urban fabric through the various "towns" that take their names: Chinatown, Little Armenia, Koreatown, etc. Here at least, some semblance of the *frisson*, mixture and "danger" of the city is reintroduced – as transnational corporations have little interest as yet in speculating on the property market in these areas, and, without state funding, they have sometimes been allowed to mutate into what some commentators have described as Third or Fourth World conditions, a quasi-medieval space of family guilds, markets, festivals, and occasionally of gangs, drugs, and guns.[21]

It is here that those colossal demographies of the postmodern that we shall examine in the next section come back to the center from the periphery and contest the "purified" postmodernism of the city with their own proliferating subjectivities and identities; even as "their" cities back home are increasingly homogenized along classically western lines. Tolerated as "minorities," the newer masses of immigrants from across the globe oblige the jaded white postmodern urbanite to readjust his or her spatial experience in an increasingly relativistic way. What used only yesterday to be a "Chicano" district is now divided between Korean, Salvadorean, and Black constituencies; the older landmarks are rapidly replaced; the look, feel, and smell of the area change overnight; and what it means exactly to "be oneself" amid this demographic upheaval is ever more acutely in question. Thus, inevitably, racism is back at the heart of urban politics today, the incipient terror of the possessing white class that these waves of otherness will eventually swamp their precious identity and property in an urban meltdown. No wonder, then, that the most significant political episode in postmodern urban history – the Los Angeles riots of 1992 – broke out in that canonically postmodern city in response to the racist battering of a black man by white police, and the subsequent acquittal of the offending officers by an all-white jury.[22]

There is, however, a sense in which all of this "difference" is vestigial and secondary; for, when seen in the context of the actual economic function of what is increasingly being called the "world city" today, these visible factors of demography, cultural confusion, and politics seem rather divorced from the invisible truth of postmodern urbanism. What Manuel Castells calls the "informational city" is one whose economy is predicated not only on the inrush and concrete investment of multinational capital, but on the flows through it of that capital and of those "knowledges" that ensure the growth and maintenance of the global money market.[23] Finance capital: the world city does not so much "ground" itself in this ethereal and abstract element as raise itself up to it; so that, in the new spatiality of this economy, London is "closer" to Tokyo than it is to Hull; Miami is meshed more with Sydney and Seoul than it is with Havana. This unheard-of transcendence of old spatial barriers in a new system of simultaneities may have been prepared for in the modern (by telegraphy, radio, telephony); but its perfection today, the flawless circulation, via satellite and cable, of funds and information between urban concentrations of technology and capital renders the nonurban and physical geography *per se* irrelevant as never before, and impacts with extraordinary abstraction on the spatial form of the cities themselves.

For if the point of the world city today is no longer industrial, or residential, or cultural, or even commercial in any overt sense (as all of these things can be relocated properly to the suburbs and beyond), but to enable the ever greater accumulation of wealth through financial speculation on the stock market, then the production of urban space takes on entirely new meanings. John Fitch's book *The Assassination of New York* examines the eviction of classical production from that city, and its replacement by FIRE (finance, insurance, and real estate) industries.[24] The reasons for this are straightforward: a 1,000 percent increase in the rate of rental return on office space over factory space. What are the spatial consequences of this "shift from investments in production to speculation on the stock market, the globalization of finance and...the new level of a frenzied engagement with real estate values"? Fredric Jameson answers thus: "the building [in the world city] will no longer have any aura of permanence, but will bear in its very raw materials the impending certainty of its own future demolition."[25] Isometric space and enclosed skin volumes lift the built environment of the postmodern city beyond the realm of spiritual values and older kinds of architectural "humanism," into a free-floating world of abstraction, ephemerality, the reflection of reflection. These buildings are no longer meant to be lived or worked in, but merely bought, sold, and rented; as a result, their architectural aesthetic has become directly meshed with political economy. As David Harvey has written:

> Whereas the modernists see space as something to be shaped for social purposes and therefore always subservient to the construction of a social project, the postmodernists see space as something independent and autonomous, to be shaped according to aesthetic aims and principles which have nothing necessarily to do with any overarching social objective, save, perhaps, the achievement of timeless and "disinterested" beauty as an objective in itself.[26]

It being understood, of course, that in this context beauty is as "interested" as iron girders in the accumulation of value.

What seems incontestable and inevitable is the expansion of the city, hitherto circumscribed by the great agricultural systems of yesteryear, to limits of properly global proportions. It seems of little moment today to feel oneself to be urbanite as opposed to a "countrysider," when the rural itself is increasingly being redefined simply as a mode of retreat from the urban. The government, economy, and culture of our planet is centered as never before in the cities that house more than half the world's inhabitants, and the classical conception of the city as an exceptional, future-oriented concentration of the social (very much like the modern itself) has tended to lose its significance. "Rather, the urban becomes the social in general, and both of them constitute and lose themselves in a global that is not really their opposite either (as it was in the older dispensation) but something like their outer reach, their prolongation into a new kind of infinity."[27]

Globalization

And so we reach that confusing point of transition between the world city and the world system itself, no longer strictly distinguishable given the extension of urban forms and communications over the spaces of the vanishing other of the modern: agriculture, peasantries, traditional societies, the wilderness. The postmodernization of space has to do with this steady erasure of everything "not modern," and its absorption into our mode of production, to the point where the social so saturates the global object that it is increasingly difficult to imagine any outside to it. And tourism (the leisure industry) cynically claims for itself those vestigial spaces of otherness hitherto feared and desired as the "heart of darkness," so that literally nothing is beyond our ken in the context of an adventure holiday.

Yet there is no tidy break between a modernist conception of world space and a postmodernist one, and the history of the twentieth century was one of broadening horizons of global consciousness. As early as 1904, the Oxford geographer Halford J. Mackinder was arguing that developments in communications and transportation, and the vanishing of the frontier, dictated the necessity and advantage of viewing the world as a single, integrated system. "For the first time we can perceive something of the real proportion of features and events on the stage of the whole world, and may seek a formula which shall express certain aspects . . . of geographical causation in universal history."[28] As Stephen Kern has written of Mackinder's thesis, the idea that the world was now "a single organism that will respond as a whole to power shifts anywhere on the globe" was controversial, but not atypical of "a number of observations made at that time."[29] In the arena of political economy, Karl Marx had already speculated tentatively on the implications of the extension of the world market: increasing development of productive forces and individuals, universalization of the "civilizing" tendency, and incipient crisis once geographical saturation point was reached.[30] As a result, the contours of what David Harvey has called the "limits to capital" came into view by virtue of the finite resources and places available for such expansion. The short-term expansionism that was imperialism was summed up by Lenin: "the characteristic feature of the period under review is the final partitioning of the globe . . . in the sense that the colonial policy of the capitalist countries has *completed* the seizure of the unoccupied [sic] territories of our planet. For the first time the world is completely divided up, so that in the future *only* redivision is possible."[31]

A passage from Virginia Woolf's 1931 novel *The Waves* finely summarizes what is at stake in the imperialist shattering of old national spatial frames and the vertiginous entry into a newly global one:

> And look – the outermost parts of the earth – pale shadows on the utmost horizon, India for instance, rise into our purview. The world that had been shrivelled, rounds itself; remote provinces are fetched up out of darkness; we see muddy roads, twisted jungle, swarms of men, and the vulture that feeds on some bloated carcass as within our scope, part of our proud and splendid province.[32]

The twentieth century was characterized by the dissolution, in a decentering dilation of known space of the sense of luminous centrality surrounded by shadows. So much of what we now think of as modernism springs from the crisis in cognition and representation precipitated by this new global object. The problem is, of course, how we are to adjust the lens mechanism on "our scope" so as to take in the extraordinary panorama on offer. If history has "gone spatial" and space has gone global, then how exactly does the humble human subject propose to reorient her or his perceptual machinery so that nothing will be missed? Few strategies seem available that are grounded in the precious basis of bourgeois art and culture – *experience*. For a single social atom cannot possibly "experience" the global sweep of imperial administration, commodity circulation, nascent geopolitics; it is by definition what is beyond anyone's experiential capabilities.

How much more inaccessible, then, is the world since imperialism, whose geopolitical brush had at least organized the vastness of the colonial system into those reliable patches of red, blue, green, orange, purple, and yellow on Conrad's map.[33] With the processes of decolonization and neo-imperialism, the awakening of an unguessed-at number of new national sensibilities, and thus the emergence on the world scene of an unprecedented variety of world-historical "identities," the confidence of Woolf's "proud and splendid province" is shattered. All the various ex-colonies are now centers in their own right, albeit most often on the economic margins of an ever more integrated global market. What happens when the imperial system is dismantled is the greatest challenge to situational thought since the discovery of the New World. Indeed, after the Asian–African Bandung Conference of 1955, there were Three Worlds, each composed of its own system of relatively autonomous states, and all animated by competing modes of political thought and struggle. Waves of national liberation swept the so-called "Third World" convulsively between 1945 and 1975, inflected by either socialist ideology or capitalist statism, and each success obliged the world citizen to factor in yet another national entity in the roster of states whose highly complex pattern of relations defined the horizon of her or his world. Geography – borders, access to key materials, distance from nodes of accumulation, proximity to neo-imperial centers, rapid urbanization, the ability to manage pollution, the rise of the tourism and heritage industries – mattered as never before in the new world system. If the imperialist order had simply seen colonial space as an arena for unfettered expansionism and exploitation, the consolidation of a world of nation states ideally meant the delicate management of a global space now fully "occupied" by responsible agents, and supervised by an abstract supranational authority that was once called "The Bomb," and is now known as the United Nations.

Yet, especially since the fall of the Soviet bloc, the deeper story has been one of what Aijaz Ahmad calls "Super Imperialism": a rigidly patrolled global system, with power concentrated overwhelmingly in the USA, in German-centered Europe, and Japan, "largely unified in its will to weed out all opposition in all parts of the globe and to dominate collectively the backward capitalist countries."[34] Sherif Hetata describes the existing geopolitical order of things in starkly familiar terms:

> Never before in the history of the world has there been such a concentration and centralization of capital in so few nations and in the hands of so few people. The countries that form the Group of Seven, with their 800 million inhabitants, control more technological, economic, informatics, and military power than the rest of the approximately [5] billion who live in Asia, Africa, Eastern Europe, and Latin America. Five hundred multinational corporations account for 80 percent of world trade and 75 percent of investment.[35]

The fallout of the global epoch of imperialism has been a veritable deconstruction of the old political maps of Empire, but within the context of a now almost incontestable stranglehold over planetary space by a single mode of economic organization. Postmodernism is, in this spatial sense, the completed modernization of a hitherto unevenly modernized world, bringing previously extrinsic, "wild" and "backward" spaces within one integrated system of exchange and accumulation. When Marx wrote that industrial capitalism was unlike any previous mode of production precisely in its universalizing tendency, it is unlikely that even he could have foreseen the limits to which his prophecy has been fulfilled.

The command over global space exercised, let us say, by the Shell corporation, or Microsoft, or any number of other elite multinational companies, far exceeds the wildest dreams of any Kublai Khan from history, or the national government of any state but the USA today. How has this command been established, but through an escalation of their ability to control a congeries of places within an overarching regime of financial abstraction? "It is now possible for a large multinational corporation like Texas Instruments to operate plants with simultaneous decision-making with respect to financial, market, input costs, quality control and labour process conditions in more than fifty different locations across the globe."[36] Such "simultaneous decision-making" enabled by digital technologies and communications evades the jurisdiction of any particular nation state, even as its results affect particular places within those states with often severe consequences: job losses, environmental degradation, etc. Only the tentacles of the Pentagon and the decision-makers of the World Bank and International Monetary Fund themselves have more abstract command over space than corporations such as these. What is postmodern about this is precisely the degree of freedom such corporations enjoy from those regulatory and diplomatic mechanisms with which states have previously had to curtail their own ambitions for total spatial control (or face war).

If the modern was, in retrospect, the great period of class upheaval and the industrial division of labor, then the postmodern can be seen as the spatialization of that division of labor, with the attenuations of class struggle consequent upon a geographical displacement and reification of hitherto merely sociological divisions. Slavoj Žižek has intriguingly speculated that Americans no longer think in terms of class, not because, as so many speculators in the post-Marxist camp have urged, the traditional working class has disappeared or been absorbed into white-collar services; but because the American working class is now – China![37] With the messy business of production magically transported to convenient territories out of sight and out of mind, the First World, thus "cured" of the most potent threat to its internal equilibrium, can congratulate itself on having solved the problem of history. When Francis Fukuyama entitled his famous work *The End of History and the Last Man*, his covert and unspoken premise was that such an opportune "end of history" had been enabled precisely by the spatial displacement of previously historical antagonisms. History, as Marx said, had always been the history of class struggle; only now, with a global division of labor, it has become a *geography* of class struggle, whose forms, dimensions, and modes of engagement have yet to be fully defined. History is thereby stalled, and what the West calls "globalization" is the resultant intensification of capital in the meantime, a sweeping away of obstacles and impediments to its rates of profit.

And yet, an implicit destabilization is part of the system's consolidation. As a vital corollary of economic globalism there has been a colossal expansion of the very numbers of human beings who overrun and exceed stable spatial territories. Space is swarming as it has never swarmed before, with movement, difference, color, polyphony. Summing up the entire process with strikingly prophetic cadences, Michael Hardt and Antonio Negri write:

> Through circulation the multitude reappropriates space and constitutes itself as an active subject. When we look closer at how this constitutive process of subjectivity operates, we can see that the new spaces are described by unusual topologies, by subterranean and uncontainable rhizomes – by geographical mythologies that mark the new paths of destiny.[38]

Of course these new spaces and pathways are quickly mapped and integrated by capital, but even so the multitude, this vast mobile army of people, is one shaky step ahead of power, trekking out anew, laying new paths, forming new alliances, and challenging spatial orthodoxies – especially the Heideggerian orthodoxies of "home" and "belonging." If postmodern space has so far "contained" this explosive dynamic, that is not to say that it will do so forever.

"Globalization," then, is that integrated circuitboard of contemporary capitalism that has divided the globe into so many distinct spatial segments, the better to organize and squeeze profits from the flows between them of objects, people, data, and money. In everyday life it seems increasingly impossible not to find oneself caught within a worldwide web of spatial threads: eating Thai food, wearing garments made in China, vacationing in Cuba, driving a Korean car, singing karaoke, drinking Australian wines. It is often as though our every act of consumption draws us into a palimpsest of places we may never visit, but whose effects and determinations are now inescapable and, at least at a subliminal level, call out for their own cartography – which never comes.

> The general implication is that through the experience of everything from food, to culinary habits, music, television, entertainment, and cinema, it is now possible to experience the world's geography vicariously, as in a simulacrum. The interweaving of simulacra in daily life brings together different worlds (of commodities) in the same space and time. But it does so in such a way as to conceal almost perfectly any trace of origin, of the labour processes that produced them, or of the social relations implicated in their production.[39]

The implicit expansion of spatial awareness, the diversification of cultures, exfoliation of migration patterns, increasing numbers of people and groups on the world stage, relative democratization and hybridization of practices, may all be thought of as a cultural counterpoint of *differentiation* to the "economic" groundnote of *identity* already sketched. "Globalization" is, somehow, both these rather incompatible, even contradictory, things at once, and much of our contemporary theoretical crisis springs from these colossal contradictions in social space: homogeneous and fragmented, same and different. It was the great French philosopher Henri Lefebvre who first began thinking about space in these terms. What he called the "production of space" is at first sight a simple and transhistorical concept. It is incontestable that human beings collectively produce their social spaces, in concrete and imaginary ways. But the more radical hypothesis is that in our world the "production of space" has become an end in itself, manifest at every level from the pliable body, through the hyperreal spaces of everyday life, to the intensely abstract production of urban space and the outer limit of our very global system.

Space, not simple commodities, is what contemporary or "late" capitalism has most interest in producing, regulating, representing, and marketing. And this is pushed through the straits of a contradiction, between an abstract representation of space on the one hand (maps, charts, graphs, plans, statistics, and all the other means of reducing spatial qualities to figurative quantities), and an intensifying differentiation on the other (territoriality, new social movements, "multiculturalism," ethnic partitioning, etc.). While everyday life appears actively engaged in the spatial diversity and micropolitics of this latter moment, the direction and logic of the system is governed by the former, which, because the "encircling networks of multinational capital that actually direct the system exceed the capacities of any perception," eludes representation and everyday consciousness.[40] If we detect this glacial, abstract "production of space" at all, it is only allegorically, in those very buildings, cityscapes, fortuitous television and internet conjunctions, and cinematic narratives of conspiracy, through which some dim trace of the true proportions of the totality is glimpsed.

The lesson of this, according to Lefebvre, is that late-capitalist society desperately needs to command space, and does so by parcelizing and equalizing its multitude of places. It can thus always "control the politics of place even though, and this is a vital corollary, it takes control of some place to command space in the first instance."[41] The distinction drawn here between "space" and "place" is of the first importance and opens up the presiding spatial contradiction between abstract homogeneity and diversifying fragmentation to a political possibility. For if spatial abstraction works only *through* particular places, then those places have the capacity to resist or frustrate the very abstraction into which they are being compelled. The restitution of memory to place is here of particular salience, since the past is the first casualty of spatial abstraction; the "crisis of historicity" of the postmodern can be partially resisted through the telling of stories which reinscribe places with their lived pasts. Dolores Hayden's inspired work on *The Power of Place* is of particular interest in this regard, describing as it does the varied means by which working-class, women's, and ethnic histories can be reintroduced to areas in the postmodern city that have long since fallen victim to the spatial amnesia of its glittering surfaces.[42] From Lefebvre's point of view, this kind of practice hits on a conflict between two distinct conceptions of space, one of which he calls the "representation of space" (maps, knowledges, power), and the other – somewhat confusingly – "representational spaces" (passions, affects, memories, rituals, all of which inhere in and give life to social space). If Lefebvre had ever countenanced the notion of "postmodernism," he would have described it in terms of a virtual eclipse of "representational space" by the superficial "representations of space" we have addressed throughout this chapter.

The reinvigoration of politics today will have everything to do with the reinvestment of place by memories, histories, and passions, by grassroots practices and transnational collectivities that enable the concept of citizenship to transcend a mere abstract sense of membership, and ground it concretely in the conduct of everyday life. This is why those movements of indigenous peoples, in Mexico, Australia, South America, Canada, India, and elsewhere, against the abstract and imperial administration of their "native" habitats by neocolonial powers (including their own national governments) is potentially so inspiring for the practice of politics in our time. For such movements depend upon the reclamation of an imaginary sense of solidarity with place itself, fleshed out with differential practices, rituals, religious personae, etc., all of which are unassimilable to the rationalized conceptions of society emanating from the West. It is sobering for "us" to see that "our" abstractions, concepts, entertainments, values, and systems are not everywhere welcome, and not everywhere very good for people. The struggle for the local control of and respect for "place," in Chiapas and elsewhere, brings home what that system means for those few remaining who see it from the outside, as an enemy.

And we who reside within it: are we doomed to nothing but dispassionate immersion in the superficial stimulations of the postmodern? Space, having become for us so truly monolithic in its inscription and mastery by capital across the world, appears as a surfeit, inexhaustible, replete, and perfect. Yet, and for that very reason, we are discontented. It is hard to feel at home in a space such as this; the *heimlich* (homely, familiar) means something only in relation to an *unheimlich* (foreign, uncanny) against which it shelters us. Our cultural figurations reach again and again for some conception of ourselves over and against a sublime "outside," coded as a threat yet alive with excitement in its yawning extrinsicity to what is. The resurgence of science-fictional representations of alien hordes or asteroids descending from on high and shattering our cities would be curious, given the collapse of the Cold War hysterias of which they are mechanical revisions; but the thrill of the idea of an "outside" to our space, which would catastrophically bring the achieved surfeit and seeming perfection of our social space to ruins, seems an irresistible fantasy – or did so before the events of 9–11. We may not be able to imagine an alternative to capitalism, but we can enjoy imagining being destroyed by an apocalypse visited from without. In all our similitude, we still feel the need to be different, special, unique; it is part of the program of modernity. But modernity becomes meaningless when it is not displacing and bringing to their knees more archaic and traditional social orders. When it loses an exterior to its own space, it floods the entirety of space with its own image. It becomes postmodern, and yearns for the very destructive outside which *it* must have been for Africa, Asia, and the island nations.

In one of his late publications, the philosopher Jean-François Lyotard sketched out a "postmodern fable." There he imagines that "liberal democracy," having proven itself as the most workable political and economic system the human species is ever likely to produce, sucessfully manages to reproduce itself for millions of years into the future, managing the ecological and political government of the planet for countless generations – until finally, the Sun nearing the end of its expected life-span, the descendants of "man," still existing in the perfect, untrammelled equilibrium of liberal democracy, design and construct a spacecraft that hurtles our brilliant descendants into the void of deep space, that they may spread the gospel across the entire universe.[43] Lyotard meant this as a secular vision of paradise. It may, however, strike some of us as a vision of living hell. Liberal capitalism *per se* is only three hundred years old in its oldest bases; elsewhere it is but a generation away from having supplanted despotisms and feudal monarchies, or lives in uneasy symbiosis with forms of clerical fundamentalism. Its primary value has been to rationalize social space, sweep out the feudal cobwebs, and reduce quality to quantity, for the purposes of instrumental reason and the profit motive. But everywhere it imposes homogeneity and standardization, liquidates the past, and ruins collective identities. Lyotard's glib refusal to accept this terrible abstraction of space as the price paid for capitalism's perpetuity signals his blindness to what will surely be a period of worldwide political upheaval now that the gospel of the New World Order is being squared by billions of people with the poverty of everyday life in a system entirely dedicated to consumption. The contradictions inherent in postmodern space will eventually dictate a global political reckoning; whether or not the final result of this is "liberal democracy" or something as yet unimagined remains to be seen.

NOTES

1. Fredric Jameson, *Postmodernism, or, The Cultural Logic of Late Capitalism* (Durham, NC: Duke University Press; London: Verso, 1991), p. 22.
2. Michel Foucault, "Of Other Spaces," trans. Jay Miscowiec, *Diacritics* 16 (1986), p. 23.
3. John Frow, *Time and Commodity Culture: Essays in Cultural Theory and Post-modernity* (Oxford: Clarendon, 1997), p. 15.
4. Henri Lefebvre, *The Production of Space*, trans. Donald Nicholson-Smith (Oxford: Blackwell, 1991), p. 98.
5. Jean Baudrillard, *America*, trans. Chris Turner (London: Verso, 1988), p. 77.
6. Ibid., p. 60.
7. E. L. Doctorow, *The Book of Daniel* (New York: Random House, 1971), p. 295.
8. Ibid.
9. Sharon Zukin, *Landscapes of Power: From Detroit to Disney World* (Berkeley, CA, and Oxford: University of California Press, 1991), p. 222.
10. See Andrew Ross, *The Celebration Chronicles: Life, Liberty and the Pursuit of Property Values in Disney's New Town* (London: Verso, 2000).
11. Edward W. Soja, "Los Angeles, 1965–1992: From Crisis-Generated Restructuring to Restructuring-Generated Crisis," in Allen J. Scott and Edward Soja (eds.), *The City: Los Angeles and Urban Theory at the End of the Twentieth Century* (Berkeley, CA, and London: University of California Press, 1996), pp. 451–2.
12. David Harvey, *The Condition of Postmodernity: An Inquiry Into the Origins of Social Change* (Oxford: Blackwell, 1989), p. 92.
13. Jameson, *Postmodernism*, p. 9.
14. Perry Anderson, *The Origins of Postmodernity* (London: Verso, 1998), pp. 88–89, 56.
15. Marc Augé, *Non-Places: Introduction to an Anthropology of Supermodernity*, trans. John Howe (London: Verso, 1995).
16. Lewis Mumford, *The City in History: Its Origins, Its Transformations, and Its Prospects* (New York: Harcourt, Brace and World, 1961), p. 622.
17. Mike Davis, *City of Quartz: Excavating the Future in Los Angeles* (London: Verso, 1990), p. 257.
18. Ibid., p. 231.
19. Michel de Certeau, *The Practice of Everyday Life*, trans. Steven Rendall (Berkeley, CA, and London: University of California Press, 1988), p. 123.
20. Steven Connor, *Postmodernist Culture: An Introduction to Theories of the Contemporary*, 2nd edn. (Oxford: Blackwell, 1997), p. 256.
21. David Rieff, *Los Angeles: Capital of the Third World* (London: Cape, 1992).
22. See, on this subject, Robert Gooding-Williams (ed.), *Reading Rodney King/Reading Urban Uprising* (New York and London: Routledge, 1993).

23. Manuel Castells, *The Informational City: Information Technology, Economic Restructuring, and the Urban-Regional Process* (Oxford: Blackwell, 1989).

24. John Fitch, *The Assassination of New York* (London: Verso, 1993).

25. Fredric Jameson, *The Cultural Turn: Selected Writings on the Postmodern, 1983–1998* (London: Verso, 1998), p. 185.

26. Harvey, *Condition of Postmodernity*, p. 66.

27. Fredric Jameson, *The Seeds of Time* (New York: Columbia University Press, 1994), pp. 28–9.

28. Halford J. Mackinder, "The Geographical Pivot of History," *The Geographical Journal* 23 (1904), p. 422.

29. Stephen Kern, *The Culture of Time and Space 1880–1918* (Cambridge, MA: Harvard University Press, 1983), p. 228.

30. Karl Marx, *Grundrisse* (Harmondsworth: Penguin, 1973), pp. 524, 540–3.

31. V. I. Lenin, from "Imperialism, the Highest Stage of Capitalism," in Robert C. Tucker (ed.), *The Lenin Anthology* (New York and London: Norton, 1975), p. 234.

32. Virginia Woolf, *The Waves*, in *Four Great Novels* (Oxford: Oxford University Press, 1994), p. 489.

33. Joseph Conrad, *Heart of Darkness*, in *Youth / Heart of Darkness / The End of the Tether* (Harmondsworth: Penguin, 1995), p. 56.

34. Aijaz Ahmad, *In Theory: Classes, Nations, Literatures* (London: Verso, 1992), p. 313.

35. Sherif Hetata, "Dollarization, Fragmentation, and God," in Fredric Jameson and Masao Miyoshi (eds.), *The Cultures of Globalization* (Durham, NC: Duke University Press, 1998), p. 274.

36. Harvey, *Condition of Postmodernity*, p. 293.

37. Slavoj Žižek, "Why We All Love to Hate Haider," *New Left Review* NS 2 (2000), p. 40.

38. Michael Hardt and Antonio Negri, *Empire* (Cambridge, MA: Harvard University Press, 2000), p. 397.

39. Harvey, *Condition of Postmodernity*, p. 300.

40. Anderson, *Origins of Postmodernity*, p. 56.

41. Harvey, *Condition of Postmodernity*, p. 234.

42. Dolores Hayden, *The Power of Place: Urban Landscapes as Public History* (Cambridge, MA, and London: MIT Press, 1995).

43. Jean-François Lyotard, *Postmodern Fables*, trans. Georges van den Abbeele (Minneapolis, MN: University of Minnesota Press, 1997), pp. 97–110.

7

URSULA K. HEISE

Science, technology, and postmodernism

Postmodernism and the legacy of the enlightenment

Between the 1970s and the late 1990s, the concept of the "postmodern"
was associated with a wide range of different meanings. It could designate
a chronological period, a particular style found in some contemporary art-
works and literary texts, a property of social structures at the end of the
twentieth century, a change in the values of certain societies, or a specific
way of thinking theoretically about such issues as language, knowledge, or
identity. Different interpretations of these basic meanings further add to the
complexity. Understood as an historical period, the postmodern could either
follow a *modernity* defined by political, social, cultural, and economic institutions that had emerged in the late eighteenth century, or succeed the
cultural and artistic *modernism* that had characterized the era from approximately the 1850s to World War II. Viewed as an aesthetic style, the
postmodern could refer to quite different features depending on whether it
was studied in an old historical art form such as architecture, which had developed a distinctive "modern" style beforehand, or a very young art form
such as film, which had evolved only during the modernist period.[1] Some of
this terminological ambivalence also attaches to the relationship between science, technology, and postmodernism. On the one hand, one can designate as
"postmodern" some of the latest scientific and technological achievements,
particularly those that are culturally perceived as ushering in a different
historical era and type of society. On the other hand, scientific knowledge
and technological rationality have been seriously challenged by postmodern
modes of thought that more generally question fundamental Enlightenment
assumptions about human subjectivity, knowledge, and progress.

In the second half of the twentieth century, some scientific insights
and technological innovations have particularly contributed to shaping the
sense of a new historical age. Nuclear technology (both bombs and power
plants), journeys to the Moon and Mars, television, global communications

networks, the discovery of DNA, *in vitro* fertilization, the cloning of animals, the human genome project, digital technology from the personal computer to the World Wide Web, and environmental disasters such as those at Seveso, Bhopal, and Chernobyl have all contributed to defining the postmodern period. The intensive push of technoscientific innovation in the decades following World War II opened up new fields whose impacts have been perceived, experienced, and vigorously discussed among a broad public: computer technology and biotechnology are two of the most salient areas that have given rise to utopian hopes as well as to apocalyptic fears, and that have most strikingly created the sense of an epochal break. The widespread resistance to nuclear technology and the emergence of environmentalism as a perceptible social and political force point to a different dimension of technoscientific postmodernism: the rise of popular ambivalence *vis-à-vis* science and technology as unequivocally positive forces, and toward the narratives of progress and mastery of nature with which they have conventionally been associated.[2] These developments will be discussed in the next section of this essay ("Postmodern technologies").

The ambivalence in the general population of industrialized nations, combined with resistance to particular technological innovations among some parts of the population, took the form of skepticism and criticism of modernity and science in scholarly circles. Postmodernist currents of thought developed in philosophy, history, sociology, and cultural study that share a fundamentally critical perspective on many of the philosophical concepts, social institutions, and traditions of thought that evolved out of the European Enlightenment of the eighteenth century, from notions such as individuality and rationality to institutions such as the nation state. Science, one of the most important institutions and modes of thought with cultural roots in the Enlightenment, has not remained exempt from such criticism. In the third and fourth sections of this essay, I shall examine the broad claim that science, at the turn of the millennium, finds itself in a "crisis of legitimation," and shall survey some of the major issues and controversies that have arisen in the debate over its nature and history.

The postmodern moment, then, is characterized by two distinct tendencies with regard to science and technology. On the one hand, scientific insights and technological applications are advancing at a more rapid pace than ever, and some of their more spectacular developments have changed the material environment and a vast range of values, beliefs, and expectations, along with the very meaning of the words "science" and "technology" for average citizens. On the other hand, science and technology are met with ambivalence, skepticism, or resistance not only because of some undesirable "side effects" their rapid evolution has generated, but in terms of some of their most basic assumptions about nature, progress, human observation, appropriate methodologies for creating knowledge, and the role this knowledge should play in shaping public policies.

Postmodern technologies

When one considers the development of science and technology over the course of the twentieth century, what leaps to mind are some of the most spectacular technological achievements such as the exploration of the Moon and Mars (which is admired by many) or the invention of the atomic bomb (deplored by many), as well as path-breaking theoretical revolutions such as relativity theory, quantum mechanics, or the discovery of DNA. Important as these highly visible achievements may be, what is perhaps even more remarkable is the extent to which science and technology, through a long series of much less spectacular innovations, have ended up reshaping all areas of life from the most specific and technical activities to the most trivial and everyday experiences.[3] Few of us, as we go about our daily routines, think about the extremely complex substances and processes that go into the making of such basic staples as building materials, hygiene products, or foods, and even more perceptibly "technological" artefacts such as refrigerators, television sets, and cars have become so much a part of daily life in industrialized nations that they are no longer visible as products of quite recent innovation processes. Neither are we usually aware of the vast networks of complex technologies, institutions, social practices, and modes of thought that produce, manage, and deliver these artefacts to us.[4] For most us, most of the time, science and technology form part of a daily background that has come to seem "natural" and indispensable.

Against this taken-for-granted background, some areas of science and technology stand out with much more visible innovations that have variously generated enormous enthusiasm and utopian hopes or evoked deep-seated anxieties and rejection. In the second half of the twentieth century, three of the areas around which such hopes and fears crystallized were information and communication technologies, biotechnology, and ecology.[5] Each of these areas has also come to be associated with ideas about the legacies of modernity in particular ways, and therefore illuminates some facets of postmodernism in its relation to science and technology.

Among these three, computer technology is no doubt the one that for large parts of the population in industrialized societies is most clearly associated with the idea of technological progress, and the one that has transformed daily life most radically. In the 1930s and 1940s, when computers were first invented, they found their primary uses in military and highly specialized scientific purposes and, by the late 1950s, in business. Their enormous size, their ability to perform complex calculations very rapidly, and their control by a small group of highly trained specialists inspired popular fears about scenarios of totalitarian surveillance and control, either through the power of a technocratic elite or through the possibility of a "reign of machines" in which computers' intelligence would outpace that of humans and allow them to dominate their creators. More mundanely, the use of computers in the industrial sector and later in the service sector fueled worries over whether they would in the end destroy employment for humans. But even when it turned out, in subsequent decades, that computers were destined to become smaller rather than larger as their processing power increased, and that they could be made to perform a wide variety of tasks other than mathematical calculations, futurologists and science-fiction writers did not foresee just how common a device the computer would become in the 1980s. In fact, even when the possibility of building "personal computers" emerged in the 1970s, some computer designers themselves doubted that the general public outside a small circle of experts would have any interest in acquiring such devices.[6]

The enthusiasm with which millions of non-experts adopted the personal computer once it became available is hard to explain only in terms of its practical uses, especially when one considers that it initially required some familiarity with programming, operating systems, and hardware. For quite a few new users, the computer remained little more than an extremely advanced form of typewriter for years before they discovered its more sophisticated and wide-ranging applications. For many, the computer also was an icon of progress, autonomy, and individual empowerment (quite the opposite of the electronic mammoths that had been owned by the government, the military, and big corporations earlier), and the idea that one could personally own such a piece of futuristic technology seemed to promise access to a different world. Businesses, initially overtaken by the fast pace of innovation in digital technology, also began to adopt computers in large numbers to carry out a wide range of tasks from record-keeping and accounting to inventory control, production, and advertising. In a mere two decades, the computer turned from a specialized research tool to a universal machine that can be adapted to the most varied uses, from number-crunching all the way to creative experimentation with sound and images.

What contributed crucially to the success of the computer in professional as well as private contexts was the merging of information with communications technologies. The computer came to function, not only as a sophisticated device for storing and managing varied types of information efficiently, but also as an innovative means of communication. Electronic mail and bulletin boards brought about a first shift in communicative habits, allow-ing communities of geographically far-removed individuals and institutions with shared interests to interact without the intermediary of the printed word or the telephone. In the 1990s, the emergence of the internet from ear-lier networks of computers that had been dedicated to specific military and academic purposes brought about an explosion in electronic communica-tions. More than individual computers or even electronic mail, the internet helped to create a sense that the computer was not so much a tool as an entirely new medium, an alternative environment or space in which many daily activities would take place in the future. Transcending the modernist association of technology with machines, the networked, communicating computer promised access to a virtual space in which an abundance of infor-mation sources, commercial opportunities, and places for social encounter awaited the user. Reinforced by the "cyberpunk" images, popular in the 1980s, of a future in which virtual space has become a far richer and more interesting environment than real space, the globally networked computer as a "postmodern" technology seemed to open the door to a realm beyond the physical limitations of modernist machines.

The rise of digital technology was accompanied by utopian hopes for the transformation of social structures. It was claimed that marginalized indi-viduals and communities would be empowered by easier and cheaper access to information, that the new medium would enable greater democratization of political processes, and that it would transform education and allow new types of social communities to emerge.[7] The figure of the cyborg, originally a physical amalgam of human and machine, simultaneously emerged as a tan-talizing metaphor that signaled potential new relationships between body and mind and the possibility of endlessly transformable identities.[8] Some of these hopes have been at least partially realized (many types of information have become more easily accessible, at least for those who can use comput-ers, and new groups have formed via email and the World Wide Web), while others continue to exist as aspirations for the future.[9]

But during the 1990s, drawbacks and fears about the new medium also began to emerge: in many western countries, individuals, consumer organi-zations, and legislators became increasingly concerned that private informa-tion about individuals might have become too easily accessible and could no longer be protected from undesired uses; fears about invasions of pri-vacy, control, and surveillance that had been voiced in the early days of the computer resurfaced. At the same time, it became clear that, while digital technology provided easy access to the most varied sources of knowledge, it also made it difficult to distinguish accurate from inaccurate information, or statements that had been arrived at through some sort of expert review process from those that were simply expressions of opinion. Since internet documents can be published without the oversight of editors, referees, and publishing houses, it became harder to know which information derived from reliable sources and represented authenticated knowledge, and which did not. Education via digital technology, it turned out, would require a good deal more tutoring to address these problems than had initially been assumed. More generally, some scholars and critics worried that, even if information conveyed through the computer were accurate, there was simply too much of it for any individual to digest; while information had been a scarce resource throughout most of history, the internet was triggering an information explosion. This "information glut," as it was called, might not lead to any genuine increase in knowledge unless some filtering and shaping structure were provided.[10] In addition, some of those who had first viewed the internet as an alternative medium that would enable different social configurations to emerge through online communities without spatial barriers, were discouraged by signs of a digital divide reinforcing social differences. The internet, in this view, was turning into yet another corporate-dominated sphere, a "virtual shopping mall" and entertainment space that expanded the reach of consumerism and reinforced social isolation. By the turn of the millennium, therefore, the utopian hopes connected with the new technology had not entirely disappeared, but had certainly been mitigated by the experience of its real uses.

But while digital technology did not lead to the wholesale social revolution that early enthusiasts had anticipated, it did contribute to a transformation that is often referred to as paradigmatically postmodern: namely, the transition of societies in the West but also in other parts of the world from goods-based to service-based economies. This transition implies that a large part of what is produced, sold, and bought in a particular economy is no longer physical objects, but services of various kinds, and in particular services that provide the consumer with specific sorts of information. Indeed, it has often been argued that information is *the* most important commodity in postmodern society in that it is the production of and access to knowledge rather than material goods that ultimately shape social and economic structures.[11] This "postindustrial" or "knowledge economy" came to be referred to as the "new economy" in Europe and the United States in the 1990s, an economy that, it was argued, did not obey the same principles as economies that rely principally on the manufacture and distribution of material goods. The idea that such economies would lead to sustained rates of high growth, low inflation, the disappearance of "up-and-down" business cycles, and the transfer of business from physically rooted to internet-based companies, however, began to seem more doubtful when many "dot.coms" failed and economies across the globe returned to low growth at the turn of the millennium. While it remains to be seen, therefore, whether the functioning of the "new economy" differs as fundamentally from the old one as has sometimes been claimed, it is clear that services have an unprecedented prominence in its functioning, and that access to information does function as a pivotal commodity.[12] That it can do so is in no small part due to digital technology, one of the most central media for the postmodern "information society."

Computers in their various forms are undoubtedly one of the late twentieth-century technological changes that are most immediately experienceable for average citizens. But other areas of science, which do not touch upon their lives quite so directly, have also exerted great influence on the cultural imagination. In the early twentieth century, the discipline that most captured the popular imagination was physics; new paradigms such as relativity theory and quantum mechanics, while poorly understood by the great majority, nevertheless conveyed a sense that our understanding of the world had changed profoundly, and the sense of excitement as well as of uncertainty that accompanied this change reached far beyond the circle of trained physicists. In the aftermath of World War II, however, this admiration for the power of physics became more and more mixed with fear and revulsion: not only had the detonation of two atomic bombs in Hiroshima and Nagasaki alerted the world to a whole new scale of technological destruction, but the Cold War turned nuclear annihilation into a permanent fear for populations in the East and the West even during peacetime. While some areas of physical research, such as cosmology, continued to captivate widespread interest, another scientific discipline gradually moved into the limelight of public attention: biology.

The discovery of DNA by Watson and Crick in 1953 marked a point of departure as important as physical theories had been earlier in the century. But while this discovery was widely discussed, public controversy over biological advances did not surface in full force until two decades later. During the 1970s, scientists succeeded in fertilizing ova and creating human embryos outside the maternal body for the first time. Most immediately, this advance enabled doctors to help some infertile couples in conceiving children, in that the embryo created *in vitro* in a lab could be implanted in the woman's body and then evolve through a normal pregnancy; the first "test-tube baby," Louise Brown, was born in Britain in 1978, and was soon followed by tens of thousands of others. Through the same procedures, multiple human embryos could be created – and, indeed, had to be created for the repeated implantation attempts that were often necessary for a single successful pregnancy. Biologists and medical researchers were keenly interested in doing research on these embryos; for families affected by genetic diseases, embryos could be screened before implantation to ensure a healthy baby, and this research could also give clues to the causes of miscarriages and other problems in human reproduction. But, for a part of the public and not a few politicians, the idea of turning human embryos into objects of scientific experiment seemed abhorrent. If human life starts at conception, they believed, then performing experiments on humans that are a few days old is as profoundly immoral as performing them on mature beings. Genetic screening, they feared, might be only the prelude to more radical and sinister interventions into humans' genetic make-up, an idea that conjured up visions of mass-produced humans as Aldous Huxley had described them in his novel *Brave New World*. In addition, it was feared that techniques of assisted reproduction that were not confined to married couples would pose a threat to stable family structures. This perception that scientific advances were putting the value of individual human lives in question and opening the way for an insidious subversion of social structures led to acrimonious debates over whether fetal research should be allowed at all, and, if so, how much it should be regulated. More recently, similar debates have surged up again around the issue of stem-cell research, which also involves the use of human embryos for experiments that might potentially lead to therapies for currently incurable diseases. In these debates, potential gains in knowledge and human health have to be weighed against fundamental questions about the definition and value of human life, and the extent of humans' right of intervening into its natural processes.[13]

Since the 1980s, related concerns about the possibilities and limits of human manipulations of nature have reverberated in public debates that revolve around the large-scale introduction of genetically engineered crops and foods, the widely publicized cloning of Dolly the sheep in 1996, and the mapping of the human genome. Genetically modified fruits and vegetables entered the US market without much discussion, but met with enormous resistance among European consumers.[14] The genetic alteration of animals for research purposes and for transplantation of their organs to humans provoked less controversy, in part because it was more shielded from public view in specialized laboratories. But ample media coverage of Dolly the sheep, cloned by Scottish biologist Roger Wilmut and his team, did bring the actual genetic manipulation of animals and the possible genetic alteration of humans to the fore of public debate. Even though animal cloning has so far been successful with only a few species, human cloning seemed to move instantly into the realm of the possible. Unlike the emergence of personal computers, cloning and, more generally, the creation of human beings by technological means had a long prehistory in the cultural imagination. Not only had science-fiction writers explored its implications for decades before any sort of cloning was scientifically possible, but a long literary tradition had imagined the consequences of the chemical or mechanical creation of humans by humans, from the conversion of Pygmalion's statue into a woman in Ovid's *Metamorphoses* (*ca.* AD 8) and the Jewish legend of the Golem all the way to figures of the Romantic era such as E. T. A. Hoffmann's puppet-woman Olympia (in the short story "The Sandman") or the artificial human created by Dr Victor Frankenstein in Mary Shelley's famous novel (1818).

With the rapid advance of genetic research and engineering, such uncanny but remote fantasies seemed for the first time within the reach of science.[15] But opinions about how far genetic manipulation should go diverged radically. While even critics conceded that humans have for a long time manipulated the genetic evolution of plants and animals through selective breeding, modern genetic engineering was judged by some to be much more radical and unpredictable in its consequences. Fears regarding the uncontrolled spread of genetically modified plants through wind-borne and insect-borne pollination emerged, as did concerns about the health consequences of mingling the genes of unrelated species in plants and animals consumed by humans. But the possibilities of human genetic manipulation and cloning continue to provoke the most violent controversies, with advocates expressing hopes for much more effective cures for human diseases, and detractors pointing to the dystopian scenario of "designer humans" that would turn sociocultural prejudices into biological realities and degrade human life to yet another commodity that can be produced at will. In some respects, these debates echo the fears and fascinations around the cyborg: partly real and partly imagined possibilities of reshaping the human body and mind in unprecedented ways lead to futuristic hopes for humans' liberation from physical limitations, but also to deep-seated anxieties about what "being human" or "being an individual" might still mean in such a context. Such concerns about whether the boundaries between human and animal and between human and machine might have become too technologically permeable are hardly new or particular to the early twenty-first century. But the fact that technoscientific advances are beginning to make such border crossings more than mere hypotheses, combined with a willingness, at least in some quarters, to put in question conventional definitions of humanness, do mark a point of departure from the modernist conviction that human beings stand apart, and should remain apart, from other forms of existence.

Questions about the limits and desirability of human interventions into nature also shape, in a very different way, the varied strands of environmentalist thought that have emerged since the 1960s. While environmentalism encompasses an enormous diversity of visions, it is fair to say that a critique of modernization forms an integral part of many environmentalist approaches to the question of humans' relationship to nature. Environmentalists charge that modernizing processes have increased and accelerated uses of natural resources that damage ecosystems in ways that are extremely difficult or impossible to reverse later on; science and technology, in this view, have contributed to human population growth that is exhausting global resources, have enabled agricultural and industrial production and distribution processes that are not sustainable in the long run, and have led to reckless consumerism, which takes a heavy toll on nature. Many of the transformations that have led to what we consider "modern societies," therefore, have serious consequences for the environment as they cause large-scale loss of natural habitats and species, disrupt the proper functioning and aesthetic appeal of those ecosystems that manage to survive, and gradually lead to the disappearance of spaces not created and managed by humans. But they also, environmentalists argue, have negative effects on humans themselves: they threaten sustainable growth through the depletion of natural resources that humans rely on (such as drinkable water, unpolluted air, or arable soil), produce hazards to human health (through pollution), and, through persistent population growth, put in question whether and how humans as a species can survive in the long-term future.

In their critique of modernization, environmentalists tend to question not only particular destructive developments, but also the attitude or code of ethics that could have led to such flourishing of humanity on one hand, but to such disregard for the nonhuman world on the other. This attack on modernist ways of approaching nature often implicitly criticizes a technoscientific rationality that reduces nature to a mere object to be analyzed and used in the service of an endless array of human needs and desires, and those economically based modes of thought that would turn nature into nothing but a set of commodities to be bought and sold. It remains true, however, that many strands of environmentalist thought are fundamentally ambivalent in their relation to science and technology. On the one hand, scientific insights about interventions in nature have given environmentalism much of what public authority and credibility it has; from Rachel Carson's trenchant and detailed analysis of the effects of agricultural chemicals in the 1960s to the discovery of the ozone hole and global warming in the 1980s and 1990s, environmentalism has relied on the sciences – principally biology, ecology, and chemistry – to deliver precise descriptions of humans' deleterious impact on the natural world. On the other hand, as mentioned earlier, environmentalists have also often felt that science and technology were the forces that made humans' destruction of nature on a large scale possible in the first place. In the environmentalist critique of science, it is not only particular technologies or the uses to which they are put that are faulted for ecological devastation; more fundamentally, some environmentalists see science's rationalist and instrumentalist conception of nature as the basic problem, that is, the culture and values associated with science. In this more radical view, simply eliminating some technologies or changing the way in which they are deployed does not address the underlying problem, which is humans' conviction of their right to use, change, and exploit nature in whichever way they see fit to further their own goals.

Environmentalists also frequently charge scientists for framing their research in far too specialized a way, focusing on the detailed analysis of tightly defined and circumscribed problems, but losing track of the networks and interconnections that really make living ecosystems function. What we need in the face of planet-wide ecological devastation, some environmentalists argue, is more synthetic research that brings together different areas of specialization to develop a clearer image of how nature is bearing up to human impact. Other environmentalists consider science incapable of transcending its analytical bent, and turn to alternative perspectives instead to gain a more "holistic" or global insight into nature.[16]

In this context, environmentalists who are even more radical have sought to develop a vision of nature that would be "ecocentric" or "biocentric" rather than anthropocentric. In this view, which is often referred to as "deep ecology," nature would not be considered in terms of how it ensures the survival and well-being of humans no matter what the cost to other species, but would be valued in its own right, independently of its human uses. Obviously, such a perspective would entail a very different relation to nonhuman species, one that many human cultures would currently not be willing to accept. Unquestionably, as ecocentrists themselves admit, the attempt to value nature "in its own right" is beset with paradox, since it is humans who bestow this value on the nonhuman world. Nevertheless, the basic idea that nature is, or should be, more than a mere human resource is central to environmentalist thought, and it questions humans' right to manipulate nature for their own gain, even (or perhaps particularly) if this gain is in knowledge rather than in material well-being. It is easy to see how such "biospherical egalitarianism" also challenges science, which has conventionally assumed that even mere increases in knowledge (let alone practical advances) justify serious intervention into natural processes, and that the rights of other species play little or no role in this justification.[17]

Even though only a minority of the populations of western societies would call themselves "environmentalists," awareness of environmental problems has become relatively widespread since the 1960s. This broadly understood awareness that modernizing processes in general, and scientific and technological advances in particular, have had serious adverse effects on nature and, in some cases, on humans themselves, forms part of a more general disenchantment and ambivalence about technoscientific progress that gradually gained momentum in the second half of the twentieth century. This skepticism led to a sustained questioning of science and its roots in European and North American modernity, which we shall examine in more detail below. The developments in science and technology that we have surveyed so far, however, already point to one of the pivotal paradoxes in the emergence of the postmodern moment. On the one hand, this moment is characterized by unprecedented technoscientific advances, especially but not only in digital technology, biology, and ecology, that catalyze great enthusiasm and seem to transcend the limits of what seemed possible even in the early half of the century. On the other hand, precisely at this moment doubts and questions emerge, not only about certain applications of science and technology, but about their very nature – doubts that put their sociocultural legitimacy in question.

Science and the crisis of legitimation

Several factors have contributed to this rise of ambivalence toward science and technology. Awareness of the environmental damage that technologically advanced societies inflict on natural ecosystems figures as one cause of the gradual loss of trust. The perception that much scientific insight and technological ingenuity went into the manufacture of ever more destructive weapons of war, leading ultimately to a nuclear regime of "mutually assured destruction" for large parts of the globe, has also contributed to public disenchantment, as did a sense that technoscientific advances helped to improve the lives of people in some privileged regions, but left the rest of the globe in abject misery. In some circles, such perceptions led to the suspicion that science might essentially be a tool of oppression at the service of the powerful. It was pointed out that science had in the past been used to justify sexist and racist forms of domination through biological theories allegedly proving the inferiority of women and nonwhite peoples. Of course, such theories were subsequently repudiated by science itself; still, even in the present, scientists have often been perceived as experts who serve as mere mouthpieces for governments or business companies rather than for the common people. Science, it was suspected, might not be as beneficial to the majority as Enlightenment philosophy had claimed through its general belief that increased knowledge furthers the individual's emancipation and liberation.

Such perceptions form part of a set of factors that from the 1960s led to a weakening of the cultural belief in historical progress in western societies.

The idea that history evolves according to an underlying logic that brings about the gradual betterment of human societies had emerged from Enlightenment thought and nineteenth-century philosophies of history. It became one of the defining marks of modernist thought, a widespread background assumption that was not questioned most of the time. At the same time, it turned into a strong ground of legitimation for those groups, institutions, and currents of thought that claimed progress as their goal. Science and technology, two of the areas in which the idea of continuous advance and improvement were most clearly manifest, seemed justified and desirable to many precisely because of their association with progress, in the sense that they provided greater knowledge of the world as well as increased material well-being.

The gradually increasing skepticism about the idea that history would bring about ever more progress led to a parallel questioning of the justification for many modern institutions; in particular, it led historians and philosophers to postulate a *crisis in the legitimation of science* as one of the pillars of western thought and society.[18] This idea attracted particularly widespread attention in the English-speaking world after the translation of French philosopher Jean-François Lyotard's work *The Postmodern Condition: A Report on Knowledge*. In this report for the Québecois Government's Conseil des universités, Lyotard argued that the two most important narratives that had served to legitimate the pursuit of scientific knowledge throughout the nineteenth and early twentieth centuries were losing much of their persuasive force in the late twentieth century. One of these overarching arguments, or "metanarratives" as Lyotard calls them, is the Hegelian idea that the human spirit itself progresses over the course of history, and that the expansion of knowledge is one of the most visible tokens of this progress. The other one is the Enlightenment belief that the acquisition of knowledge contributes to the liberation and emancipation of individuals and communities. Neither of these legitimations commands widespread adherence, Lyotard argues, in an age when science itself has disintegrated into highly specialized research projects that maintain only scant communication with one another. Echoing a term developed by the language philosopher Ludwig Wittgenstein, Lyotard sees contemporary science as no longer a coherent, truth-oriented pursuit of knowledge, but as an assemblage of a variety of independent "language games" in which facts no longer count, but only "performativity," instrumental functioning. As critics of Lyotard have pointed out, this account falls far short of a convincing portrayal of contemporary science.[19] Perhaps for this reason, his argument did not provoke any great resonance among scientists at the time of its publication, but it became enormously popular among scholars in the humanities and social sciences who saw its argument about the demise of large-scale metanarratives of legitimation as a defining feature of postmodernism across a whole range of sociocultural phenomena.[20]

From the 1970s onward, a protracted, intense controversy among historians, philosophers, sociologists, cultural critics, and natural scientists over the basic nature and the social functions of scientific knowledge became one of the most visible manifestations of the crisis of scientific legitimation. This controversy, which has affected above all American, British, and French universities, led to what is now commonly referred to as the "science wars": violent disagreement among scholars and scientists over the relationship between scientific knowledge, truth, and reality, the kinds of ideological and political uses to which science and technology are or should be put, as well as the distinction between scientific experts and the lay public and the roles each should play in shaping public policies about issues involving science and technology. In the US, the debate heated up with the publication of *Higher Superstition* (1994) by biologist Paul Gross and mathematician Norman Levitt, a book that brought postmodernist critiques of science to the broad attention of scientists for the first time and triggered a wave of controversy. Two years later, the science wars reached an even more intense peak with the so-called "Sokal hoax." In 1996, the physicist Alan Sokal submitted a paper purporting to establish connections between quantum mechanics and various strands of postmodern philosophy to a journal named *Social Text*, which had repeatedly published articles questioning the superiority of scientific over other kinds of knowledge, and whose editorial committee included some scholars who had taken a skeptical stance toward science. The editors accepted and published the article, and Sokal simultaneously went public with the revelation that the article was a mere hoax intended to expose the ignorance about scientific matters that in his view characterized the work of many scholars who questioned science. In the weeks and months that followed, responses, accusations, and counter-accusations were published in major American and international newspapers by eminent scholars from a wide variety of disciplines.[21] This extended and highly visible controversy brought academic debates about the legitimation of scientific knowledge to the attention of a broader public. The issues that have arisen in this debate illuminate in an exemplary fashion what is at stake in "postmodern" philosophy, and what problems arise within this framework of thought.

The postmodern critique of scientific knowledge

Critiques of science have emerged in various fields influenced by postmodern thought, such as anthropology, sociology, philosophy, gender studies, and cultural studies. These critiques do not form a homogeneous body of argument. They differ substantially and sometimes contradict one another, and it would be futile to attempt to summarize all of them here in their nuances. Nevertheless, certain basic lines of reasoning recur frequently enough across these different approaches that they can convey the conceptual backbone of many postmodernist critiques of science. Critics of science argue, first, that scientific method and knowledge have no special cognitive status and, like many other practices, cannot be detached from the sociocultural context in which they arise; this "social constructedness" limits the claims for objectivity and universality that can be made on their behalf. Second, the critics claim that scientific research is not value-neutral, as its advocates maintain, but that fundamental beliefs and even ideological assumptions are hardwired into the definition, goals, and procedures of scientific inquiry. In some authors' view, this ideology has served the interests of dominant social groups at the expense of knowledge that would benefit the common people. In their search for a science that would be more responsive to democratic and progressive political goals they suggest, third, that the relationship between science and other modes of knowledge needs to be rethought so as to open the way for more pluralist and in the end more "objective" kinds of inquiry about the world. All forms of knowledge are socially constructed, and none of them can claim superior cognitive validity; therefore representations of the natural world are open to negotiation among scientists themselves, as well as between the scientific community and the public. The boundaries between experts and lay people, "insiders" and "outsiders," have to be redefined, and the institutional mechanisms that have shielded the scientific community from lay people need to be redesigned so as to open up new channels for public participation in shaping scientific applications and technologies.

Advocates of science have responded to such charges by pointing out how, among other things, many of them are trapped in the pitfalls of relativist thought even when the critics claim not to take a relativist stance. They have asked how a "politically responsible" science could be realized in the absence of universally agreed-upon political aims, and how the findings and theories of such a science would in practice differ from those proposed by conventional research, considering the constraints that the givens of the natural world impose upon any scientific investigation.[22] They have also defended the specificity of scientific knowledge, and the stringent procedures as well as logical and empirical controls that are applied to establish the validity of a particular knowledge claim. These procedures, they argue, account for both the changing character of scientific knowledge and its gradual progress in the understanding of nature.

Many of the perspectives that foreground how science is historically and culturally constructed derive from the seminal 1962 work *The Structure of Scientific Revolutions* by historian of science Thomas Kuhn.[23] In this book, Kuhn distinguishes between "normal science" and "scientific revolution" or "paradigm shift." In periods of "normal science," a particular theoretical framework has been established in a specific area of scientific research, and most scientists working in this area focus on exploring its implications and applications, expanding scientific knowledge by accretion. At moments of revolutionary paradigm shift, however, explanatory models are proposed that are at least in part irreconcilable with the established paradigm, and that lead scientists to expand knowledge by fundamentally rethinking and redirecting their research, including asking what questions can meaningfully be asked and what counts as a criterion for a successful theory. This account of scientific history does not lead Kuhn to take a relativist view of science or to reject the notion of scientific progress; but he insists that the normal understanding of scientific progress as a gradual incrementation of knowledge that will someday lead to a full and complete account of the natural universe does not hold up in view of the historical evidence. Rather, he proposes, scientific progress should be understood as an evolution that leads from simple beginnings to more detailed, complex, and specialized accounts without any ultimate goal, and without approximation to any universally defined truth.

In partial disregard of Kuhn's own views, many of his followers have taken *The Structure of Scientific Revolutions* as a point of departure for considering science more radically as an activity rooted in particular socio-historical and cultural contexts, the authority of which derives from social consensus rather than from any privileged grasp of reality. It is this consensus, they argue, rather than the verification or falsification of hypotheses through empirical findings or the replication of results by independent researchers, that makes for the special status of scientific knowledge. "Social constructivism," as this view is commonly called, does not in and of itself imply radical relativism; it is possible to admit that science is socially conditioned in multiple ways without giving up the claim that science's particular set of social constructions provides a type of access to the natural world that is more accurate or successful, from a cognitive or explanatory perspective, than other constructions. Indeed, even scientists would not deny that some dimensions of scientific inquiry are clearly dependent on social and historical circumstance: which general areas and specific topics are researched, how much funding is made available for particular projects, what general research strategies are selected, and how well the results are disseminated and applied all depend on a particular society's structure of interest.

This structure manifests itself in cultural biases that pervade the culture at large (for example, greater interest in men's health than in women's), in the institutions that finance research and their interests (for example, a preference for research on either basic science or specific applications), the schools that train and certify scientists, and the number and quality of publishing venues through which results can be communicated and thereby influence the work of other scientists. But once a particular issue has been selected for research, scientists and some philosophers of science would argue, scientific methodology – the "shared grammar" or "*lingua franca*...that binds together most of the [scientific] community in a tacit consensus as to 'what science is all about'"[24] – ensures that the results can be replicated by independent researchers outside of the social context from which they originally emerged. Kuhn would agree with this so long as the same scientific paradigm persists, but he would point out that such replication may become pointless after a fundamental change of paradigm. Some of his followers argue, more radically, that what counts as a result or as replication may itself be subject to change, which in their view shows the difficulty of arriving at any universal criteria of scientific validity. Social constructivism, in this perspective, means not only that scientific procedures are shaped by social context, but that this social conditioning implies that science has no privileged access to reality.

In this radical perspective, even as apparently basic and uncontroversial a term as "fact" comes under scrutiny. While scientists readily admit that facts are "theory-laden" – that is, that they cannot be established without some theoretical framework that determines which dimensions of a given situation are relevant – postmodern critics of scientific rationality develop this noncontroversial point by arguing that facts are actually not "discovered" but "created" by scientific procedures. This point has been argued most forcefully by the Edinburgh School of sociology of knowledge, and by the French sociologist Bruno Latour. Both argue that the truth or falsehood of scientific claims is not established by reference to the "real world" itself, but by complex mechanisms that pertain to the social and cultural world. The Edinburgh School sociologists claim that scientific knowledge needs to be understood in terms of the societies that produce it.[25] Latour, in his turn, analyzes laboratory life and scientific controversies from an ethnographic perspective. What interests him about such scientific practices is not primarily whether they deliver accurate descriptions of the world or not, but how something comes to be called a "fact," and what consequences the usage of this term entails. In his empirical studies, he therefore focuses particularly on time periods when claims that were later accepted as scientific facts were still being investigated and fought over by different scientists and laboratories. In his view, it is a complex network of references to instruments, institutions, and individuals that gradually leads to the consensual crystallization of facts (his theory is often referred to as "actor-network theory" for this reason); but once a fact is accepted, this network of connections drops out of sight, and facts come to seem self-evident and fixed where they were fluid and debatable earlier on.[26]

In this perspective, "truth," "fact," and "objective knowledge" are the terms commonly attributed to those knowledge claims that command a large degree of consensus among researchers or a larger social community. This viewpoint has also been argued with particular force by the influential American philosopher Richard Rorty, whose seminal book *Philosophy and the Mirror of Nature* has become one of the cornerstones of postmodern philosophy.[27] Talking about facts and external realities makes sense, Rorty argues, but only within the framework established by a particular social community; we cannot claim any foundations for factuality beyond social consensus. Other scholars would add that how this consensus is established depends in large measure on the relations of power in the social community.[28] Such fully fledged relativism, however, leads to conceptual difficulties and self-contradictions that many critics of Rorty in particular, and of postmodern approaches to science in general, have pointed out: how can we ascertain that the claim that facts are valid only within a social consensus framework is itself factual? If this claim is itself valid only within a certain social framework, there is no reason to privilege it over other claims – such as the one, for example, that facts are independent of consensus. If, conversely, the claim is valid independently of the particular framework, it contradicts its own rule, and we should need some explanation as to why claims about how factual claims are established are more factual than fact claims themselves: "Is the belief that everything is culturally relative itself relative to a cultural framework? If it is, then there is no need to accept it as gospel truth; if it is, it undercuts its own claim," as Marxist literary critic Terry Eagleton sums it up.[29]

A related problem that emerges within the relativist framework is that it shifts a heavy burden of explanation to concepts such as "society" and "culture," without clarifying what epistemological tools would make the analysis of these phenomena any more reliable or "factual" than those of the natural world. If the realities of nature do not exist except as socio-cultural constructions, do society and culture exist beyond such constructions? If not, it is difficult to see how these concepts could offer any solid ground for explaining scientific findings. Eagleton points to this problem when he remarks, somewhat flippantly, "Why is everything reducible to culture, rather than to some other thing? And how do we establish this momentous truth? By cultural means, one assumes; but is this not rather like claiming that everything boils down to religion, and that we know this because the law of God tells us so?"[30] Bruno Latour, who does not share Eagleton's opposition to relativism, points up the same inconsistency when he takes fellow scholars to task for not being relativist enough: "If nature and epistemology are not made up of transhistoric entities, then neither are history and sociology – unless one adopts some authors' asymmetrical posture and agrees to be simultaneously constructivist where nature is concerned and realist where society is concerned."[31] Jean Bricmont and Alan Sokal, staunch defenders of science, similarly argue that the attempt to account for science purely in terms of cultural and social factors forces one to claim that sociological or anthropological theories have greater explanatory force than scientific ones.[32] These and related arguments have led scholars such as philosopher Paul Boghossian to assert that the postmodern critique of science is merely another one of many historical versions of relativism, and not a particularly coherent one at that, and Eagleton calls culturalism "one of the great contemporary reductionisms" along with biologism, economism and essentialism.[33]

But not all critical perspectives of science that build on postmodernist strands of thought are relativist and "culturalist" in this sense. On the contrary, some critics of science reject relativism and insist that some form of objective knowledge is necessary and desirable. In their argument, contemporary science is in fact not objective enough, and needs to be fundamentally changed and complemented to attain anything like objectivity. In particular, they claim that the notion of "objectivity" needs to be detached from the concept of "value-neutrality"; scientific observers and methods, in their view, do not and never have operated outside of specific value frameworks, and the goal in attaining objectivity is not to rid them of such values but to examine them critically and substitute better ones where necessary.

Some feminist perspectives provide a good example of why some postmodernist critics do not want to adopt a radically relativist viewpoint on science. The feminist approach to science, like a good deal of other postmodern criticism, is motivated by a perception that scientific activity excludes the interests and perspectives of large groups of populations, as well as by sociopolitical engagement to change such patterns of exclusion. A completely relativist stance *vis-à-vis* scientific descriptions of the world would not serve that interest well: after all, pointing out that certain assumptions about women are scientifically inaccurate has often been one of the strongest arguments on behalf of feminist approaches. Relativism disables this kind of argument and makes it difficult to claim that one's own perspective offers a better description of the world; if all descriptions of the world are *nothing but* social constructions, then there are no factual grounds for choosing between them. But feminist theorists would like to preserve a basis for indicting mistaken assumptions about women or gender. Furthermore, they claim that in fact a feminist perspective in science offers greater objectivity because it uncovers some of the hidden prejudices in standard science. Feminist philosopher Sandra Harding, for example, points out that "no critics of racism, imperialism, male supremacy, or the class system think that the evidence and arguments they present leave their claims valid only 'from their perspective'; they argue for the validity of these claims on objective grounds, not on 'perspectivalist' ones."[34] Feminist historian of science Donna Haraway similarly argues that "feminists have to insist on a better account of the world; it is not enough to show radical historical contingency and modes of construction for everything."[35]

This desire to ground their feminist projects in factual claims leads both theorists to reject relativism as what Haraway calls "the perfect mirror twin of totalization,"[36] and to insist instead on what they variously call "standpoint epistemologies," "partial perspective," "local knowledge," or "situated knowledges." (The emphasis on the epistemological importance of local, situated, and partial kinds of knowledge is generally one of the hallmarks of postmodern thought across a variety of disciplines such as anthropology, philosophy, and cultural studies.) All of these terms refer to searches after knowledge that do not abandon claims of fact, but acknowledge with self-critical awareness that such claims can only ever be made from standpoints that are shaped by historical, social, and cultural contingencies. For Harding in particular, such awareness leads to an alternative account of objectivity: one that does not postulate that the observer has to be neutral, but on the contrary that she or he has the ability to recognize and think through rival positions. Neutrality, according to Harding, usually conceals how much dominant positions do in fact owe to particular social interests, and this becomes especially visible when they are viewed from socioculturally marginalized positions. Since such marginalized perspectives allow one to perceive and address distortions that are caused by the dominant investment in a particular set of social values and interests, they in fact lead to a stronger rather than a weaker notion of objectivity.[37] Haraway similarly asserts that "situated knowledges" should be pursued with the goal of achieving "enforceable, reliable accounts of things."[38] Cultural-studies scholar Andrew Ross echoes this call to go beyond relativism from a generally progressive rather than a specifically feminist perspective:

> If the practice of cultural studies is to preserve its activist direction, then it cannot afford to give up a public voice that goes beyond the relativism of respectfully recognizing and appreciating all cultural differences equally... In science, probably more than in "humanist" culture, there remains the challenge of providing... "better accounts of the world," that will be publicly answerable and of some service to progressive interests... If the rallying-cry for a "science for the people" is still to stand for something that resembles an objective vision of the social good, then it depends on salvaging workable strategies from the vertiginous relativism that often results from culturalist analyses of science's day-to-day workings.[39]

At first sight, such proposals seem to offer an alternative to the conflict between scientific realism and postmodernist relativism by rejecting the strong forms of both. But relativism does emerge as a problem again when one asks what would allow a situated knowledge-claim to be judged "reliable," and what would make it "enforceable." What enables a subject in one sociocultural location to agree with or contest the knowledge produced in another one? On the basis of what criteria would conflicts between contradictory knowledge claims be resolved? It is difficult to see how these questions could be answered without resorting either to some sort of realism that would allow facts to constrain what counts as legitimate knowledge, or to a relativism that would make facts dependent on value judgments. Haraway seems to tend toward the latter solution when she argues that, "admitted or not, politics and ethics ground struggles over knowledge projects... Moral and political discourse should be the paradigm of rational discourse."[40] Advocates of scientific realism such as Gerald Holton or Paul Gross and Norman Levitt respond to such privileging of ideological discourse by pointing out that this makes it difficult to find grounds for resisting the self-consciously "situated knowledge" of, for example, the German Nazis, who openly rejected objectivity in favor of a specifically German, non-Jewish science.[41] Harding and Haraway might answer this objection by arguing that, indeed, the crucial reasoning against Aryan science has to be based on questions of political goals and desirability rather than on those of factual accuracy.[42] This may be a plausible argument as far as it goes, but it is not one that can appeal to objective knowledge or "reliable accounts of the world" against Nazism. If facts cannot ground or constrain arguments about political ideology, it is unclear how Harding and Haraway's pluralism of situated knowledges in the end differs from the relativism they so vigorously reject.

This is the problem that underlies Harding's disagreement with physicist Steven Weinberg over whether she should be called a relativist; as Weinberg indicates, Harding criticized a draft of his book *Dreams of a Final Theory* that labeled her as such by pointing to her explicit rejections of relativism;

Weinberg dropped the term, but continued to argue that her reasoning made sense only within a relativist framework.[43] In this context, it is curious that the work of philosopher Paul Feyerabend is mentioned only in passing in Harding and Haraway's work; in a note, Harding accuses him of being an "example of apolitical postmodernist philosophy."[44] Yet in his central book, *Against Method*, Feyerabend outlines an ideological framework that does not sound fundamentally different from the pluralism of knowledges proposed by Harding and Haraway:

> I want to make two points: first, that science can stand on its own feet and does not need any help from rationalists, secular humanists, Marxists and similar religious movements; and, secondly, that non-scientific cultures, procedures and assumptions can also stand on their own feet and should be allowed to do so, if this is the wish of their representatives... My main motive in writing the book was humanitarian, not intellectual. I wanted to support people, not to "advance knowledge." People all over the world have developed ways of surviving in partly dangerous, partly agreeable surroundings... Today old traditions are being revived and people try again to adapt their lives to the ideas of their ancestors. I have tried to show, by an analysis of the apparently hardest parts of science, the natural sciences, that science, properly understood, has no argument against such a procedure.[45]

Once again, then, theorists who advocate a plurality of situated knowledges may be closer to radically relativist positions than they perceive themselves to be.

Leaving aside the question of whether any of the postmodernist critiques of science offer a genuine alternative to realism and relativism, one might want to explore some of their more pragmatic dimensions. Thomas Kuhn's account of scientific history focuses almost exclusively on the internal dynamics of the scientific field as it moves through transitions from one paradigm to another. Much work in sociology of knowledge, by contrast, has attempted to set the scientific knowledge of a particular historical and cultural moment in relation to its social context, and in particular to the ideological interests and configurations that went into its shaping. In such analyses, some sociologists of science (for example, those of the Edinburgh School) have deliberately set aside a basic distinction that was established by the philosopher Hans Reichenbach earlier in the twentieth century. Reichenbach argued that science operates in a "context of discovery" and a "context of justification." Social and historical factors can be invoked, he argued, to explain how scientists first arrive at ("discover") particular insights and theories; but subsequently, these theories need to be justified in terms of their internal logic and the empirical evidence so that their validity can be established. This epistemological core, Reichenbach claimed, is independent from sociohistorical contingencies. Such a distinction is no longer accepted by some

contemporary sociologists of science, who argue that the basic epistemological properties of science are not exempt from beliefs and values shaped
by sociohistorical contexts. This claim has led them to merge the cognitive
and sociohistorical dimensions of scientific research and to propose an entirely new explanation of scientific procedures in terms of social factors (an
example of such an analysis is Latour and Woolgar's *Laboratory Life*).

Often, the gist of such analyses is to relativize dominant scientific claims
by showing their politically motivated underside, and in some cases to reha-
bilitate minority claims that might have had comparable legitimacy. (Steve
Fuller has noted a certain asymmetry that tends to characterize these analyses, in that sociologists of knowledge rarely undertake to deliver a revin-
dicating account of knowledge claims on the part of groups whose political
ideology is fundamentally opposed to that which tends to prevail among the
sociologists; Aryan science and the creationism of Christian fundamentalists
in the USA, for example, have so far been exempt from such arguments.)[46]
While this framework lends itself well to explaining why scientific successes
may have occurred, it is not equally persuasive in accounting for the difficulties and failures that even dominant scientific strains frequently confront.
The failure of cold fusion or the search for the elusive cure for cancer come
to mind as contemporary borderlines of science that should be susceptible to
an explanation in the same theoretical terms as, say, the invention of nuclear
energy generation or the discovery of penicillin. It is not clear, however, at
least at present, what such an explanation would look like, and this raises the
more general question regarding what factors might function as constraints
in constructivist and relativist approaches.[47]

One last question that arises in the debate over postmodernist critiques
of science is how standpoint epistemologies or situated knowledges would
change the actual principles and procedures of science. Advocates of science
sometimes dismiss the claims of situated knowledge by arguing that, in such
highly abstract areas as mathematics or theoretical physics, it is difficult to
envision what difference a feminist approach, for example, would make. But
in scientific fields with more immediate social relevance, situated knowledge
is less easy to set aside. Ecological or medical investigations, for instance,
sometimes do undergo fundamental shifts when the lived experience and
local expertise of those immediately exposed to the problem are considered.
The sociologist Brian Wynne, to give an example, has shown how the pre-
dictions and instructions of scientists in charge of investigating the effects
of radioactive fallout from Chernobyl on some of the uplands of Northern
England missed their mark because the scientists were unacquainted with
the local ecology and economy, and ignored the suggestions of farmers who
had lived and worked in the area for many decades.[48] Medical diagnoses

and therapies sometimes similarly vary depending on how much contextual knowledge is brought to bear on particular types of cases. In these instances, it is harder to determine conclusively to what extent situated knowledges could be integrated into the existing theories and methodologies of science, and to what extent they would transform them.

Even if situated knowledges turn out not to challenge basic scientific protocols, their integration would by no means be a minor accomplishment in practical terms. Postmodernist critics of science are surely right to inquire after the institutional interests and funding sources that currently propel research into certain directions at the expense of others. It is equally legitimate to ask for whose benefit scientific knowledge is being generated, and what social groups have access to the institutions and management of science. But while a critique of science in these social terms is surely justified and, if implemented, might lead to significant changes in some aspects of scientific research, the argumentative difficulties and self-contradictions discussed above do remain when the critique is taken to the epistemological core of scientific research. Since sociopolitical and epistemological criticisms of science became inextricably fused with each other in the heyday of postmodernism, at any rate, it is unlikely that the argumentative inconsistencies of the epistemological critique will in and of themselves lead to its rejection. Instead, the urgency of the sociopolitical critique will most likely continue to bolster the attempt to seek out grounds for a more socially responsible science, not only in its institutional framework and its sociocultural uses and functions, but in the theoretical and methodological structure of scientific research itself.

The science wars after postmodernism

In its questioning of rationality, late twentieth-century postmodernism has often been compared to the Romantic era, another historical moment in which a strong technoscientific push – the wave of industrialization in England at the turn of the nineteenth century – was met with intense cultural skepticism and resistance. As Patricia Waugh writes:

> Postmodernism can be understood...as the culmination of an aestheticist tradition deriving from Romantic thought...This tradition has consistently viewed Enlightenment reason as complicit in its instrumentalism with industrial modernity...It has drawn on the aesthetic in order to offer both a critique of social rationalization and the restriction of definitions of knowledge to what can be consciously and conceptually formulated.[49]

Undeniably, there are family resemblances between Enlightenment critiques of the early nineteenth and the late twentieth centuries. Yet it is not insignificant that the science wars erupted with full force only in the mid-1990s, at a time when many of the main currents of postmodernist thought were already being vigorously criticized and sometimes even rejected within the disciplines that had most eagerly embraced them in the 1970s and 1980s, such as literary criticism and anthropology. That the conflict over the nature and social functions of scientific rationality has persisted into a period in which "postmodernism" has been replaced by "globalization" as a key concept around which debates about the legacies of modernity revolve suggests that issues other than academic postmodern thought might underlie it.

One of these issues is clearly visible in the concerns many science critics voice over the relationship between rationality, science, and political power structures. Their target of criticism in this context is not so much rationality as such as the belief that science is the only, or any rate the privileged, embodiment of rationality. This belief, they argue, is compromised by the oppressive political uses to which scientific rationality has been put; therefore, as a way of opening up scientific research to more democratic politics, they suggest that there are different types of rational inquiry, a variety of which should be represented in the search for knowledge. Sociologist Stanley Aronowitz, for example, argues that scientific rationality is "*a* but not *the* form of reason" (original emphasis), and that, as such, "it may occupy no privileged position with respect to knowledge of nature."[50] Instead, he concludes, "an alternative science would have to imagine, as a condition of its emergence, an alternative rationality which would not be based on domination."[51] Sandra Harding similarly suggests that several different types of science might and should coexist and should be brought together in a "knowledge collage" or "borderlands epistemology."[52] One of the goals of such pluralist knowledge, in her view, would be to "distinguish ... between those values and interests that block the production of less partial and distorted accounts of nature and social relations ('less false' ones) and those – such as fairness, honesty, detachment, and ... advancing democracy – that provide resources for it."[53] Donna Haraway, likewise, articulates hopes for a science committed to democratic politics: "I want to argue for a doctrine and practice of objectivity that privileges contestation, deconstruction, passionate construction, webbed connections, and hope for transformation of systems of knowledge and ways of seeing," as does cultural-studies scholar Andrew Ross: "Workable strategies [emerging from the cultural analysis of science] ... must ... be addressed to the desire for personal responsibility and control that will allow nonexperts to make sense of the role of science in their everyday dealings with the social and physical world."[54] What motivates many of the postmodern science critics, then, is the concern to open up to democratic participation a science that they consider politically oppressive.

In this context, the question arises how such democratic participation might function practically, given the fact that the majority of the population even in industrialized countries has very limited knowledge of the science that is relevant in processes of public decision-making about technological and scientific matters. French physicist Jean-Marc Lévy-Leblond argues that democratic countries do not usually require their citizens to acquire specialized political or legal knowledge before asking them to vote or serve on a jury; why, then, should such expertise be expected in matters of a scientific or technological character? "Democracy is a *bet*: the bet that conscience should take precedence over competence," Lévy-Leblond claims.[55] Most scientists and experts on the public understanding of science take a more moderate position, arguing that democracies need to work on improving citizens' scientific literacy so that decision-making can be based on the best available knowledge.[56] Mathematician Norman Levitt, by contrast, points out that genuine scientific literacy takes so much time and effort to acquire that it can hardly be a realistic goal for the majority of citizens; in most cases, their knowledge will of necessity remain extremely limited, and will not attain a level where they can make truly informed decisions. While he grants the public authority to decide what kinds of broad purposes science should serve and what kinds of scientific projects should be prioritized, decisions that involve expert knowledge should in his view be left to the specialists. The task of the public, in this context, is not to aspire to expert knowledge but to learn how one distinguishes experts from nonexperts, and how one seeks out their opinion in case of need.[57]

My point here is not to argue for one of the various sides in this debate, but to foreground how both critics and advocates of science focus on the relationship between a broad public that may possess only rudimentary forms of scientific knowledge and training, and political processes that play a crucial role in determining how scientific insights and technological innovations will be socially implemented. In democratic societies, such processes are supposed to be shaped by the participation of citizens. To what extent can and should citizens with limited technoscientific competence be called upon to participate in decisions about science and technology that involve a good deal of technical detail? This question obviously has considerable urgency in societies where issues such as computer privacy, genetically engineered foods, or pollution standards come up constantly on the political, legislative, and juridical agenda, and it is one of the acute political issues that has given the science wars and the controversy over scientific rationality and its possible alternatives some of their argumentative violence.

In this context, it is significant that German sociologist Ulrich Beck has suggested the term "risk society" as a substitute for "postmodern society," since debates over technoscientifically generated risk, which are primary sites of conflict between scientific expertise and public participation, are in his view fundamental to understanding the global society of the present and future.[58] If this is so, it is unclear whether the gradual shift away from the concept of the postmodern and toward that of globalization will mitigate the vehemence of the conflict over scientific rationality.[59] On one hand, the more frequent and intimate contact between different cultures that accompanies globalization might be expected to reinforce calls for the consideration of different sorts of research and knowledge. On the other hand, it might reinforce the demand for the products of western science and technology and thereby relegate to the background any questioning of its dominance (as is the case, for example, in the urgent international call to make western-developed AIDS drugs available to affected populations across the globe). What is certain, however, is that the "postmodern" forms of science and technology that evolved over the course of the twentieth century are already exerting a shaping influence on those societies around the planet that are still struggling to shape their own forms of the modern.[60] Western debates over the fate of postmodernism are most fruitfully approached in this global context of emergent modernities, in which science and technology will unquestionably continue to play a central role.

NOTES

1. The best survey of the different meanings of "postmodernism" and "postmodernity" is Hans Bertens, *The Idea of the Postmodern: A History* (London: Routledge, 1995), ch. 1. On the value changes that characterize postmodernity, see John Gibbins and Bo Reimer, "Postmodernism," in Jan W. Van Deth and Elinor Scarbrough (eds.), *The Impact of Values* (New York: Oxford University Press, 1995), pp. 301–31, and Ronald Inglehart, *Modernization and Postmodernization: Cultural, Economic, and Political Change in 43 Societies* (Princeton, NJ: Princeton University Press, 1997). The divergent shapes that postmodernism takes in different art forms is explained in Steven Connor, *Postmodernist Culture: An Introduction to Theories of the Contemporary*, 2nd edn. (Oxford: Blackwell, 1997).

2. On public ambivalence toward science, see Oscar Handlin's "Ambivalence in the Popular Response to Science," in Barry Barnes (ed.), *Sociology of Science* (Harmondsworth: Penguin, 1972), pp. 253–68, and Jon D. Miller and Rafael Pardo, "Civic Scientific Literacy and Attitudes to Science and Technology: A Comparative Analysis of the European Union, the United States, Japan, and Canada," in Meinolf Dierkes and Claudia von Grote (eds.), *Between Understanding and Trust: The Public, Science and Technology* (Amsterdam: Harwood, 2000), pp. 131–56. On progress and nature, see Leo Marx, "The Domination of Nature and the Redefinition of Progress," in Leo Marx and Bruce Mazlish (eds.), *Progress: Fact or Illusion?* (Ann Arbor, MI: University of Michigan Press, 1998), pp. 201–18.

3. In *The Economics of Industrial Innovation*, 3rd edn. (Cambridge, MA: MIT Press, 1997), Chris Freeman and Luc Soete distinguish these "incremental innovations" from the more obvious "radical innovations."

4. On these networks, see Thomas P. Hughes, *American Genesis: A Century of Invention and Technological Enthusiasm, 1870–1970* (New York: Viking, 1989), and *Rescuing Prometheus: Four Monumental Projects that Changed the Modern World* (New York: Pantheon, 1998).

5. Two other areas, nuclear energy and space exploration, have undergone profound changes in public perception; nuclear energy became an object of social controversy and a symbol of public resistance to technology; space exploration, a focus of public excitement in its first decades, has lost much of its prominence and attracts attention mainly when accidents occur.

6. Computer pioneers in the late 1940s and early 1950s believed that fewer than ten computers would satisfy all the computing needs of the time, as Paul E. Ceruzzi has pointed out in "An Unforeseen Revolution: Computers and Expectations, 1935–1985," in Joseph J. Corn (ed.), *Imagining Tomorrow: History, Technology, and the American Future* (Cambridge, MA: MIT Press, 1986), pp. 188–201. For a survey of the evolution of digital technology, see Ceruzzi, *A History of Modern Computing* (Cambridge, MA: MIT Press, 1998).

7. For examples of such enthusiasm, see Richard A. Lanham, *The Electronic Word: Democracy, Technology, and the Arts* (Chicago, IL: University of Chicago Press, 1993); George P. Landow, *Hypertext: The Convergence of Contemporary Critical Theory and Technology* (Baltimore, MD: Johns Hopkins University Press, 1992); and Howard Rheingold, *The Virtual Community: Homesteading on the Electronic Frontier* (Reading, MA: Addison-Wesley, 1993).

8. For engagements with the cyborg, see Donna J. Haraway, "A Manifesto for Cyborgs," ch. 8 of *Simians, Cyborgs, and Women: The Reinvention of Nature* (New York: Routledge, 1991), pp. 149–81; and Chris Hables Gray (ed.), *The Cyborg Handbook* (New York: Routledge, 1995).

9. For example, Michael Dertouzos, *What Will Be: How the New World of Information Will Change Our Lives* (New York: HarperEdge, 1997) offers an optimistic assessment of information technologies and their impacts.

10. See, for example, David Shenk, *Data Smog: Surviving the Information Glut* (New York: HarperCollins, 1997).

11. Daniel Bell, *The Coming of Post-Industrial Society*. 2nd edn. (New York: Basic, 1999).

12. See Erik Brynjolfsson and Brian Kahin (eds.), *Understanding the Digital Economy: Data, Tools, and Research* (Cambridge, MA: MIT Press, 2000).

13. For analyses of the debates surrounding embryo research, see Dorothy Nelkin, "Science, Technology, and Political Conflict," and Steven Maynard-Moody, "The Fetal Research Dispute," in Dorothy Nelkin (ed.), *Controversy: Politics of Technical Decisions*, 3rd edn. (Newbury Park: Sage, 1992), pp. ix–xxv, 3–25; Dorothy Nelkin and M. Susan Lindee, *The DNA Mystique: The Gene as a Cultural Icon* (New York: Freeman, 1995); Peter Singer *et al.* (eds.), *Embryo Experimentation: Ethical, Legal and Social Issues* (Cambridge: Cambridge University Press, 1990); and Michael Mulkay, *The Embryo Research Debate: Science and the Politics of Reproduction* (Cambridge: Cambridge University Press, 1997).

14. Cf. George Gaskell, Martin W. Bauer, John Durant, and Nicholas C. Allum, "Worlds Apart?: The Reception of Genetically Modified Foods in Europe and the U.S.," *Science* 285 (16 July 1999), pp. 384–7.

15. Jon Turney reads the current resistance to genetic engineering and other biological advances against the background of the Frankenstein story in *Frankenstein's Footsteps: Science, Genetics and Popular Culture* (New Haven, CT: Yale University Press, 1998).

16. Cf. Leo Marx's discussion of the countercultural critique of science in the 1960s in *The Pilot and the Passenger: Essays on Literature, Technology, and Culture in the United States* (New York: Oxford University Press, 1988), pp. 169–78.

17. A good introductory survey of the many varieties of environmentalist thought is David Pepper, *Modern Environmentalism: An Introduction* (London: Routledge, 1996). One of the most influential proponents of deep ecology is the Norwegian philosopher Arne Naess; see, for example, his seminal book *Ecology, Community, and Lifestyle*, trans. David Rothenberg (Cambridge: Cambridge University Press, 1989). See also Bill Devall and George Sessions, *Deep Ecology: Living as if Nature Mattered* (Salt Lake City, UT: Smith, 1985), and George Sessions (ed.). *Deep Ecology for the 21st Century: Readings on the Philosophy and Practice of the New Environmentalism* (Boston, MA: Shambhala, 1995).

18. For an analysis of how legitimation crises affect other modern institutions, see Jürgen Habermas, *Legitimation Crisis*, trans. Thomas McCarthy (Boston, MA: Beacon, 1975).

19. Connor, *Postmodernist Culture*, pp. 30–1.

20. A much more solidly argued account about how the unspoken contract between scientists and the society they work in changed from the nineteenth to the late twentieth century and brought about an erosion of public trust and legitimation is David H. Guston and Kenneth Keniston, "Introduction: The Social Contract for Science," in Guston and Keniston (eds.), *The Fragile Contract: University Science and the Federal Government* (Cambridge, MA: MIT Press, 1994), pp. 1–41. This argument has not been given similar attention in the humanities.

21. Alan D. Sokal, "Transgressing the Boundaries: Toward a Transformative Hermeneutics of Quantum Gravity," *Social Text* 46–7 (1996), pp. 217–52; the text of this article, Sokal's revelation, the *Social Text* editors' response, as well as numerous comments on both sides of the controversy are assembled in *The Sokal Hoax: The Sham that Shook the Academy* (Lincoln, NB: University of Nebraska Press, 2000), edited by the editors of the journal *Lingua Franca*. Sokal elaborated his critique in more detail in the book he co-wrote with French physicist Jean Bricmont, *Fashionable Nonsense* (in the UK: *Intellectual Impostures*): *Postmodern Intellectuals' Abuse of Science* (New York: Picador, 1998; London: Profile, 1999).

22. By talking about "critics" and "advocates" of science, I do not mean to suggest that there are two well-defined, homogeneous camps opposing each other. Each of these groups consists of a variety of scholars with different disciplinary backgrounds and argumentative interests who have proposed various lines of reasoning; cf. Michael Lynch, "Is a Science Peace Process Necessary?," in Jay A. Labinger and Harry Collins (eds.), *The One Culture? A Conversation about Science* (Chicago, IL: University of Chicago Press, 2001), pp. 50–4. In summarizing

these arguments, however, it is necessary to describe the different sides of the controversy by some overarching term.

23. Thomas S. Kuhn, *The Structure of Scientific Revolutions*, 3rd edn. (Chicago, IL: University of Chicago Press, 1996).

24. Norman Levitt, *Prometheus Bedeviled: Science and the Contradictions of Contemporary Culture* (New Brunswick: Rutgers University Press, 1999), p. 14. Levitt borrows the term "shared grammar" from the geneticist Steve Jones.

25. See, for example, David Bloor, *Knowledge and Social Imagery*, 2nd edn. (Chicago, IL: University of Chicago Press, 1991).

26. See Bruno Latour and Steve Woolgar, *Laboratory Life: The Social Construction of Scientific Facts*, 2nd edn. (Princeton, NJ: Princeton University Press, 1986), and Bruno Latour, *Science in Action: How to Follow Scientists and Engineers through Society* (Cambridge, MA: Harvard University Press, 1987) for the best-known presentations of this approach.

27. Rorty explicitly discusses the relation of his argument to Kuhn's in ch. 7 of *Philosophy and the Mirror of Nature* (Princeton, NJ: Princeton University Press, 1979), pp. 315–56.

28. See, for example, Andrew Ross, *Strange Weather: Culture, Science, and Technology in the Age of Limits* (London: Verso, 1991), p. 25, and Stanley Aronowitz's exploration of the relationship between the rise of science and that of capitalism in *Science as Power: Discourse and Ideology in Modern Society* (Minneapolis, MN: University of Minnesota Press, 1988).

29. Terry Eagleton, *The Idea of Culture* (Oxford: Blackwell, 2000), p. 92. A very concise and clear exposition of this argument can be found in Paul A. Boghossian, "What Is Social Constructivism?," *Times Literary Supplement* (23 February 2001), pp. 6–8. The inconsistencies of culturalism are also discussed with great perspicacity in Kate Soper, *What Is Nature? Culture, Politics and the Non-Human* (Oxford: Blackwell, 1995).

30. Eagleton, *Idea of Culture*, p. 92.

31. Bruno Latour, *We Have Never Been Modern*, trans. Catherine Porter (Cambridge, MA: Harvard University Press, 1993), p. 27.

32. Jean Bricmont and Alan Sokal, "Science and Sociology of Science: Beyond War and Peace," in Labinger and Collins (eds.), *The One Culture?*, pp. 42–43.

33. Boghossian, "What Is Social Constructivism?," p. 8; Eagleton, *Idea of Culture*, p. 92.

34. Sandra Harding, "After the Neutrality Ideal: Science, Politics, and 'Strong Objectivity,'" *Social Research* 59 (1992), p. 576.

35. Haraway, *Simians, Cyborgs, and Women*, p. 187.

36. Ibid, p. 191.

37. Harding, "After the Neutrality Ideal," pp. 578–80.

38. Haraway, *Simians, Cyborgs, and Women*, p. 188.

39. Ross, *Strange Weather*, p. 29.

40. Haraway, *Simians, Cyborgs, and Women*, pp. 193–4.

41. Gerald Holton, *Einstein, History, and Other Passions: The Rebellion against Science at the End of the Twentieth Century* (Reading, MA: Addison-Wesley, 1996), pp. 30–1; Paul R. Gross and Norman Levitt, *Higher Superstition: The Academic Left and Its Quarrels With Science* (Baltimore, MD: Johns Hopkins University Press, 1994), p. 129.

42. This argument is made explicitly in Barbara Herrnstein Smith's *Belief and Resistance: Dynamics of Contemporary Intellectual Controversy* (Cambridge, MA: Harvard University Press, 1997), pp. 26–31.

43. Steven Weinberg, *Facing Up: Science and Its Cultural Adversaries* (Cambridge, MA, and London: Harvard University Press, 2001), p. 149.

44. Sandra Harding, *The Science Question in Feminism* (Ithaca, NY: Cornell University Press, 1986), p. 194 n. 42.

45. Paul Feyerabend, *Against Method*, 3rd edn. (London: Verso, 1993), pp. viii, 4.

46. Steve Fuller, *Thomas Kuhn: A Philosophical History for Our Times* (Chicago, IL: University of Chicago Press, 2000), p. 360.

47. Katherine N. Hayles attempts to give just such a theoretical account of constraints in her remarkable essay "Constrained Constructivism: Locating Scientific Inquiry in the Theater of Representation," in George Levine (ed.), *Realism and Representation: Essays on the Problem of Realism in Relation to Science, Literature, and Culture* (Madison, WI: University of Wisconsin Press, 1993), pp. 27–43.

48. Brian Wynne, "Misunderstood Misunderstandings: Social Identities and Public Uptake of Science," in Alan Irwin and Brian Wynne (eds.), *Misunderstanding Science? The Public Reconstruction of Science and Technology* (Cambridge: Cambridge University Press, 1996), pp. 19–46.

49. Patricia Waugh (ed.), *Postmodernism: A Reader* (London: Edward Arnold, 1992), p. 4. See also Philip S. Baringer, "Introduction: The 'Science Wars,'" in Keith M. Ashman and Philip S. Baringer, *After the Science Wars* (London: Routledge, 2001), p. 5.

50. Aronowitz, *Science as Power*, p. 27.

51. Ibid., p. 352.

52. Sandra Harding, "Science Is 'Good To Think With,'" in Andrew Ross (ed.), *Science Wars* (Durham, NC: Duke University Press, 1996), pp. 21, 23–4.

53. Harding, "After the Neutrality Ideal," p. 580.

54. Haraway, *Simians, Cyborgs, and Women*, pp. 191–2; Ross, *Strange Weather*, p. 29.

55. Jean-Marc Lévy-Leblond, "About Misunderstandings about Misunderstandings," *Public Understanding of Science* 1 (January 1992), p. 20.

56. Kenneth Prewitt, "Scientific Illiteracy and Democratic Theory," *Daedalus* 112 (1983), pp. 49–64; Jon D. Miller, *The American People and Science Policy: The Role of Public Attitudes in the Policy Process* (New York: Pergamon, 1983).

57. Levitt, *Prometheus Bedeviled*, pp. 187–8, 315.

58. Ulrich Beck's book *Risk Society: Towards a New Modernity* (London: Sage, 1992) was originally published in German in 1986 (*Risikogesellschaft: Auf dem Weg in eine andere Moderne*), and attained considerable popularity in western Europe far beyond academic circles. The literature on risk assessments and risk perceptions in contemporary societies is vast; a good introduction can be found in Ragnar E. Löfstedt and Lynn Frewer (eds.), *The Earthscan Reader in Risk and Modern Society* (London: Earthscan: 1998).

59. The tone of the debate, to be sure, has changed in some of the more recent publications; both Ashman and Baringer, *After the Science Wars*, and Labinger and Collins, *The One Culture?*, anthologies that include contributions by critics as well as defenders of science, reflect a more reasoned and conciliatory

stance toward the debate of the crucial issues than the one that prevailed in the 1990s. It is not clear, however, that the *substance* of the arguments has changed fundamentally.

60. For two important discussions of the different forms that modernization takes in different regions, see Arjun Appadurai, *Modernity at Large: Cultural Dimensions of Globalization* (Minneapolis, MN: University of Minnesota Press, 1996); and Néstor García Canclini, *Hybrid Cultures: Strategies for Entering and Leaving Modernity*, trans. Christopher L. Chippari and Silvia L. López (Minneapolis, MN: University of Minnesota Press, 1995) (originally published in Spanish under the title *Culturas híbridas: Estrategias para entrar y salir de la modernidad*, 1990).

8

PHILIPPA BERRY

Postmodernism and post-religion

"All that is solid melts into air"

The society and culture we inhabit today, at the start of the third millennium, appear at first glance to be the most secular that the world has yet known. As traditional conceptions of knowledge and religion appear increasingly redundant in the context of a postmodern pluralism, so an increasingly frenetic pursuit of this-worldly pleasures, along with an ever higher standard of living – with the attendant pressures not just to work harder and to play harder but, above all, to consume – seems definitively to have replaced that emphasis upon otherworldly and religious forms of comfort, or "salvation," that was accorded social and cultural legitimation in precapitalist society. When Marx and Engels published *The Communist Manifesto* in the middle of the nineteenth century they declared that the relentless logic of capitalist economics would ultimately dislodge "all fixed, fast-frozen relations, with their train of ancient and venerable prejudices and opinions," with the result that "all that is solid melts into air, all that is holy is profaned."[1] It was a statement that proved to be eloquently prophetic, not simply of modernity, but also of the paradoxical (and notoriously difficult to define) cultural and economic phase that has succeeded it, which can very generally be described as postmodern and late-capitalist. For what Marx and Engels so astutely anticipated was the advent of a hyperactive society of "everlasting uncertainty and agitation," driven ceaselessly onwards by technological advance, in which the desire for the new is so intense that new fashions and new ideas "become antiquated before they can ossify into custom."[2] A century and a half later, in remarks whose bitter skepticism echoes the proleptic disillusionment of Marx and Engels, a contemporary critic has described what he sees as "our all but consumed, consumptive society" as follows: "a time of massive cynicism and universal lying, in which all qualities have been devalued, or rather suspended in a wave of reactive consumer populism that seems both inescapable and never-ending...This is an age in which one must be

168

classifiable, so that everything one says can be dismissed as mere point of view."[3]

It is hardly surprising, of course, that not only orthodox religion but even the more general concept of "value" appears to have reached a critical impasse within a cultural and economic climate where traditional modes of both knowledge and exchange are being rapidly superseded, on the one hand, by the dissemination of increasingly populist cultural forms and "hyperintelligent" sources of information, and on the other, by the advent of global, computer-based networks of trading. How is it possible, then, for a leading British specialist in religious studies, Ursula King, to express the view that "postmodernism can ... be seen positively as a challenging task, an opportunity, even a gift for religion in the modern world"?[4] And even more perplexingly, how can we relate the following cryptic formulation by Jacques Derrida, taken from his influential *Specters of Marx*, to what we *think* we know about our postmodern culture?

> There is then *some spirit*. Spirits. And *one must* reckon with them. One cannot not have to, one must not not be able to reckon with them, which are more than one: the *more than one/no more one* [*le* plus d'un].[5]

The return of religion(s)

The apparent incompatibility of the contrasting responses to late capitalist culture and society cited above has not prevented them from becoming peculiarly interwoven in the complex cultural mesh which is postmodernism. Thus, alongside the oft-stated conviction that our society's brash ephemerality and greed are utterly meaningless, inimical not simply to religious belief but also to conventional ideas of an interior quality of life, there have begun to be voiced less usual but nonetheless compelling opinions: expressions of an apparently irrational hope in the possibility of a different future, which may be informed by reference to conventional religion on the one hand (King) or, alternatively, by cryptic allusion to a numinous and nonhuman force that is loosely called "spirit" (Derrida).

From the vantage point of a postmodern relativism, of course, neither of these contrasting perspectives, of despair and of hope, can be unequivocally dismissed, since each represents a relative form of truth or value. In Thomas Pynchon's *The Crying of Lot 49* (1965), often described as a seminal postmodern novel, his female protagonist, Oedipa, finds herself hesitating between two radically contrasting conceptions of meaning:

> It was now like walking among matrices of a great digital computer, the zeroes and ones twinned above, hanging like balanced mobiles right and left, ahead,

thick, maybe endless. Behind the hieroglyphic streets there would either be a transcendent meaning, or only the earth . . . Ones and zeroes . . . Another mode of meaning behind the obvious, or none.[6]

Oedipa's dilemma is of either/or, zero or one – either there is one transcendent meaning, or there is none. But of course postmodern thought has consistently claimed that the hyperrational mind's urge constantly to discriminate between "truth" and "falsehood" is itself urgently in need of revision. And certainly the political necessity of articulating new ethical as well as critical positions in relation to polarized paradigms of belief and nonbelief has become vividly apparent after the events of 11 September 2001 (9–11) and their equally tragic aftermath.

In his meditation upon the relationship of different forms of "religion" to our contemporary culture, which builds on his lifelong critique of the illusions inherent in western dualistic thought, Jacques Derrida has stressed once again the futility of continuing to draw absolute distinctions such as that between belief and doubt. Indeed, Derrida claims that our exaggerated secularism is invisibly bound to and attracted by its purported opposite or antithesis. And he poses the following rhetorical question:

> Why is this phenomenon, called "the return of religions," so difficult to think? Why is it so surprising? Why does it particularly astonish those who believed naively that an alternative opposed Religion, on the one side, and on the other, Reason, Enlightenment, Science, Criticism . . . as though the one could not but put an end to the other? . . . *In this very place*, knowledge and faith, technoscience ("capitalist" and fiduciary) *and* belief, credit, trustworthiness, the act of faith will always have made common cause, bound to one another by the band of their opposition.[7]

According to this viewpoint, the putative cultural triumph of secular reason is necessarily haunted or shadowed by its presumed opposite – by that very absolutism of belief which nihilism's prophet, Nietzsche, so fervently renounced. But this cultural haunting is not singular. Instead, like the ghost/spirit that Derrida describes as *le plus d'un* – the more than one/no more one – it assumes manifold and different forms – including *phantasmatic* effects whose imaginative difference is especially uncanny because less substantial and familiar, because both like and *unlike* what is remembered as religion. It is now more than a sociological cliché, but a startling political reality, of course, that the recent acceleration of postmodern culture has coincided with the often violent revival of fundamentalist religious attitudes, as the technological achievement of a virtual experience of planetization is peculiarly inverted or shadowed by parallel movements towards retribalization. The quality of historical belatedness and stark anachronism that seems to distinguish fundamentalist reiterations of traditional faith in relation to postmodern culture invests them with a quality of cultural strangeness or uncanniness whose implicit violence has regularly been enacted, whether in Jonestown in Guyana, in Waco, Texas, or more recently in New York and Washington. Yet in that they purport to be restatements of the "fundamental" forms of established religions, these fundamentalist stances are also peculiarly familiar or homely (*heimlich*), as part of our collective cultural memory system.

In his provocative response to the terrorist attack on America of 9–11, an essay first published in *Le Monde*, Jean Baudrillard alluded, not directly to religious fundamentalism, but instead to

> that (unwittingly) terroristic imagination which dwells in all of us . . . Which explains all the counter-phobic ravings about exorcizing evil: it is because it [evil] is there, everywhere, like an obscure object of desire. Without this deep-seated complicity, the event would not have had the resonance it has, and in their symbolic strategy the terrorists doubtless know that they can count on this unavowable complicity.[8]

Yet Derrida has strongly implied that the "return of the religious" should not be "reduced to what the *doxa* confusedly calls 'fundamentalism,' 'fanaticism,' or, in French, 'integrism'" and has suggested in his reference to "some spirits" that the cultural haunting we are experiencing is not singular.[9] Like Pynchon's Oedipa, many members of our society may experience themselves as trapped between the apparently irresolvable binarism of belief and doubt; yet postmodern culture is also imprinted with the traces of other, more ambiguous and elusive, modes of spirituality, or of what might best be described as a post-religious, post-skeptical, and, crucially, post-dualistic consciousness. If these are signs of what Richard H. Roberts has called a "quasi-religious" state, they appear to differ significantly both from the dominant secularism and from the often impassioned and even violent re-presentations of the tenets of dogmatic religion(s).[10] This second group of symptoms – a cluster of asymmetrical rifts or flaws that not only runs suggestively through popular culture, but that also informs key contemporary philosophical, theological, and literary texts – attests to the widespread dissemination of heterodox and highly diffuse forms of belief, if not of religion. These cultural rifts are unsettling or *unheimlich* in a sense importantly different from the re-presentation of the dogmas of traditional religions; not only do they typically draw on (both populist and elite) ideas of pre-Christian or non-Christian religious experience, but in some respects they are also more expressive of a postmodern sensibility. Hence, while re-presentations of faith – whether it be that of dissident cults or of orthodox religion – typically appear at the edges or on the borderline of our postmodern culture, several of these different signs of spirituality fissure its confident secularism and materialism rather less obtrusively, or as it were from within. Like the cracks in the earth that form the central metaphor of a recent novel by Salman Rushdie, *The Ground Beneath Her Feet*, these "post-religious" or "quasi-religious" phenomena direct our attention, not to a putative spiritual *depth* that is concealed behind or underlies our culture, but rather to the way in which unexpected fusions of materiality with "spirit" are constantly appearing on its most ephemeral surfaces. At the same time, these often highly quotidian effects can arguably be compared to what Zgymunt Bauman, writing of postmodernity, has termed "the reenchantment of the world."

In an attempt to define "modern post-Protestant consciousness" at the end of the twentieth century one journalist observed:

> People have moved away from 'religion' as something anchored in organised worship and systematic beliefs within an institution, to a self-made 'spirituality', outside formal structures, which is based on experience, has no doctrine and makes no claim to philosophical coherence.[11]

More specifically, theologian James R. Lewis observed as early as 1992 that

> Gallup Poll statistics indicate that one out of every four Americans believes in astrology, and that one out of every five Americans believes in reincarnation. Similar statistics taken in the United Kingdom turn up the interesting statistic that 30–35 percent of the British population hold a belief in reincarnation.
>
> Statistics of this magnitude indicate that we are no longer talking about a marginal phenomenon. Rather, we appear to be witnessing the birth of a new, truly pluralistic mainstream.[12]

Some elements of the discursive formation that Lewis is describing here, which can very approximately be termed New Age culture, seem highly anomalous in relation to postmodern culture; others, however, afford quite distinctive parallels to the cultural motifs and products of postmodernism. In economic terms the postmodern condition is generally defined as the complete commodification of experience; New Age culture apparently signals the extreme commodification of the religious impulse, if not of religion. The American theologian Carl Raschke has stressed the exaggerated "materiality" of New Age culture, a seeming paradox (given its spiritual agendas) that he defines as "the *commodification of the arcane and obscure*."[13] The fluid juxtaposition of elements of erudite and mass culture that distinguishes New Age commodities (from self-help books to crystals, pendulums, and divination packs) – along with their syncretic mixing of time periods and cultural sources – results in a discursive *bricolage* in which both the appropriation of earlier cultural materials and the (typically unintentional) pastiching of these fragments parallels the deliberate aesthetic techniques of postmodern art.[14] At the same time (and in spite of its late-humanist emphasis upon concepts of self-realization or fulfilment) the impact upon this trend of concepts of voidness chiefly derived from Buddhism affords a suggestive analogue to the deconstruction of substantive models of identity and knowledge within postmodern thought.

It is presumably not in response to the surprising multiplicity of new modes of popular belief that Derrida has asked, evoking Kierkegaard, "How dare we speak of it [religion] in the singular without fear and trembling?"[15] But it is clear that, like the ghost/spirit that he represents in *Specters of Marx* as *le plus d'un* – the more than one/no more one – the haunting of our secular culture by something like yet unlike religion is now assuming manifold different forms. And in contrast to the frequent banality of New Age commodity culture, a range of much more demanding cultural statements – including several significant artistic, literary, and filmic productions as well as theoretical and philosophical texts – have begun to stage the paradoxical return(s) of a spirit or spirits not yet imagined. Several of these "spirits" may plausibly be read, not simply as seeming antitheses to secularism and hyperrationality, but also as tentative relocations of something like spirit within an emergent epistemology and ontology that is not founded on binary methods of thought.[16]

Conceptual deserts

It has been acknowledged for several years, of course, that a philosophical concern with religion – or with the post- or quasi-religious – is explicit in the works of a number of continental philosophers, notably Emmanuel Levinas, Edmond Jabès, Michel de Certeau and Luce Irigaray. Yet there has been only gradual comprehension of the extent to which, albeit less overtly, comparable motifs inform the work of other continental thinkers: notably Georges Bataille, Maurice Blanchot, Julia Kristeva, Hélène Cixous, Jean-Luc Nancy, and – perhaps most importantly – Jacques Derrida himself. Although aspects of Derrida's thought were compared by him to negative theology as early as the late 1960s, it is only in the last decade that some of the wider cultural implications of the quasi-religious or post-religious themes in both his work and that of this second group of thinkers have begun to be elucidated, by readers long attuned to secular modes of thought.[17]

What has made it easier both to identify and to decipher the quasi-religious or spiritual aspects of this new intellectual nexus is our recent reassessment of the work of German phenomenologist Martin Heidegger, which influenced all of these postmodern thinkers to different degrees. Heidegger famously observed of the late-modern condition that "Only a god can save us now" – a remark recently retranslated by one critic as "Only *another* god can save us now" (my emphasis).[18] And Derrida has noted the paradox inherent in the "dechristianizing" trajectory of Heidegger's thought, alluding to a "Heidegger who seems unable to stop either settling accounts with Christianity or distancing himself from it – with all the more violence in so far as it is already too late, perhaps, for him to deny certain proto-Christian motifs in the ontological repetition and existential analytics."[19] But along with other critics of Heidegger Derrida has also stressed the extent to which Heidegger's rejection of that "Roman" mode of thinking and of religiosity, both pagan and Christian, that is implicit in the Latin word *religare* (to bind again) was integral to his aim of reawakening, however allusively, a different "experience of the sacred, the holy or the sacred (*heilig*)." What has been gradually effected both by Derrida's own *oeuvre* and by that wider intellectual current in which he is a major voice is a deconstructive reweaving of Heidegger's Greekness, with its acknowledged taint of anti-Semitism, into its seeming antitheses. Thus, commenting on the semantic history of the German word for the "holy," *heilig*, much used by Heidegger, Derrida observes that it "seems to resist the rigorous dissociation that Levinas wishes to maintain between a natural sacredness that would be pagan, even Graeco-Christian, and the holiness <*sainteté*> of Jewish law, before or under the Roman religion."[20] In this reconfiguring of the holy as an imperfectly differentiated ("jewgreek") mode of the "sacred," Derrida articulates a recurring theme in the postmodern thinking of "religion." And in the contributions of other thinkers to this emergent discourse, not only are Jewish conceptions of the mysterious unrepresentability, withdrawal, and absence of the divine interwoven with Greek motifs – of a quasi-divine *ekstasis*, and of a mysterious place of nonorigin, Plato's *chora* – other religious and quasi-religious elements also resonate: recurring echoes of Christianity, but also more distinctly (near-oriental) ideas of spirit or the holy, from Egypt, India, and China. Yet, perhaps unsurprisingly, there is one repeated and now very telling omission from this post-religious or quasi-religious *bricolage*: the religion of Islam. Of course, it is that very absence that seems now (although only, I must confess, with the advantage of hindsight) to accord Islam an aporetic potency in relation to these postmodern (theoretical) assemblies of bits and pieces of spirit: these fragments or synecdoches of different models of belief.

In a review in the *New Statesman* of a rash of books analyzing the events of 9–11, sociologist John Gray made some provocative but intriguing claims, observing among other things that "Al-Qaeda's closest affinities are with 19th-century revolutionary nihilism, not medieval religion" – a combination that "does not square with any of the theories of modernization that we have inherited from the Enlightenment." Gray's most telling observation in the context of this essay is that "The western intelligentsia as a whole is more confused and marginal than it has been for generations" – primarily, because it is still dominated by thinkers who subscribe to "the Enlightenment faith that as societies become more modern, they become more alike, accepting the same secular values and the same view of the world. That faith was always questionable. Today it is incredible. If now we reach to our shelves for books that can help us to understand what happened on 11 September, we find almost nothing."[21]

But perhaps it is appropriate as well as somewhat ironic that it is the ethical and religious meditations of two Jewish thinkers that may provide us with some vital clues as to how we should begin to read and respond to this representational aporia, as a conceptual desert or Ground Zero that has suddenly become the locus of a terrifyingly violent resistance to the festive excesses of both global capitalism and postmodern secularism. Emmanuel Levinas's writing, vitally shaped by his reflections upon the Holocaust as a Jewish thinker, stresses that after this seminal ethical crisis it is "the absolutely foreign [that] alone can instruct us." In the process Levinas redefines subjectivity as well as ideas of God. The Levinasian subject becomes the locus of a new spaciousness and decenteredness as it discovers the need to found a new ethical relationship to the "other" in the *infini* (infinity) that is experienced in the midst of an ethical exchange. The result is that one is required "to open oneself as space" – or, put another way, to create a space for some direct or indirect form of communication.[22] In the last few decades, the sometimes violent "opening" of the human to forms of radical alterity has become a recurring motif in art and literature. Writing of the alchemical implications of the powerful "electro-technology" works produced by the artist Anselm Kiefer, for example, Matthew Biro has noted that both spirit and matter are understood here as forms of energy, as these paintings

> bind together a series of binary oppositions relating to the transformation of "spirit" and matter into energy and vice-versa. Among these oppositions, the two most consistently emphasized are the opposition between the human and the non-human or divine and the opposition between solid materials that liquefy and solid materials that transmit energy but do not themselves change state.[23]

Since the ethical relationship is always understood by Levinas as an encounter with the divine, in this respect it must always elude rational comprehension: "It is through its ambivalence which always remains an enigma that infinity or the transcendent does not let itself be assembled."[24] And Edmond Jabès places a parallel or complementary emphasis upon the spatiality of this (non)relationship to a divine other that is precisely defined by its lack of definition, its absence. It was Jabès, most importantly, who seems to have been the first of these thinkers to select the "non-place" of the desert as a highly suggestive metaphor for our postmodern, post-religious situation. This nonspecific site is spatially situated between all oppositions, yet through its emptiness and radical dereliction it is also temporally differed from such polarities (as both predialectical and postdialectical). Jabès observes: "And what is the desert if not a place denied its place, an absent place, a non-place?"[25] Commenting upon the Jewish as well as early Christian resonances of this motif, Jean-Luc Nancy observes that now, "our experience of the divine is our experience of desertion. It is no longer a question of meeting God in the desert: but of this – and this *is the desert* – : we do not encounter God, God has deserted all encounter."[26] For Baudrillard, the desert that is metonymically adjacent to postmodernism, as in the desert surrounding what he sees as the postmodern city *par excellence*, Las Vegas, is always already a site of potential violence. In a half-acknowledgment of the location's affinity with archaic attempts to communicate with the divine (an impulse to which, in antiquity, sacrificial ritual was central), Baudrillard observes in *America* that "you always have to bring something into the desert to sacrifice."[27]

It seems that, in order to explore the significance of this post-religious void-like intellectual and cultural location, the human subject is required to *desert* or sacrifice any idea of himself or herself as substantive, fixed, or central. He or she must become instead the site in which *something else*, whether this be nonhuman Being, or the nonhuman materiality of "place" itself, can become manifest. After 9–11, however, this emphasis upon a subjective and individual experience of the postmodern desert of negation and emptiness or of nihilism seems curiously naive. Instead, it now seems necessary to reflect upon the extent to which the secular confidence of an entire society has suddenly foundered as it experiences itself as vulnerable to being fissured, torn, and even secretly invaded – virus-like – by radical modes of alterity. Slavoj Žižek notes the spectral, uncanny character of the events of 9–11 in *Welcome to the Desert of the Real*:

> The virtualization of our daily lives, the experience that we are living more and more in an artificially constructed universe, gives rise to an irresistible

urge to "return to the Real", to regain firm ground in some "real reality". The Real which returns has the status of another semblance: *precisely because it is real, that is, on account of its traumatic/excessive character, we are unable to integrate it into what we experience as our reality, and are therefore compelled to experience it as a nightmarish apparition.*[28]

Reason beyond itself

On closer observation, therefore, the cultural boundaries of the postmodern appear to be extremely fragile as well as porous, in respect of both religion and the quasi-religious. So Baudrillard has commented of global capitalism:

> In a sense, the entire system, by its internal fragility, lent the initial action [of 9–11] a helping hand.
> The more concentrated the system becomes globally, the more it becomes vulnerable at a single point (already a single little Filipino hacker had managed, from the dark recesses of his portable computer, to launch the "I love you" virus, which circled the globe devastating entire networks). Here it was eighteen suicide attackers who, thanks to the absolute weapon of death, enhanced by technological efficiency, unleashed a global catastrophic process.[29]

From the perspective of a postmodern ethics, the very fragility and porousness of the West's global power structures will ultimately require a much more thoughtful and measured interpretative response than the violent policing of our cultural and economic difference that we have seen since 9–11. Suffice it to say that the vital contribution of deconstruction or poststructuralism to postmodern theory has not yet revolutionized the much less reflective field of international relations. Yet through their repeated interrogation of the centrality to western thought of polarized categories such as light/dark, good/evil, atheism/belief, these discourses remind us of the need to reflect upon our ontological and epistemological deserts, as we reopen the shadowy and liminal terrain *between* opposing concepts. In contrast to Pynchon's Oedipa, the postmodern *flâneuse* or *flâneur* who can move intelligently amid the shimmering commodities and the peculiarly ephemeral, inherently non-referential images (or *simulacra*) of our superficial and superaffluent culture is now being invited to experience the uncanny *coexistence* of contrasting systems of meaning. Responding to these differences requires a seemingly perverse admixture of reason (though now of an impure, post-Kantian kind) with a revitalized imaginative faculty. This postmodern *flâneuse* or *flâneur* has, one hopes, learned from deconstruction to unravel the both/and that is inherent in the subtle texture of all signification, by directing her or his attention not primarily to the signs themselves but also to the spacing *between* signs.

Contemporary postmodern thinkers such as John Sallis and Mark C. Taylor have elaborated some highly suggestive metaphors for those points of tension or undecidability within signification where seeming antitheses coexist, by alluding to nodes within meaning that are also (k)nots, and which, in the words of Sallis, "open reason beyond itself."[30] It is precisely negation – imaged by Taylor as the (k)not – that is central to this epistemological shift: "Neither something nor nothing, the not falls *between* being and non-being ... the not is not just resistance but something other that simultaneously emerges and withdraws at the elusive point where the religious and ethical inevitably intersect."[31]

During the crisis of *The Satanic Verses* Salman Rushdie declared: "Unable to accept the unarguable absolutes of religion, I have tried to fill up the hole with literature."[32] And in the penultimate chapter of his infamous novel, the episode of Ayesha's pilgrimage uses the techniques of magical realism to deconstruct the apparent binarism of doubt versus (an unorthodox mode of) belief. For Rushdie's Ayesha introduces an heretical difference into the traditional tenets of Islam. The literal pilgrimage she leads, in its objectively deluded aim of reaching Mecca by walking through the Arabian sea, ends in death by drowning for the faithful. Nonetheless, the otherwise sceptical survivors who lacked the faith to follow Ayesha under the water still think they have seen a miracle – a parting of the waters. At the very end of this chapter, as Sara Suleri has pointed out, Rushdie replaces the Islamic idea of faith as submission with a vivid imaginative experience of the postmodern motifs of "listening" and "opening" that also perceptively allies this experience to a disturbing combination of violence and ecstasy. For at this point, a final memorial differing of the disastrous pilgrimage informs the dying moments of a surviving sceptic, Mirza Saeed.

> Before his eyes closed he felt something brushing at his lips, and he saw the little cluster of butterflies struggling to enter his mouth. Then the sea poured over him, and he was in the water beside Ayesha, who had stepped miraculously out of his wife's body ... "Open," she was crying. "Open wide!" Tentacles of light were flowing from her navel and he chopped at them using the side of his hand. "Open," she screamed. "You've come this far, now do the rest" ...
>
> His body split apart from his Adam's apple to his groin, so that she could reach deep within him, and now she was open, they all were, and at the moment of their opening the water parted, and they walked to Mecca across the bed of the Arabian Sea.[33]

When reimagined in this way, far from being antithetically opposed to "absolute" concepts such as faith, it seems that it is precisely through its negation of traditional beliefs and values that postmodern culture is currently encountering disturbingly aporetical locations or positions which traumatically disturb our sense of the "real" along with our rational responses. Yet there is still a chance that western society may start to explore its conceptual deserts – as well as those real deserts upon which it is currently seeking to reimpose its political, economic, and cultural hegemony – more thoughtfully. Precisely because these locations are currently the locus of violent conflicts, they indicate the extreme urgency of elaborating a new understanding of these potent aporias within western thought. For if we are to negotiate new relationships between the polarized concepts upon which our culture has formerly grounded itself, then both religion and nihilism will have to be thought "otherwise" – precisely by being thought together.

NOTES

1. Karl Marx and Friedrich Engels, *The Communist Manifesto*, trans. Samuel Moore (1888) (Harmondsworth: Penguin, 1989), p. 83.
2. Ibid.
3. Thomas Pepper, *Singularities: Extremes of Theory in the Twentieth Century* (Cambridge: Cambridge University Press, 1997), p. xii.
4. Ursula King (ed.), *Faith and Praxis in a Postmodern Age* (London: Cassell, 1998), "Introduction," p. 7.
5. Jacques Derrida, *Specters of Marx: The State of the Debt, the Work of Mourning, and the New International*, trans. Peggy Kamuf (New York: Routledge, 1994), "Exordium," p. xx.
6. Thomas Pynchon, *The Crying of Lot 49* (London: Vintage, 1996), pp. 125–6.
7. Jacques Derrida, "Faith and Knowledge: The Two Sources of 'Religion' at the Limits of Reason Alone," trans. Samuel Weber, in Jacques Derrida and Gianni Vattimo (eds.), *Religion* (Cambridge: Polity, 1998), p. 2. Reprinted in Derrida, *Acts of Religion* (London: Routledge, 2002), pp. 42–101.
8. Jean Baudrillard, *The Spirit of Terrorism and Requiem for the Twin Towers*, trans. Chris Turner (London: Verso, 2002), pp. 5–6.
9. Derrida, "Faith and Knowledge," p. 5.
10. Richard H. Roberts, "Time, Virtuality and the Goddess," in Scott Lash, Andrew Quick and Richard H. Roberts (eds.), *Time and Value* (Oxford: Blackwell, 1998), pp. 112–29. Roberts observes that, currently, among social theorists, "there is a growing awareness of the increasing salience of the religious (or *quasi-religious*) factor in contemporary social and cultural change" (my emphasis) (p. 114).
11. Clifford Longley, "A Spiritual Land with Little Time for Church," *The Daily Telegraph*, Friday 17 December 1999, p. 31.
12. James H. Lewis, "Approaches to the Study of the New Age Movement," in James H. Lewis and J. Gordon Melton (eds.), *Perspectives in the New Age* (Albany, NY: State University of New York Press, 1992), p. 4.
13. Carl Raschke, "Fire and Roses, or, The Problem of Postmodern Religious Thinking," in Philippa Berry and Andrew Wernick (eds.), *Shadow of Spirit: Postmodernism and Religion* (London: Routledge, 1992), pp. 93–108, quotation from p. 104.

14. Fredric Jameson defines pastiche as a key device of postmodernism in *Postmodernism, or, The Cultural Logic of Late Capitalism* (Durham, NC: Duke University Press; London: Verso, 1991), pp. 16–19, 21, 25, 34. See also Donald Kuspit, "Archaeologism: Postmodernism as Excavation", in *The New Subjectivism: Art in the 1980s* (Ann Arbor, MI: UMI Research Press, 1988), pp. 531–7. For affinities to these techniques in New Age discourse see David J. Hess, *Science in the New Age: The Paranormal, Its Defenders and Debunkers, and American Culture* (Madison, WI: University of Wisconsin Press, 1993), p. 39.

15. Derrida, "Faith and Knowledge," p. 1.

16. Postmodernism is the heir to symbolism and modernism in this respect, through its philosophical expansion of the (often neglected) mythological and quasi-religious motifs used by writers such as Mallarmé, Joyce, Eliot, and Pound. A modernist anticipation of a new/old, *both* modern *and* Greek, synthesis of spirit with materiality is articulated in Ezra Pound's "The Return" – a poem written just after World War I, where he imagines the returning ghosts or *revenants* of the dead soldiers in relation to the advent of archaic "souls of blood," in a poetic evocation of the Greek concept of the "blood-soul" or *thymos*.

17. See, for example, the introduction by Gil Anidjar to Derrida's *Acts of Religion*, which traces a complex development in Derrida's discursive "acts" of religion, from early meditations upon negative theology to "the unsettling problematic of the theologico-political" (p. 39).

18. Pepper, *Singularities*, p. 82.

19. Derrida, "Faith and Knowledge," p. 12.

20. Ibid., p. 15.

21. John Gray, "Why Terrorism Is Unbeatable," *New Statesman*, 25 February 2002, pp. 50–3.

22. Emmanuel Levinas, *Otherwise than Being, or, Beyond Essence*, trans. A Lingis (The Hague: Martinus Nijhoff, 1979), p. 150.

23. Matthew Biro, *Anselm Kiefer and the Philosophy of Martin Heidegger* (Cambridge: Cambridge University Press, 1998), p. 207.

24. Ibid., p. 161.

25. Edmond Jabès, *The Book of Questions: El, or the Last Book*, trans. Rosemarie Waldrop (Middletown, CT.: Wesleyan University Press, 1984). Cited in Mark C. Taylor, *Disfiguring: Art, Architecture, Religion* (Chicago, IL: University of Chicago Press, 1992), p. 269.

26. Jean-Luc Nancy, cited in Taylor, *Disfiguring*, p. 269.

27. Jean Baudrillard, *America*, trans. Chris Turner (London: Verso, 1988), p. 14.

28. Slavoj Žižek, *Welcome to the Desert of the Real: Five Essays on September 11 and Related Dates* (London: Verso, 2002), p. 19.

29. Jean Baudrillard, *The Spirit of Terrorism*, trans. Chris Turner (London: Verso, 2002), p. 8.

30. John Sallis, *Spacings: Of Reason and Imagination in Texts of Kant, Fichte, Hegel* (Chicago, IL: University of Chicago Press, 1987), p. xv. For nodes and (k)nots of meaning, see Kenneth Maly, "Reading Sallis: An Introduction," in Maly (ed.), *The Path of Archaic Thinking: Unfolding the Work of John Sallis*, pp. 1–19 (quotation from p. 7), and Mark C. Taylor, *Nots* (Chicago: University of Chicago Press, 1993), *passim*.

31. Taylor, *Nots*, pp. 1–4. Elucidating the nodal/knotting metaphor in Sallis's work, Kenneth Maly observes that "in physics, a node is the point or surface of a vibrating thing where there is no vibration – a stillness" ("Reading Sallis," p. 7).

32. Salman Rushdie, "The Book Burning," *New York Review of Books*, 2 March 1989, p. 26.

33. Salman Rushdie, *The Satanic Verses* (London: Viking, 1988), pp. 506–7. See Sara Suleri, "Contraband Histories: Salman Rushdie and the Embodiment of Blasphemy," in M. D. Fletcher (ed.), *Reading Rushdie: Perspectives on the Fiction of Salman Rushdie* (Amsterdam: Rodopi, 1994), pp. 221–35.

9

ROBERT EAGLESTONE

Postmodernism and ethics against the metaphysics of comprehension

Postmodernism, ethics and European "success"

Postmodern ethics is often described in vague terms such as "openness," "otherness'" and "fracture" and an "opposition to totalizing systems." In this chapter, I aim to explain, in one way, why these terms are vague and why they have come to mean so much for postmodern thought. I also argue that postmodernism is first an ethical position before anything else.

Mary Midgley writes that

> the strong unifying tendency that is natural to our thought keeps making us hope that we have found a single pattern which is a Theory of Everything – a key to all the mysteries, the secret of the universe . . . A long series of failures has shown that this can't work. That realisation seems to be the sensible element at the core of the conceptual muddle now known as postmodernism.[1]

Midgley's comment is clearly right about postmodernism: it is a "conceptual muddle" (just *what* does it mean?) and there is some form of "core element," however expressed. She is also right that there is (more than) a tendency in western thought (but perhaps not a *natural* tendency) to reduce everything to a system. Is she also right that this tendency has failed to work and that the "sensible element" of postmodernism is the "realisation" of this failure?

Zygmunt Bauman and Jacques Derrida both argue that the different and murderous totalitarian regimes of the twentieth century grew from European thought: "Nazism was not born in a desert," after all.[2] Perhaps these systems, these "theories of everything," did not fail quite enough. Hannah Arendt suggests that both anti-Semitism and colonial expansion stem from European thought. She cites Rhodes's insight into the secret of European power, that expansion "is everything . . . I would annex the planets if I could," while – from the other side, as it were – Fanon writes that it is "in the name of the spirit of Europe that Europe has made her encroachments, that she has justified her crimes and legitimised the slavery in which she holds four fifths of humanity."[3] Simone de Beauvoir identifies western thought as a "male activity that in creating values has made of existence itself a value; this activity has prevailed over the confused forces of life; it has subdued Nature and Woman."[4] It would be easy to argue that other forms of daily oppression are evidence too of how little western thought actually fails. The glories of science and medicine are one thing, and could and should be shared as widely as possible, but with these extraordinary inventions of western thought are interwoven what Peter Winch called the "extra-scientific pretensions of science" – scientism, not science – which offer easy and implicitly unpalatable answers to a huge array of problems. ("Science plays its own game; it is incapable of legitimating the other language games. The game of prescription, for example, escapes it," writes Lyotard.)[5] Fanon again: "Europe has been successful in as much as everything that she has attempted has been successful."[6]

Postmodernism is not a response to failures of western thought, but – perhaps horrified – to its successes. Postmodernism, implicitly or explicitly, is about ethics before it is anything else. Before it is a style in art and architecture; before it is a description of an era ("late-capitalist" or "postindustrial" or "globalized" or "postcolonial"); before it is a philosophical movement, however vaguely defined (as "poststructuralism" or as "nomadic"); before it names a situation of knowledge ("incredulity about metanarratives," say) it is concerned with ethics. It is an ethical response to exactly the idea of a "single pattern" that characterizes western thought and the activity that stems from that "single pattern."

"Western thought" is one of those vague terms at which, rightly, people look askance; to define it here in detail, even if this were possible, would take too long. The "West" is a geographic term designating a space, roughly the same as the "First World" but no longer all in Europe. It is also a chronological term designating a time – perhaps the last 2,500 years, since Greek philosophy created a path of thought; perhaps the last 400 years, since the Renaissance, colonialism, and the rediscovery of this thought; perhaps the last 130 or so, since the exponential growth of scientism, science, and technology, imperialism and postimperialism, and the totalitarian states. It is an intellectual term, marking philosophical paths that can be seen to have a "family resemblance." It is all these terms at once. By "western thought," I mean roughly something like a *tradition* – which is not just philosophy, but is also made up of art, literature, politics, the culture of everyday life, everything that relies on thinking to make it so – which is part of a recognizable and "fundamental conceptual system,"[7] most powerfully but not exclusively stated in language, located geographically, chronologically and intellectually in what is called (calls itself?) the western world. Wittgenstein makes a very illuminating remark that gets at what I call here "western thought":

> We keep hearing the remark that philosophy does not progress, that we are still occupied with the same philosophical problems as were the Greeks. Those who say this, however, don't understand why it is so. It is because our language has remained the same and keeps seducing us into asking the same questions. As long as there is still a verb 'to be' that looks as though it functions in the same way as "to eat" and "to drink", as long as we still have the adjectives "identical", "true", "false", "possible", as long as we continue to talk of a river of time and an expanse of space, etc., etc., people will keep stumbling over the same cryptic difficulties and staring at something that no explanation seems capable of clearing up.[8]

By discussing "western thought," I am trying to arrive at this sense of a language – and so a matrix of problems and intellectual behaviors and practices – that has remained the same: very close to what Derrida calls the logos.

Postmodernism – whatever it is understood to be – does not offer a new system of ethics or explicitly endorse older ethical systems based on duty or on virtue or on use and ends. Rather, in prying through these explanatory systems, it can be seen as an attempt to respond to the "primordial ethical experience" that underlies "the construction of a system, or procedure, for formulating and testing the moral acceptability of certain maxims or judgements relation to social action and civic duty."[9] This is because postmodernism is, first, *the disruption of the metaphysics of comprehension, which is the gesture that characterizes western thought. This disruption stems from an encounter with otherness.* (But, to disrupt a meeting, you have to attend it; the tools you use to break up a house are the same tools you use to build it. Postmodernism is not *outside* the metaphysics of comprehension in the way that, perhaps, nonwestern modes of thinking are.) The metaphysics of comprehension is a way of describing how western thought works. To comprehend means two things: to understand and to take hold, and to do one involves, to a lesser or greater extent, the other; they are unavoidably intertwined. This is developed from the work of Emmanuel Levinas.

The Jewish philosopher Emmanuel Levinas (1906–95) was born in Lithuania, studied philosophy with Husserl and Heidegger in Germany, and settled in France in the early 1930s. He introduced phenomenology to French intellectual life. As a French POW, he was imprisoned and escaped death at the hands of the Nazis during World War II, although all his and his wife's family were murdered (his wife and daughter were hidden first in Paris and then in a St Vincent de Paul convent in southern France). After the war, he went on to hold chairs in philosophy at Poitiers, Paris-Nanterre and the

Sorbonne. His two most significant works are *Totality and Infinity* (1961) and *Otherwise than Being: or, Beyond Essence* (1974). Perhaps most importantly in this context, his work has exercised a profound influence on a whole generation of "postmodern" French philosophers, including Derrida, Lyotard, and Irigaray. Derrida's work in particular has been very influenced by Levinas. His early essay "Violence and Metaphysics" is "a key document both in Derrida's development of deconstruction and in the reception of Levinas's own ethical thinking."[10] Derrida has returned to Levinas and recognizably Levinasian themes throughout his work; his most specific recent piece is "A Word of Welcome" (1996, trans. 1999).[11] Of course, other French thinkers have been hostile to Levinas's thought. (The account of the Face in Deleuze and Guattari's *A Thousand Plateaus* is a veiled and penetrating attack on his thought.)[12] Without accepting the whole of his philosophy, however, Levinas's analysis of the process of western thought can be seen to underlie almost all responsible work in postmodernism.

Omnivorous philosophy

"I think" comes down to "I can" – to an appropriation of what is, to an exploitation of reality.[13]

Levinas, responding to Heidegger and to the whole tradition of western philosophy, offers a way of seeing how what I have called the metaphysics of comprehension works. Let us, in a version of Hegel's master/slave dialectic, take two existents ("existents": that which exists, but before being understood as members of a genus, a class, or even understood as a being),[14] (1) the knower, and (2) that which is to be known, separate from the knower: the other. What happens when they encounter each other? The knower encounters the known as an other to itself, in such a way that respects its otherness "and without marking it in any way by this cogitative relation" (p. 42). (I shall return to this.) But at the same time, and more importantly in this context, the knower – and here the knower is one from the West, steeped in the "logos of being" (p. 42) – cannot but *comprehend* the known. This comprehension strips the known existent of its otherness because of the way it works. Comprehension works by understanding, by grasping, the known existent though a third, neutral term. This third term may be "thought," in which case the particular known existent becomes not a concrete particular but an abstract general. It may be sensation, in which the "objective quality and the subjective affection are merged" (p. 42). Or, most significantly, this third term may be Being. For Levinas, Heidegger's work is perhaps the strongest restatement of western thought and so becomes both his major exemplar and opponent. Heidegger takes the experience of being, often ignored by previous philosophers, as the grounding for thought: ontology. "Western philosophy," Levinas writes, "has most often been an ontology: a reduction of the other to the same by interposition of a middle and neutral term that ensures the comprehension of being" (p. 43). So it is that "Being is the light in which existents become intelligible" (p. 42), become "a concept" (p. 43); the "relation with Being that is enacted as ontology consists in neutralising the existent in order to comprehend or grasp it" (p. 46). An existent comes to be comprehended because it stands in relation to me, and is understood as that "standing in relation to me," not as itself. If I understand myself as a being who has Being (already reflectively but unreflective, already an implicit philosophy absorbed with my mother's milk; ideas are at their most powerful when we do not recognize that they are there), I am led to believe that any other existent must have Being as I do, and is, in this key way at least, the same as me.

Socrates' teaching, Levinas argues, was this "primacy of the same": "to receive nothing of the Other but what is in me" (p. 43). (Think of, for example, Socrates's proof of recollection in the *Meno*.) This is the "mediation . . . characteristic of western philosophy" which involves "somewhere a great 'betrayal'" of the other into the same. For things, this betrayal is a "surrender" into use by human beings (the rock becomes a useful site for extracting ore, the tree a source of timber). For people, this betrayal is "the terror that brings a free man under the domination of another" (p. 44);[15] think of Fanon on "this Europe where they are never done talking of Man, yet murder men everywhere they find them."[16] Truth and universality become "impersonal" third terms – "and this is another inhumanity" (p. 46). Other examples of this "middle and neutral term" are "Hegel's universal, Durkheim's social, the statistical laws that govern our freedom, Freud's unconscious" (p. 272), and, as I have suggested, Heideggerian "Being."

The work of ontology, then, "consists in apprehending the individual (which alone exists) not in its individuality but in its generality (of which alone there is a science). The relation with the other is here accomplished only through a third term which I find in myself . . . Philosophy is an egology" (p. 44). For Levinas, this is tied in with an understanding of freedom (not straightforwardly here political freedom). Ontology, the comprehension of the other by the same, "promotes freedom" (p. 42) because otherness – totally consumed and mediated by the third term – does not impede the subject. If there is nothing outside me, I am totally free and without limits. But the assumption that "there is nothing outside me," nothing other, stems from the form of western thought as ontology that takes the "I" as its starting point. Freedom, rooted in the "I," opposes that justice that takes the "other person" as the starting point. This is clearest in Levinas's critique of Heidegger:

> To affirm the priority of Being in relation to the existent is to already decide the essence of philosophy: it is to subordinate the relation with someone who is an existent (the ethical relationship) to a relation with the being of the existent, which, impersonal, permits the seizure, the domination of the existent (a relationship of knowledge) and subordinates justice to freedom. If freedom denotes the mode of staying [in the sense of both remaining and delaying] the same in the midst of the other, knowledge (where the existent hands itself over through the medium of impersonal being) contains the ultimate sense of freedom. It would be opposed to justice, which involves obligations with regard to an existent that refuses to give itself, the Other... In subordinating every relation with existents to the relation with Being, Heideggerian ontology affirms the primacy of freedom over ethics.[17]

Once a philosophy of Being has established itself, implicitly or explicitly, an existent can appear only in, or as a part of, that philosophy. This means that the "I" thinks that it is not delimited in any way as everything it knows is part of itself. It is totally free; knowledge is freedom. Moreover, this leads to what Levinas calls the "thematization and conceptualisation of the other" that is the "suppression or possession of the Other" (p. 46).[18] This means that western thought, which begins with (or has always been, despite forgetting it) ontology, is a "philosophy of power... a philosophy of injustice" (p. 46).

Levinas has pointed out, however, that, as this process of comprehension takes place, there is also an encounter between a knower and a known that respects the alterity of the existent and does not "mark" it. In this, the very nature of the encounter between the same and the other, both concretely there, calls into question the "exercise of ontology" and critiques it. He writes that a "calling into question of the same – which cannot occur within the egoist spontaneity of the same – is brought about by the other" and that we "name this calling into question of my spontaneity by the presence of the other ethics." Ethics here means the way that the "strangeness of the Other, his irreducibility to the I, to my thoughts and possessions" occurs; this inability to comprehend and to grasp the other leads to the way in which ethics, although not a sort of knowledge, "accomplishes the critical essence of knowledge" (p. 43): ethics critiques knowledge.[19]

Thus, there are two movements or moments. One is the movement or moment of the thought of the West, understood (*pace* Heidegger) as ontology. Beginning with the "I" and the Being of being, western ontology as knowledge leads to the comprehension of the other as the same by taking possession, or comprehending, the other as a neutral term that comes from the same; this, of course, has shades of the Hegelianism that Levinas distrusts so utterly. Its otherness, its difference from the same, the "I," is suppressed. This claims to reveal the freedom of the "I," which is not limited by the relation to the other, since, in this view and if this view was all there was, there is no other with which to be in relation. But this movement or moment in fact depends on a relation with the other, that which is outside of me, in order to happen. (There would be no need to comprehend or grasp the other if the other was not outside the "I" in the first place.) This relation is unavoidable. "I cannot disentangle myself from society with the Other" (p. 47), and it constantly reemerges: the "comprehension of Being in general cannot dominate the relationship with the other" because this relationship, despite the ontology of western thought which flies for a radical freedom and loneliness, "precedes all ontology" (p. 48). Indeed, for Levinas, the very need for ontology, for "I" philosophy, is predicated on the relation with the other. Thus, ethics – the relation with the other – is first philosophy. Levinas returns to this in a later work, *Otherwise than Being*, where he asks: why "does the other concern me? What is Hecuba to me? Am I my brother's keeper?" His answer to this question is to suggest that these

> questions have meaning only if one has already supposed the ego is concerned only with itself, is only a concern for itself. In this hypothesis, it indeed remains incomprehensible that the absolute outside-of-me, the other, would concern me. But in the 'pre-history' of the ego posited for itself speaks a responsibility, the self is through and through a hostage, older than the ego, prior to principles.[20]

Here, he uses the terms "responsibility" and "hostage" to stress that we do not have the freedom that western thought would have us believe we do.

Western thought and otherness

The aim of his work, then, is to show how, at the same time as western thought comprehends the other and makes it into the same, there are also ways in which western thought is, unawares, based on the relation with the other and how the other can be encountered in a "non-allergic relation" (p. 47), through the cracks and boundaries of western thought. This means that western thought *per se* is not to be totally rejected. (This would also mean rejecting the fruits of science and the use of rationality to, for example, resolve conflicts of interest.) Rather, it is to be put into question through its encounter with otherness. Indeed, Levinas writes that this

> putting into question of the same by the Other...is, beyond knowledge, the condition of philosophy...[It is] not only attested by the articulations of

Husserlian thought...but also appears at the summits of philosophies: it is the beyond-being of Plato, it is the entry through the door of the agent intellect in Aristotle; it is the idea of God in us, surpassing our capacity as finite beings; it is the exaltation of theoretical reasoning in Kant's practical reason; it is the study of the recognition by the Other in Hegel himself; it is the renewal of duration in Bergson; it is the sobering of lucid reason in Heidegger.[21]

The other both is the foundation of western thought and also marks its limit. This putting into question or thinking of the limits can, however, happen only in the "conceptual language available...that of the Greek *logos*": for the West, no other conceptual language is easily to hand.[22] To critique ontology, to critique the metaphysics of comprehension, the only language available is the language of comprehension. And this critique is begun by an encounter with the other.

This means that there are two kinds of other: (1) the "other" that is within the system of "same/other," whose "otherness" is really an inverted projection of the same, and (2) the other that is outside and underlies the system. This structure is visible in, for example, the way Edward Said suggests that western thought created a discourse of orientalism through which it understood the inhabitants of the Middle East. Regardless of their otherness, they were – in the eyes of the West, at least – transformed into exemplars of the opposite of "western virtues." Yet it was the very existence of "nonwestern" peoples that made "the west" the West. It can also be seen in Hélène Cixous's essay "Sorties," which shows how the binary oppositions (such as man/woman, father/mother, day/night) leave unthinkable and unthought the existence of a woman.

Postmodernism begins when the mainstream of western thought encounters otherness and does not – or tries not to – consume it but instead responds to it, using the only language it can, its own "Greek" language.[23] Thus, postmodernism begins in ethics, in a response to otherness; but it can only respond through precisely the language that denies otherness and attempt to fracture that language. Who are these others? In one way, they are personal others, other existents. But perhaps more importantly, the others whom western thought encounters are those with other sociocultural ways of thinking or existing in the world. These could be "internal" to Europe (women, Jewish, Roma, Sinti; any who do not, for whatever reason, *possess*, as, for Levinas, possession "is pre-eminently the form in which the other becomes the same, by becoming mine" (p. 46) or "external," through the experiences of trade or colonialism. And this is not meant to suggest, either, that western thought is totally monolithic. It is itself made up of mixtures, different voices, reflections on encounters, things added by chance or on purpose, a combination of rational and religious traditions. All too often, however (especially when it has been "successful"), it denies these voices and is dominated by the metaphysics of comprehension. The same metaphysics, the same *urge*, underlies the desire for colonial and economic expansion, the oppression of peoples, the development of technoscience (medicines, aeroplanes, "pushing back scientific boundaries"), and the resolution of conflicting claims by putting them into the same language – if possible. The point is not that the urge is to be destroyed (which would amount not to the deconstruction of the West but to the *destruction* of the West), but that it needs to be reflected on, allowed to go only where it should, its side-effects scrupulously watched and reported on.

Totalitarianism and postmodernism

One very extreme example of the "metaphysics of comprehension" is in the working of the totalitarian states in the twentieth century. Hannah Arendt's *The Origins of Totalitarianism* is dedicated not only to uncovering the history and development of Nazism and Stalinism but also to exploring the logic of totalitarianism itself. Arendt explores the ideology of the totalitarian regimes; ideology for Arendt here means an "-ism which to the satisfaction of their adherents can explain everything and every occurrence by deducing it from a single premise"; the "logic of an idea."[24] Ideologies, as used by the Nazis and in Stalin's USSR, claim to offer a total explanation of history, of the past, present, and future. Ideological thinking "becomes independent of all experience"; this thinking is unable to encounter anything new and consumes all within it (p. 470). She continues:

> Ideological thinking orders facts into an absolutely logical procedure which starts from an axiomatically accepted premise, deducing everything else from it. The deduction may proceed logically or dialectically; in either case, it involves a consistent process of argumentation which, because it thinks in terms of a process, is supposed to be able to comprehend the movement of the suprahuman, natural or historical processes... Once it has established its premise, its point of departure, experiences no longer interfere with ideological thinking, nor can it be taught by reality. (p. 471)

As she says, the ideas with which these ideologies began were not "Plato's eternal essence... nor Kant's regulative principle of reason," but this is not central to her argument because what made the totalitarian states different was that it was "no longer primarily the 'idea'" that empowered them but "the logical processes which could be developed from it" (pp. 469, 472). These processes, the logic of argument and reason taken from a central assertion or axiom, not only aimed to "to organise the infinite plurality of human beings as if all humanity were just one individual" but also consumed all otherness into its own system (p. 438). The logic on which these states relied was omnivorous.

Science, scientism and postmodernism

The metaphysics of comprehension can also be seen in scientism. The relationship between the discourses of science and postmodernism have been fraught, especially since the Sokal affair and his subsequent book, *Fashionable Nonsense*.[25] Roger Hart suggests that science is one of the "central lacunae of poststructuralist analyses."[26] I would suggest, however, that much of the philosophy of poststructuralism is precisely about science: not, perhaps in its everyday form, but in terms of its scope and ambition. If the "post" in poststructuralism begins with the deconstruction of Saussure's project (a "science which studies the role of signs")[27] by bringing to the fore the unquestioned axioms at its center and the logic that follows from them, then the question of science has been at the heart of the postmodern project: "philosophy, as logocentrism, is present in every scientific discipline," said Derrida in an interview, and it is often forgotten that much of Lyotard's *The Postmodern Condition*, too, is concerned with the role of science.[28] The metaphysics of comprehension can be seen in the work of Daniel Dennett, one of the leading philosophers of science. He argues that science tends towards the "desire to reduce, to unite, to explain it all in one big overarching theory."[29] "Once you have explained everything that happens," Dennett writes, "you've explained everything."[30] Once the system (science, in this case) has comprehended everything on its own terms, then there is nothing more – no otherness. A less abstract example of the metaphysics of comprehension in science is the case of Richard Dawkins and "Kennewick Man." In 1996, a (possibly) 9,000-year-old skeleton was found in Kennewick in Washington State in the USA. As the scientists were beginning to do DNA tests on the bones, the five local Native American tribes demanded the return of the remains, which were exhumed on their land, for burial. Dawkins cites one as saying, "From our oral histories, we know that our people have been part of this land since the beginning of time. We do not believe our people migrated here from another continent, as the scientists do."[31] Dawkins is extremely unsympathetic to these others, to these other beliefs that he sees as clearly wrong. Indeed, he finds them laughable. His scientism has comprehended the Native American beliefs as "superstition" and as "false belief" – the opposite to his "science" and "true belief" – and so he is no longer attending to them as others to his discourse, but only as terms within his discourse. The point here is not that carbon dating itself is right or wrong, but that, as even Dennett says, "there is no such thing as philosophy-free science."[32] It is what underlies that philosophy that is open to question for precisely the ways in which it encounters otherness. Dawkins, who scorns the Native Americans, does not encounter them in any real way. Postmodernist thought is not able to proclaim science wrong or right, especially within the highly complex sets of protocols that determine changes in science and lead to the discoveries of, for example, medicines. It is, however, able to highlight where science, "fed by a philosophy it no longer admits," turns into scientism.[33] Jonathan Rée writes about the "risk that our ideas of objectivity, method and science and indeed of being 'up to date' will introduce distortions of their own" He continues: "They have their own peculiar histories after all, and they too can carry unsuspected biases. That is why there is a standing cultural necessity for philosophy – for philosophy as a critique of metaphysics (though not necessarily distinct from it) and for philosophy as distinct from science (but not necessarily opposed to it)."[34] The "bias" that lies at the heart of scientism (and perhaps of science) is the attempt to explain, and so to comprehend, everything.

Conclusion

Levinas's analysis of the "omnivorous philosophy" that underlies western thought is one way of showing how the ethical response to the events of the past and present underlies postmodernism. I would suggest that, without the need to take on board more of Levinas's thought, analogous structures are visible in the thought of other figures. Deleuze and Guattari, opposed to Levinas in many ways, are "participants in what might be described as the advent of a 'postmodern ethics'... posed in the light of the dissolution of both the rational, judging subject and the contract based, liberal accounts of the individual's allegiance to the social community."[35] Here, both the "rational, judging subject" and the contract-based community partake of the metaphysics of comprehension that reduces otherness to a third term established by that same metaphysics, and its "dissolution" – if too hopeful – certainly reflects a disruption. Foucault can be seen to be showing (perhaps in broad strokes) the ways in which western thought turned forms of otherness (which it would now call "madness," "homosexuality," "criminality") into third terms (madness, homosexuality, criminality) and so stripped their otherness from them and incorporated them within the system of itself. It can also be seen, perhaps, and at an angle, in the work of Adorno. He writes, aphoristically, that dialectical thought "is an attempt to break through the coercion of logic by its own means. But since it must use these means, it is at every moment in danger of itself acquiring a coercive character: the ruse of reason would like to hold sway over the dialectic too."[36] Following Benjamin, Adorno argues that the obligation is to "think at the same time dialectically and undialectically"; that it is necessary to use reason and not to use it simultaneously.[37]

It is true that this ethics – the disruption of western thought through western thought based on a more primordial response to the other – is, as Derrida points out, "an ethics without law and without concept, which maintains its non-violent purity only before being determined as concepts and laws."[38] It could not become a law or a series of moral axioms, as this would, at once, mean that it was complicit with, rather than interrupting, the metaphysics of comprehension and would become blind to some others. This is why many postmodern thinkers and writers continue to use vague terms such as "openness" or "fracture"; the specificity of, say, an axiom would immediately betray the ethical intention. But, by the same token, it cannot be forever free-floating, since, first, we live in a world and, for Levinas, our subjectivity arises from our ethical responsibilities in it; second, there are obvious ethical needs; and third, in order to respond it is necessary to do so through recognition and reorganization of older thoughts and moments of culture. Thus, the ethical interruption must become, cannot but be, codified in a politics, a morality, a position, an identity. But this must also be always ready to interrupt itself again in the name of the obligations to which it responds. The ethics of postmodernity is not an ethics of freedom: for Levinas, for postmodernists, we can never be free from obligations and from responsibility.

NOTES

1. Mary Midgley, *Utopias, Dolphins and Computers: Problems in Philosophical Plumbing* (London: Routledge, 1996), pp. 10–11.
2. Jacques Derrida, *Of Spirit: Heidegger and the Question*, trans. Geoffrey Bennington and Rachel Bowlby (London: University of Chicago Press, 1989), p. 109; Zygmunt Bauman, *Modernity and the Holocaust*, 2nd edn. (Cambridge: Polity, 1993).
3. Hannah Arendt, *The Origins of Totalitarianism* (London: Harcourt Brace, 1973), p. 124; Franz Fanon, *The Wretched of the Earth*, trans. Constance Farrington (Harmondsworth: Penguin, 1990), p. 252.
4. Simone de Beauvoir, *The Second Sex*, trans. H. M. Parshley (London: Picador, 1988), p. 97.
5. Peter Winch, *The Idea of a Social Science, and Its Relation to Philosophy*, 2nd edn. (London: Routledge, 1991), p. 3; Jean-François Lyotard, *The Postmodern Condition: A Report on Knowledge*, trans. Geoffrey Bennington and Brian Massumi (Manchester; Manchester University Press, 1986), p. 40. For an example of the "extra-scientific pretensions of science," see Edward O. Wilson, *Consilience: The Unity of Knowledge* (London: Little, Brown, 1998).

6. Fanon, *The Wretched of the Earth*, p. 251.

7. Jacques Derrida, "Violence and Metaphysics," *Writing and Difference*, trans. Alan Bass (London: Routledge and Kegan Paul, 1978), pp. 79–153; quotation from p. 82.

8. Ludwig Wittgenstein, *Culture and Value*, rev. edn., ed. G. H. von Wright and Alois Pichler, trans. Peter Winch (Oxford: Blackwell, 1994), p. 22e.

9. Simon Critchley, *The Ethics of Deconstruction: Derrida and Lavinas* (Oxford: Blackwell, 1992), p. 3.

10. Robert Bernasconi, *Heidegger in Question: The Art of Existing* (Atlantic Highlands, NJ: Humanities Press International, 1993), p. 213.

11. Jacques Derrida, *Adieu to Emmanuel Levinas*, trans. Pascale-Anne Brault and Michael Naas (Stanford, CA: Stanford University Press, 1999).

12. Gilles Deleuze and Félix Guattari, *A Thousand Plateaus*, trans. Brian Massumi (London: Athlone, 1988), pp. 167–91.

13. Emmanuel Levinas, *Totality and Infinity: An Essay on Exteriority*, trans. Alphonso Lingis (London: Kluwer, 1991), p. 46. All references are to this edition.

14. These are terms developed in Levinas's earlier work, *Existence and Existents*, trans. Alphonso Lingis (London: Kluwer, 1988).

15. Animals, rarely Levinas's concern, are clearly a borderline case here; for this case made again recently in a powerful way, see J. M. Coetzee, *The Lives of Animals* (London: Profile, 2000).

16. Franz Fanon, *The Wretched of the Earth*, p. 251.

17. Levinas, *Totality and Infinity*, p. 45. Translation slightly modified.

18. He continues his attack on Heidegger by suggesting that he, "with the whole of western philosophy, takes the relation with the other as enacted in the destiny of sedentary peoples, the possessors and builders of the earth. Possession is pre-eminently the form in which the other becomes the same, by becoming mine" (p. 46).

19. Compare Wittgenstein: "What it [ethics] says does not add to our knowledge in any sense," in "A Lecture on Ethics," *Philosophical Review* 74 (1965), p. 12.

20. Emmanuel Levinas, *Otherwise than Being, or, Beyond Essence*, trans. Alphonso Lingis (The Hague: Martinus Nijhoff, 1981), p. 117.

21. Emmanuel Levinas, "Philosophy and Awakening," trans. Mary Quaintance, in Eduardo Cadava, Peter Connor and Jean-Luc Nancy (eds.), *Who Comes after the Subject?* (London: Routledge, 1991), p. 215.

22. Simon Critchley, "The Problem of Closure in Derrida (part two)," *Journal of the British Society for Phenomenology* 23 (1992), p. 140.

23. It has occasionally done this before, which accounts for the odd chronological character of postmodernism, and for the appearance – above and beyond the claims of academics mining their field – for "postmodernism" in earlier epochs.

24. Arendt, *The Origins of Totalitarianism*, p. 468. References hereafter in the text.

25. Alan Sokal and Jean Bricmont, *Fashionable Nonsense* [in the UK: *Intellectual Impostures*]: *Postmodern Intellectuals' Abuse of Science* (New York: Picadar, 1998; London: Profile, 1999).

26. Roger Hart, "On the Problem of Chinese Science," in Mario Biagoli (ed.), *The Science Studies Reader* (London: Routledge, 1999), p. 197.

27. Ferdinand de Saussure, *Course in General Linguistics*, 2nd edn., trans. Roy Harris (London: Duckworth, 1983), p. 15.

28. Richard Kearney, *Dialogues with Contemporary Continental Thinkers: The Phenomenological Heritage* (Manchester: Manchester University Press, 1984), p. 114.

29. Daniel Dennett, *Darwin's Dangerous Idea: Evolution and the Meanings of Life* (Harmondsworth: Penguin, 1995), p. 83.

30. Daniel Dennett, "Back from the Drawing Board," in Bo Dahlbom (ed.), *Dennett and his Critics: Demystifying Mind* (Oxford: Blackwell, 1993), p. 210.

31. Richard Dawkins, *Unweaving the Rainbow: Science, Delusion and the Appetite for Wonder* (London: Penguin, 1998), p. 19.

32. Dennett, *Darwin's Dangerous Idea*, p. 21.

33. Michael de Certeau, *The Writing of History*, trans. Tom Conley (New York: Columbia University Press, 1988), p. 342.

34. Jonathan Rée, *I See A Voice: A Philosophical History of Language, Deafness and the Senses* (London: HarperCollins, 1999), pp. 384–5.

35. Elizabeth Grosz, "A Thousand Tiny Sexes: Feminism and Rhizomatics," in Constantin V. Boundas and Dorothea Olkowski (eds.), *Gilles Deleuze and the Theatre of Philosophy* (London: Routledge, 1994), pp. 187–210, quotation from p. 196.

36. Theodor Adorno, *Minima Moralia*, trans E. F. N. Jephcott (London: Verso, 1978), p. 150.

37. Ibid., p. 152.

38. Jacques Derrida, *Writing and Difference*, trans. Alan Bass (London: Routledge and Kegan Paul, 1978), p. 111.

10

COSTAS DOUZINAS

Law and justice in postmodernity

An apparent paradox characterizes contemporary law. The legal system is going through a serious crisis while jurisprudence is enjoying something of a renaissance. At the turn of the millennium, law faces a crisis of form and a demand for ethics. To start with ethics, over the last twenty years a widely felt sense that justice has miscarried has been evident. In the United Kingdom, justice has been aborted in miscarriages of justice and denials of access to justice, in racial and gender discrimination, in institutional violence and legal dogmatism. Many recent legal reforms, most importantly the introduction of the Human Rights Act 1998 and various measures against institutional racism in the police and other state agencies, aim at removing the worst cases of abuse, but they have been criticized for timidity. But, for the legal scholar, the question is somewhat different. How is it that we came to the point where the legal system appears to be almost divorced from considerations of morality? Michel Foucault has called the great eighteenth-century civil lawyers who stood against the autocratic state "universal intellectuals": the "man of justice, the man of law, he who opposes to power, despotism, the abuses and arrogance of wealth, the universality of justice and the equity of an ideal law."[1] Postmodernity has undermined our belief in the universality of law or in the ability of an ideal equity to ground its operations. What is the meaning of justice in a world of cognitive and moral uncertainties?

The moral deficit of law goes hand in hand with the crisis of legal form. This concerns the complementary process of proliferating juridification of social and private spaces and of privatization or deregulation of hitherto public areas of concern and provision. This double move has turned the traditional divide and boundary between public and private arenas of action and regulation, upon which much of modern law rests, into an elastic line of passage, communication, and osmosis. Administrative law, to take an obvious case, keeps extending its scope to an increasing number of previously domestic areas. This regulatory colonization does not seem to represent or pursue any inherent logic, overarching policy direction, or coherent value system. Policy considerations differ between family law and planning or between criminal justice and the regulation of official secrecy, privacy, and data protection. Even worse, contradictory policies appear to motivate regulatory practices in each sphere. The fragmented legal form keeps colonizing the social, a development that goes hand in hand with the privatization of public services and deregulation.

Both sides of this extension and mutation in the governance of society have profoundly affected the nature of legal rules. Rules as normative propositions are supposed to prescribe general and abstract criteria of right and wrong, to anticipate and describe broad types of factual situations, and to ascribe legal entitlements and obligations to wide categories of (legal) subjects. Regulatory practices, by contrast, are detailed, specific, and discretionary. They change in accordance with the vagaries of the situation and the contingency of the administrative involvement; they distribute benefits, facilities, and positions according to policy choices rather than entitlement; they construct small-scale institutions, they assign variable and changing roles to subjects, they plan local and micro-relations, and they discipline people and agencies by arranging them along lines of normal behavior. In the United States, this over-legalization has led to a grave sense of unease expressed when lawyers are routinely seen as greedy money-pinchers who care about fees more than about justice.[2]

It was against this background that postmodern and critical approaches came to prominence and gave a new lease of life to a jurisprudence that had become largely irrelevant and terminally boring.[3] The decline of legal formalism and positivism, the mainstay of modernism, led to a number of new approaches to law, which include critical legal studies,[4] law and literature,[5] law and economics,[6] critical race and gender theories,[7] and psychoanalytical jurisprudence.[8] The first phase of postmodern jurisprudence addressed the form of law as a legal, moral, and political issue. Its second turned to the demand for an ethics in an attempt to develop a postmodern approach to justice and judgment. This essay follows broadly the same trajectory.

Jurisprudence and modernity

The history of jurisprudence can be described as the history of the meaning(s) of the word "law." Generations of jurisprudence writers have subdued their readers by obsessively addressing the question, "What is law?" The "concept" of law, the "idea" of law, and "law's empire" are phrases found in the titles of some of the most influential jurisprudence textbooks.[9] Jurisprudence set itself the task of uncovering and pronouncing the truth about law and approached the task by following two major approaches, the internal and external. Internal theories adopt the point of view of the judge or lawyer and try to theorize the process of argumentation and reasoning used in institutional discourse, and often deteriorate into an extended set of footnotes to judicial pronouncements, a practice useful for a certain type of pedagogy but intellectually slightly suspect. External theories, by contrast, typically the sociology-of-law and Marxist approaches, treat reasons, arguments, and justifications as "facts" to be incorporated in wider nonlegal explanatory contexts. The task here is to identify the causal chains that shape or are shaped by legal practices. External theories could be used as a corrective to the excessive formalism of jurisprudence and provided the background and methodology for empirical sociolegal research, which explored the economic and social effects of legal domination. But their interest in motives rather than intentions and in structure rather than agency kept them marginalized. Normative jurisprudence became the standard fare of the lawschool curriculum while external theories were demoted to an occasional supplement for the politically aware.

Within normative jurisprudence, legal positivism has been the dominant and typically modernist internal approach. Hans Kelsen and Herbert Hart, the two towering influences of continental and Anglo-American positivism, turned the study of law into a science. Kelsen called his approach a "pure theory of law," a discourse of truth about norms.[10] The object of study was defined as the logical hierarchy of norms, presented as a coherent closed and formal system, a legal grammar guaranteed internally through the logical interconnection of norms, and externally through the rigorous rejection of all nonsystemic normative matter, such as content, context, or history. All correct legal statements in legislation and adjudication follow a process of subsumption of inferior to superior norms and no possibility of conflict between the two exists. At the basis of the pyramid a presupposed *Grundnorm* sets the system into motion, but is an abstract imperative, an empty norm with no substantive value.

Herbert Hart, the most prominent English positivist, constructed his theory in a more pragmatic fashion. Hart calls his "concept of law" both an essay in descriptive sociology and an analytical jurisprudence. Law should be distinguished both from coercion and from morality and should be approached as a coherent and self-referential system of rules. Rules refer to other rules and their systemic interdependence determined the existence, validity, and values of any particular rule. Hart shifts the question from "What is law?" to "What is a modern legal system?" and finds the answer in the combination of primary rules of obligation, such as those of crime or tort, and secondary rules or rule-governed mechanisms that enable primary rules to be enacted, changed, and applied. Behind all, a master rule, the rule of recognition, determines whether a particular rule is legal and a legal system exists. But when Hart turns from his virulently systemic order to the actual interpretation and application of the rules, a small chink appears in the edifice. In most cases, legal terms and rules have a paradigmatic core of settled meaning that makes interpretation noncontroversial. Occasionally, however, certain terms have a linguistic or motivated indeterminacy, a "penumbra of doubt" as to their meaning. In such instances, the interpreting judge and the applier administrator must exercise a degree of discretion. Discretion reintroduced value-choices, moral, political, or policy-based, the dreaded supplement to positivism.

The political dimension of the exclusion of morality should be sought in the modern experience of relativism and pluralism and the fear of nihilism. Law is presented as the answer to the irreconcilability of value and the most perfect embodiment of human reason. Private law turns social conflict into technical disputes and entrusts their resolution to public experts and the technicians of rules and procedures. Public law imposes constitutional limits and normative restrictions upon the organization and exercise of state power. The logic of rules depersonalizes power and structures discretion by excluding subjective value; it restricts choice in the application of law by administrators and judges. The distrust of administrative discretion and of judicial creativity; the antipathy towards administrative tribunals, legal pluralism, and nonjudicial methods of dispute resolution; the insistence on the declaratory role of statutory interpretation and the "strictness" of precedent; the emphasis on the "literal" rule of interpretation that allegedly allows the exclusion of subjective preference and ideological disposition: these are key components of the rule of law as the law of rules and, at the same time, facets of the attempt to rid the law of ethical considerations.

At this crucial point, jurisprudence turned its attention to hermeneutics, semiotics, and literary theory as an aid to the ailing enterprise of positivism. The hermeneutic turn expressed the deeply felt need for a return to morality. Positivism had based the legitimacy of law on formal reason and on the consequent decline of ethical considerations. Using the strict distinction between fact and value, positivists had excluded or minimized the influence of moral values and principles in law. The effort was motivated by cognitive-epistemological and political considerations. A "science" of law could be founded only on observable, objective phenomena, not on subjective and relative values. This purified science of norms preoccupied itself with questions of validity and presented the law as a coherent, closed, and formal system guaranteed internally through the logical interconnection of norms and externally through the rigorous rejection of all nonsystemic matter such as content, value, historical provenance, or empirical context.

The importation of hermeneutics, semiotics, and literary theory in jurisprudence was motivated by the urgent need to correct the descriptively inadequate and morally impoverished theory of law as exclusively rules, and to reinscribe morality in law. The new hermeneutical jurisprudence insists that the law is a valuable source of meaning, and that it means values. We may disagree as to the meaning of any particular statute or precedent, we may even accept that judicial reasoning and justification can legitimately lead to conflicting directions, but, as a minimum, the law is about interpreting texts. We can therefore abandon the *Grundnorm* and the rule of recognition for the meaning of meaning; we can replace or supplement the technical rules of legal reasoning with the protocols of interpretation or with the study of rhetorical tropes and hermeneutical criteria; we can approach the texts of law through the law of text.

The literary and hermeneutical turn gave legal theory a long-lost sense of excitement. But another effect was to make morality an integral element of law and, in particular, of judicial interpretation. The new jurisprudence of meaning responded to the highly topical demand, as ethics became part and justification of the newly discovered interpretative character of the legal enterprise. But there is a catch. To take Ronald Dworkin's popular hermeneutical theory, the operation of law is presented as necessarily embodying and following moral values and principles. The law is no longer just about rules in the manner of Hart and certainly it is not the outcome of the untrammeled will of an omnipotent legislator, as John Austin, the nineteenth-century founder of legal positivism, had argued. Law's empire includes principles and policies, and its application involves creative acts of interpretation. Judges are asked to construct the notorious "right answer" to legal problems by developing political and moral theories that would present the law in the best possible light and create an image of the "community as integrity." Legal texts must be read as a single and coherent scheme animated by the principles of "justice and fairness and procedural process in the right relation."[11] A similar position can be found in the work of James Boyd White, the most prominent representative of the "law and literature" movement. Justice must be approached as translation.[12]

Morality and moral philosophy enter the law and are correctly recognized as an inescapable element of judicial hermeneutics. But their task is to legitimize a judicial practice that has been disassociated from the quest for justice by presenting the law as the perfect narrative of a happy community. Morality is no longer a set of subjective and relative values, as the positivists claim, nor is it a critical standard against which acts of legal power can be judged. If a right legal answer exists and can be found, even in hard cases, through the use of moral philosophy, judges are never left to their own devices and judicial choice can be exorcised. Hart had reluctantly accepted the dreaded supplement of judicial discretion at the cost of endangering the rational completeness and coherence of the law. Dworkin's hermeneutics present interpretation as both formally authorized by and replete with morality. Against the positivist lack of interest in ethics, the interpretative scholars assert that the law is all morality and that judicial interpretation implies or leads to an ethics of legal reading.

Undoubtedly, the law is interpretation, and interpretation is the life of law. The law may follow principles and further values. But there is more to it: before and after the meaning-giving act, law is force.[13] Statutes, judgments, and administrative decisions act upon people and impose patterns of behavior, attitudes, and, ultimately, sanctions. According to Robert Cover's emblematic statement, "legal interpretation takes place in a field of pain and death."[14] Law's meaning coerces and legal values constrain. This all-important aspect of the legal operation, fully acknowledged by the early positivists, was underplayed later by Kelsen and Hart and became extinct in recent hermeneutics. In their enthusiasm for the semantic component and creative interpretation, the law is presented as exclusively textual and ethical.

We are thus faced with a new paradox; power relations and practices proliferate and penetrate deep into the social, often taking a loose and variable legal form. Their common characteristics are few; an often extremely tenuous derivation from the legislative power, and more importantly their link with the increasingly empty referent "law," which bestows upon them its symbolic and legitimatory weight. If, for positivism, the "law is the law," in the sense of law's certification according to internal criteria of validity, the underlying idea becomes now fully radicalized. Power relations are law if and when they successfully attach to themselves the predication "legal," or, law is everything that succeeds in calling itself law. But the most advanced legal theory ignores these accelerating developments and continues to be preoccupied, like classical political philosophy, with sovereignty and right, representation and delegation, integrity and "right answers." It examines almost exclusively the case-law of appellate courts, the most formal and centralist expression of the legal system, which is increasingly becoming unrepresentative of the whole system. If positivism fails to understand the moral substance of law, apologetic hermeneutics becomes even more unrealistic by neglecting power or reducing and subsuming it under the operations of legal *logos*. *Auctoritas est potestas non veritas*; authority lies in power and not in truth.

It appears therefore that the presentation of law as a unified and coherent body of norms or principles is rooted in the metaphysics of truth rather than in the politics and ethics of justice. The truth of justice is justice as truth.

From this it follows that law is the form of power, and power should be exercized in the form of law. Power is legitimate if it follows law, *nomos*, and if *nomos* follows *logos*, reason. This peculiar combination of the descriptive and prescriptive, of *logos* and *nomos*, lies at the heart of modernist jurisprudence. The task postmodern jurisprudence has set itself is to deconstruct *logonomocentrism* in the texts and operations of law. The hermeneutical moral turn in jurisprudence was welcome; but the moral substance of law must be argued and fought for rather than simply assumed. Furthermore, in order to understand justice, the specifically legal facet of morality, we must link it with law's force. Postmodern jurisprudence abandons the key premises of amoral positivism and of too-moral but power-less hermeneutic jurisprudence. In a first phase, it addressed the positivist and formalist foundations of jurisprudence. The second, following the moral turn in postmodern theory, opened new ways for examining justice, judgment, and power.

Deconstructing law's formalism

The starting point of postmodern jurisprudence is the recognition that postmodern legality defies both the positivist and the moralistic image. Law is constituted through a myriad rules and regulations, of statutes, decrees, administrative legislation, and adjudication; formal judgments and informal interventions and disciplines; multiform institutions and personnel; plural nonformal methods of dispute avoidance and resolution that can no longer be seen as a coherent ensemble of rules and judgments. Legal language games have proliferated and cannot be presented as the embodiment of the public good, the general will, the wishes of the sovereign people in Parliament, or some other coherent system of principle. The distinctions between public and private and between rule and discretion, the hallowed bases of the rule-of-law ideal, are gradually becoming anachronistic as rule-makers couch their delegations of authority to administrators in wide terms, while administrators adopt policies, guidelines, and rules to structure the exercise of discretion and protect themselves from challenge. Legislative and regulatory systems are adopted to promote transient, provisional, and local policy objectives with no immediate or obvious link with wider social policy. Policy has become visible throughout the operation of law-making and administration; in many instances policy and rule-making are delegated to experts, who fill the gaps according to the latest claims of scientific knowledge. Law appears at its most imperialistic at the precise moment when it starts losing its specificity. The condition of postmodernity has irreversibly removed the aspiration of unity in law. Everything that successfully attaches the term "law" to its operations and mobilizes the coercive force of the state becomes law. In this sense, the "law" can be constituted not theoretically but only intuitively and politically. The law has no essence but only operations.

Methodologically, postmodern jurisprudence, unlike contextual approaches, carefully reads legal texts and legal history and treats them as the privileged terrain of study. But, unlike internal theories, it reads these texts not just for their normative coherence but also for their omissions, repressions, and distortions, signs of the relations of power and symptoms of the traumas created by the institution. If there is patriarchy or economic exploitation, it will be traced in the law report or the statutory provisions, in its rhetoric and images, in its certainties and omissions, which will then be followed outside of the text in the lives of people and the history of domination. Neither just in the text nor only outside of it "in the world," postmodern theory explores the textual and institutional organization of the law. The law, as a system of signs and part of the symbolic order, is both necessary and fictitious. But law's fictions operate and change the world; they help to establish the subject as free and/because subjected to the logic of the institution.

The close reading adopted as the method of early postmodernism was aimed at deconstructing logonomocentrism in the texts of law. Indeed, according to the critic Jonathan Culler, the encounter between deconstruction and law "seems nearly pre-ordained – they seem in some sense made for each other."[15] It is not difficult to see why. Jurisprudence is obsessed with order. Its task has been to present law as a system that follows a strict logic of rules or a disciplined and coherent arrangement of principles, a procedure that would, it is hoped, give law identity, dignity, and legitimacy. The corpus of law is presented almost literally as a body. It must either digest and transform the nonlegal into legality, or it must reject it. God's law in naturalism, the *Grundnorm* and rule of recognition of the positivists, the principles and the right answers of the hermeneuticians are the *topoi* of order, identity, and unity. It is not surprising that, when the question of law's legality becomes dominant, the various answers will offer a definition of essence; they will construct a system of essential characteristics and will inscribe legality within a history conceived exclusively as the unfolding of meaning. The effort to distinguish the legal from the nonlegal progresses from the search for an exhaustive list of markers that map out the whole field to the stipulation of a single law of the genre, the law of law. The law can claim its empire because it can be clearly delineated from its outside, its context and terrain of operations. But according to a forceful deconstructive principle, which receives its most compelling application in law, a field is self-sufficient only if its outside is distinctly marked so as to frame and constitute what lies inside. The exterior – morality, politics, economics – is as much part of the constitution of the field as what is proper to it.

Early postmodern jurisprudence adopted three deconstructive strategies that addressed, it turn, the concepts, the argumentation, and the discursive organization and intertextual character of legal texts. Let us examine them briefly.

Concepts and conceptual chains

The first approach focused on key jurisprudential and doctrinal concepts and, through the close reading of legal texts, showed that they cannot deliver the conceptual homogeneity or doctrinal coherence they promise. One strategy particularly popular with critical legal scholars in the United States was to show that legal texts followed a quasi-structuralist arrangement animated by conceptual juxtapositions and bipolarities. The public/private divide, for example, underpins the idea of the rule of law and supports areas of individual autonomy free of state intervention. The rule/policy opposition permeates tort and contract, while the opposition between universalism and cultural relativism or communitarianism has dominated the debate on human rights. The distinction between fact and value becomes the is/ought distinction of legal positivism, while that between form and substance and its double between principles and policies express the fault-line of legal hermeneutics. These bipolarities in theory and doctrine are presented as markers of two distinct and antagonistic forms of legal reasoning, doctrinal organization, or theoretical argumentation.

To take an obvious example: judicial reasoning is distinguished into the "grand" and "normal" styles. The former emphasizes policy concerns and discretion, claims to follow the intention of the legislator and the purpose of the rule, and examines the wider social desirability of alternative outcomes. The latter claims strict adherence to the rules, interprets literally, and promotes judicial abstinence when "gaps" appear in the legal edifice. A related and pervasive conceptual juxtaposition is that between rules and policy. Rules are said to make for certainty, predictability, and fairness, while policies and discretion are said to make for substantive justice, adaptation to the contingencies of the situation, and purposefulness in interpretation. But, while the terms of the opposition are presented as external, they depend for their existence on the difference that separates them. In the terminology of structuralism, each concept is constituted through its differential rather than its positive value. As a result, no concept can be properly constituted without a trace of its opposite inhabiting it and barring its closure. The concept and its other, rather than being opposed, are intertwined and, in this sense, legal concepts are nonidentical at their core. These bipolarities represent the dream of legal unity, totality, and order, but are undermined by what Derrida has called a "regulated incoherence within conceptuality."[16]

Doctrinal construction presents a part of law as a closed structure of norms that cohere according to formal principles of noncontradiction. Contract law, for example, or a particular doctrine in it, such as mistake or misrepresentation, is separated, and the chosen texts, case reports, or statutory provisions are treated as the vessels of a special type of rule, the *ratio decidendi* or reason for the decision. The conceptual opposition – form/substance, rule/policy, etc. – is then presented as the organizing principle of the structure and one of its poles as the dominant center. But the process of extracting agreed norms from complex texts, such as law reports, is always controversial. Rule extraction is the result of judicial institutional power rather than of textual or normative closure. Furthermore, doctrinal structures are decentered and doubly open: first, towards their outside, those areas of law excluded in the determination of the materials to be treated as relevant and, second, because of the differential value that allows the opposition to operate.

Duncan Kennedy demonstrated, for example, how common law doctrinal categories fail in their attempt to mediate a "fundamental contradiction" between self and others. This contradiction pervades the whole law, acts as the deep structure of surface doctrinal oppositions, and condemns them to endless and fruitless repetition.[17] He was followed by more specific studies, such as Gerald Frug's analysis of administrative law, which concluded that the pervasive objective/subjective opposition cannot hold. "The facets of organizational life that need to be subjective have become so constrained by objectivity that they cannot convincingly represent the expression of human individuality. Similarly the facets that need to be objective have become so riddled with subjectivity as to undermine their claim to represent common interest."[18] For Clare Dalton, too,

> within the discourse of doctrine [in contract law] the only way we can define form is by reference to substance, even as substance can be defined only by its compliance to form ... Each supposed "solution" to one of these doctrinal conundra, each attempt at a definition of line-drawing, winds up mired at the next level of analysis in the unresolved dichotomy it purported to leave behind.[19]

These studies popularized the "indeterminacy thesis," a legal expression of deconstruction's "undecidability." The indeterminacy of doctrine is logically and formally unavoidable because "there will remain in any legal dispute a logically and empirically unanswerable formal problem, that granting substantially greater discretion or limiting discretion through significantly greater rule-boundedness in the formation of the prevailing legal command is always perfectly plausible."[20]

These problems cannot be avoided by using the "context" of the rule or text. The indeterminacy is not resolved by adopting a constructive approach to interpretation and attending to the intention of the legislator or to the context of the judgment. While legal interpretation takes place in the context of a particular conflict, every "context" in itself is a text that needs further interpretation. Authorial intention, particularly when the author is a collegiate body such as the Framers of the Constitution or Parliament, is even more inscrutable than the meaning of the text. Opening the text to its context is a necessary hermeneutical operation but, if anything, it multiplies interpretative difficulties. Reading a law report in terms of its politics, as critical legal scholars tend to do, is a valuable process. But this, in turn, opens to further and often inconsistent readings of the law in terms of its economic function (as in the school of law and economics), its ideological operation (as in Marxist readings), or its aesthetic organization and psychoanalytical layers (in a law-and-literature reading). Legal texts are bound by their context but the context itself is boundless.

Argumentative inconsistencies

A second level of deconstruction moves from conceptual paradoxes to the arrangement of arguments in legal texts. Motivated by the desire for clarity, rigor, and coherence, legal argumentation moves to its conclusions in an effortless manner, in which argumentative development and closure follow naturally from the premises and any embarrassing evidence is treated as insignificant exception. Yet a close reading of the texts often reveals contradictions, disparities, and conflicts within and between argumentative lines, which frustrate the promises of closure of the text and open possibilities that the textual surface ignores.

Take, for example, the well-known rules on offer and acceptance in the law of contract, which have become a *cause célèbre* of postmodern jurisprudence.[21] An offer becomes binding when the offeree has accepted all the important terms of the offer and has expressed this acceptance to the offeror in a clear and unequivocal way. Contract law assumes a representational model of language, according to which ideas, thoughts, and the acceptance of the offer are first formed in the mind of the contractors and then communicated in linguistic form. Once the minds have "met" through the assent of the offeree, the contract has been completed and is binding on the parties. When the contractors are present, the requirement of a separate communication of the acceptance is deemed unnecessary. Under the prevalent cultural phonocentrism, in face-to-face negotiations the voice, the best expression of consciousness, will clarify intentions and prevent future disagreements as to the meaning and terms of the contract. When, however, negotiations are conducted *inter absentes*, by means of a letter, fax, telex, or email, communication is an indispensable element for the acceptance of the offer and the conclusion of the contract.

One would expect that, in such cases, an offer would be turned into a binding contract upon the delivery of the letter of the offeree and its perusal by the offeror. According to the "postal rule," a hallowed part of contract law introduced in the case of *Adams* v. *Lindsell* in 1818, however, an acceptance is binding from the moment of its posting by the offeree. It remains binding upon the unsuspecting offeror even if it is lost, destroyed, or never delivered. Contract law accepts that the moments of circulation and communication of letters and acceptances are distinct and may be temporarily or permanently disconnected. If that happens, circulation takes precedence over the "meeting of minds" and creates binding effects. This precedence is not just temporal. There is always a possibility – therefore a necessary possibility – that the letter may not arrive. In this case, the principle of the postal rule, according to which the circulation of letters and signs creates effects although there has been no communication or agreement between the parties, turns into the principle of the main rule with its demand for clear communication. These "exceptional" cases help us to understand the norm.

The standard contract-law textbook expresses surprise at the postal rule because it completely undermines the metaphysics of contract. It appears strange that the requirement of communication, which is "devoid" of all practical content in face-to-face contracts, is not applicable "in the most important arena of its application."[22] It proceeds to explain the anomaly through the history of the rule. "*Adams* v. *Lindsell* was the first offer and acceptance case in English law, and in 1818 there was no rule that acceptance must be communicated. As so often happens in English law, the exception is historically anterior to the rule."[23] The cornerstone of the law, which regulates the communication, verification, and validity of a contract is grounded on its exception. The law of communication and agreement relies on interference and disagreement. And as the textbook states, this is a common occurrence in common law. The exception, the law of the letter and of writing, puts the law and contract into circulation. The letter (the structural effect of writing) comes before the *phone* (the belief in the unmediated presence of consciousness and intention in the voice and in the possibility of uninterrupted agreements) and indicates that semiotic circulation takes precedence over semantic communication. This is the case in agreements between both absent and present contractors and throughout the written archive of the law. Writing, the privileged mode of legality, with its difference, deferral, and repetition, both facilitates and frustrates law's promise of order and closure.

Intertextual possibilities

A third type of heterogeneity results from the intertextual character of legal texts. Legal documents display discrepancies and inconsistencies arising from the fact that their various elements, parts, and layers, with their different roles, functions, and operations, are brought together with quotes and grafts from other texts, must survive in uneasy and unstable combinations, and become authoritative in various unpredicted and unpredictable new contexts. Judgments and law reports are a case in point. The evidence offered in trials and recorded in the reports is not constructed and evaluated against some "hard" external reality. On the contrary, the construction of the relevant law (the major premise of the legal syllogism) and fact-finding (the minor premise) follow standard and coherent narrative frameworks drawn from the stock of specialist and common knowledge. Events, contradictory evidence, and conflicting witness statements must be constructed into a narrative framework, which carries within it tacit evaluations.[24] Adjudication involves the choice of one coherent and plausible narrative for the emplotment of the facts of the case from those on offer, which is then "matched" with the narrative pattern of the legal rule. But there is more; the relevant law may come from many different sources and, at common law, it involves, as we saw, the extraction of an authoritative legal rule from the narrative of precedent cases and law reports. This again means that the different layers that have gone into the writing of the judgment may lead to different formulations of the rule from the most abstract and general to a concrete statement that stays close to the narrative of the earlier case. The potential for multiple formulations of facts and law of both the present and the previous cases and the continuous dialogue of legal texts with nonlegal contexts creates a fertile ground for alternative readings. These discursive discrepancies do not amount to formal contradictions and cannot be weeded out by the protocols of legal reasoning. As a result, they have largely remained hidden and have become a privileged terrain for postmodern jurisprudence.

One strategy concentrates on the discrepancy between the surface arguments of the text and its rhetorical organization. Legal texts, like a certain type of philosophy, have always aspired to a state of linguistic transparency in which the clarity and rigor of argument will not be contaminated by the "irrational" and devious figures of speech. Plato fired the opening salvo in this campaign by expelling poets from his Republic. John Locke and the early Wittgenstein followed suit by trying to imagine a fully logical language not dissimilar to mathematics. But this is both impossible and undesirable. Legal and philosophical texts as linguistic constructs and repositories of meaning are rhetorical like all texts. Indeed, the texts that most stubbornly deny their rhetorical construction are best suited to their deconstruction.

Take, for example, John Finnis's *Natural Law and Natural Rights*, an influential contemporary restatement of the naturalist tradition. Finnis attempts to ground his list of eternal and absolute goods on intuition and practical reasoning rather than on traditional or divine authority. A central trope in this endeavor is the figure of the "sceptic," who throughout the text challenges its insights and is juxtaposed to the "clear-headed and wise men." These two figures are used to cajole and put pressure on the reader to accept the "self-evidently" true character of the argument. The sceptic is presented as slightly dim and villainous; he cannot grasp the meaning of self-evidence and instead he uses rhetoric and flowery language in his attempt to misdirect the reader. The operation of self-evidence as a method of proof is not discussed, because it would have to be "embarrassingly complex"; but the "sceptic" who doubts it is "disqualified from the pursuit of knowledge" and becomes coherent only "by asserting nothing." Seductions and promises are the terrain of literature; threats and sanctions are the domain of the law. Against its claim to propose a contemporary natural-law argument, the rhetorical organization of the text shows it to be the opposite, a legal positivism. As in all positivism, a sovereign power (the author) commands the subject (the reader) using rewards (self-evidence) and punishments (putting to silence). At the end, the text admits inadvertently that its claims are "plays on meanings and references"; in other words, rhetoric.[25] The elaborate attempt to ground the good on the denial of rhetoric can be conducted only in a highly rhetorical fashion that unpicks the jurisprudential claims.

To conclude, the first deconstructive phase of postmodern jurisprudence tried to show how theoretical concepts and doctrinal structures are always "cracked and fissured by necessary contradictions and heterogeneities."[26] By the end of the 1980s the indeterminacy thesis was firmly established and accepted to such an extent that even the opponents of postmodernism had to account for it. For critical legal scholars, the deconstruction of formalism was part of the attempt to undermine the legitimacy of a law that could not deliver justice. Deconstruction revived the jurisprudential debate but did not seem to affect the ways of the law. At that point the question changed. If it is true that legal texts have many contradictory, paradoxical, and conflicting meanings, what is it that keeps texts together, authorizes one interpretation over against possible others, and gives them their power to order the world?

The urgent task was to explore the ethical dimensions, to find methods of distinguishing between the flippant and the fundamental, the worthless and the worthwhile, without in any way reinstating the modernist claims to the power of authority. This was the point at which postmodernism generally went political and ethical. In law, it meant a turn towards justice and the operation of judgment.

The ethics and justice of alterity

The classical writers presented justice as the prime virtue of the polity and the spirit and reason of law. A just constitution is legitimate and a just legal system has a valid claim to the obedience of its citizens. From Aristotle to contemporary political philosophy, justice has been related to the law and legal decision-making. Justice has been seen as the foundation, the spirit, and the end of the law. But justice is also something outside or before the law; as divine will or its expressions in nature and reason or as the present prefiguration of a future utopia, justice is also the higher tribunal or reason to which the law and its judgments are called to account. In this sense, a law without justice is a law without spirit, a dead letter, which can neither rule nor inspire.

We have traveled a long way from these classical formulations of justice. Contemporary jurisprudence identifies justice fully with the law. Legality, the rule of law, the impartiality of the judiciary, the correct following of formal procedures, are the main topics in the discussion of justice. Law is seen as the main answer to the weakening of authority and the moral polyphony of modern society. Liberal philosophy, as interpreted by Rawls, for instance, assumes a wide variety of incommensurable, even opposed conceptions of the good (life) and tries to create a framework of cooperation within which conflict can be constrained and individuals can pursue their private aims. In the absence of any widely shared vision of the good life, liberalism relies on formal procedures: on positive law and criteria of distribution of resources. Law excludes from its domain considerations of value and limits the quest for or the application of any substantive criteria of justice. The law becomes the main substitute for absent ethics and the emptied normative realm. Indeed, the very absence of ethical value, the flight of justice, ensures the morality of the law. This is the basis of the jurisprudential claim that unjust laws should be obeyed as the morality of legality overrides any local injustice.[27] Moral content may have been abstracted from law but the legal enterprise as a whole is blessed with the overall attribute of morality. On the surface, the transition from status to contract is supplemented by a parallel passage from value to norm and from the good to the right. The foundation of meaning and value has been firmly transferred from the transcendent to the social and, in this transition, normativity has forfeited its claim to substance and value and has replaced them with blanket certifications of source and of conformity with form. In the world of law, justice and injustice refer to fairness, the restoration of balance and proportion and the redress of the *status quo* between individuals. But this is a limited conception of a conservative justice, which serves our sense of fairness but also entrenches expectations and vested interests. As Anatole France memorably put it, the law in its majesty forbids both rich and poor to steal bread and to sleep under bridges.

Roberto Unger's statement that we are "surrounded by injustice without knowing where justice lies" is programmatic for postmodern approaches to justice.[28] It links our contemporary bewilderment at the failure of the theory of justice with the classical passion for the denunciation of injustice. Justice is either a critical concept that transcends the legal domain and judges its injustice, or it is redundant, if not positively harmful, by encouraging an unquestioning attitude to law and power. Postmodernity brings to an end the exalted attempts to ground moral action exclusively upon cognition, reason, or the law and marks the beginnings of a new ethical awareness. But the re-linking of ethics and politics or of justice and the law must pass through a new conception of the good, in a situation where classical teleology is historically exhausted and religious transcendence is unable to command widespread acceptance. The modern cosmos has been disenchanted and does not carry, as in classical times, meaning, purposes, and values that can ground an ethics. Natural laws are the concern of scientists, not of moral philosophers. And while we witness a return to God in the twenty-first century, this is a sign not of value-consensus and moral agreement, as in premodern times, but of disagreement and conflict between mutually exclusive religions. We need an ethical principle and an associated theory of judgment that would transcend and allow us to criticize our legal practices, while being firmly placed within our history and experience – a transcendence in immanence, which would avoid the pitfalls of Kantian moralism.

The most important philosophical influence in re-conceptualizing justice and judgment for postmodernity has been Emmanuel Levinas's ethics and their popularization in the legal academy by Jacques Derrida.[29] Levinas argues that western philosophy and ethics share a common attitude towards the world, which reduces the distance between self and other and makes the different follow the same. Classical philosophy promised to reveal the structure of reality by claiming that the realm of beings follows the laws of theoretical necessity. In modernity, individual consciousness has become the starting point of knowledge and, as a result, what differs from the self-same has turned into a question of knowledge, an exploration of the conditions under which I can know the other's existence and understand his or her mental life. The ethics of alterity challenges these ontological and epistemological assumptions. It starts with the other and challenges the various ways in which the other has been reduced to the same. The other is not the self's *alter ego*, self's extension. Nor is the other the negation of self in a dialectical relation that can be totalized in a future synthesis. Heidegger correctly emphasized the historical and social nature of self. But the other is not similar to self. Self and other are not equal partners in a Heideggerian "we" in which we share our world, nor is the other the threatening externality and radical absence of Sartrean existentialism that turns self into an object.

The other comes first. He or she is the condition of existence of language, of self, and of the law. In the philosophy of alterity, the other can never be reduced to the self or the different to the same. The demand of the other that obliges me is the "essence" of the ethics of alterity. But this "essence" is based on the nonessence of the other, who cannot be turned into the instance of a concept, the application of a law, or the particularization of the universal ego. As the face of the other turns on me, he or she becomes my neighbor, but not the neighbor of the neighbor principle in law. As absolute difference and otherness, my neighbor is also the most strange and foreign. The appeal of the other is direct, concrete, and personal; it is addressed to me and I am the only one who can answer it. The demand does not depend on universal reason or law but on the concrete historical and empirical encounter with the other. It is this situated encounter and unrepeatable unique demand that assigns me to morality and makes me a bound and ethical subject. Our relationship is necessarily nonsymmetrical and nonreciprocal as his or her unique demand is addressed to me and me alone. Equity is not equality but absolute dissymmetry.

Law and jurisprudence share the cognitive and moral attitudes of modern ontology. Cognitively, the law knows the world to the extent that it subjects it to its regulative operations. For modern jurisprudence, the law and the world are potentially coextensive. The legal system has all the necessary resources to translate nonlegal phenomena into law's arcane discourse and thus exercise its regulative function. One key strategy is the legal person. In existential terms, the subject of legal and contractual rights and agreements stands at the center of the universe and asks the law to enforce his entitlements without great concern for ethical considerations and without empathy for the other. If the legal person is an isolated and narcissistic subject who perceives the world as a hostile place to be either used or defended against through the medium of rights and contracts, he or she is also disembodied, genderless, a strangely mutilated person. The other as legal subject is a rational being with rights, entitlements, and duties like ourselves. We expect to be treated equally with the other, and reciprocity of entitlement and obligation is placed at the basis of the legal mentality. But this conception of justice as fairness must necessarily reduce the concreteness of the other; it must minimize the differences of need and desire and emphasize the similarities and homologies between the subjects. The moral worthiness of the other's demand is to be sought more in what self and other share than in those differences and specificities that make the other a concrete historical being.

Legal rules ensure equality before the law and guarantee the freedom of the parties. But this equality is only formal; it necessarily ignores the specific history, motive, and need that the litigant brings to the law in order to administer the calculation of the rule and the application of the measure. Similarly with legal freedom: it is the freedom to accede to the available repertoire of legal forms and rights, the freedom to be what the law has ordained, accompanied by the threat that opting out is not permitted, that disobedience to a legal norm is disobedience to the rule of law *tout court* and that life outside the legal form ceases. Legal rules and their mentality are strangely amoral; they promise to replace ethical responsibility with the mechanical application of predetermined and morally neutral rules, and justice with the administration of justice. But there is more. Moral philosophy in its ontological imperialism creates the generalized other.[30] The law sharing the predispositions to abstract and universalize turns concrete people into generalized legal subjects. But the legal subject, too, is a fiction and the natural (legal) subject is infinitely more fictitious than the corporate.[31] The difference between the fictions of Rawls and those of the law is that the legal subject is a *persona*, a mask, veil, or blindfold put on real people who, unlike the abstractions of moral philosophy, hurt, feel pain and suffer. It is doubly important, therefore, to remove the mask from the face of the person and the blindfold from the eyes of justice. But how can we move from the ethics of responsibility to the law?

Ethical responsibility starts with the demand of an other and the call to responsibility. But the law must also introduce the demands and expectations of the third party. "The other is from the first the brother of all the other men."[32] Coexistence places a limit on infinite responsibility. When someone comes to the law, he or she is already involved in conflict with at least one more person and the judge has to balance the conflicting requests. The judge, seen from the perspective of the litigants, is the third person, whose action removes the dispute from the domain of interpersonal hostility and places it within the confines of the institution. Because the third is always present in my encounter with the other, the law is implicated in every attempt to act morally. But the law limits our infinite responsibility for the other and introduces calculation, synchronization, and thematization; it regulates and totalizes the demands put before it. The law translates these requests into the universalizable language of rights, legal entitlements, and procedural proprieties, and makes them appear contemporaneous and comparable. Almost by definition and necessity, the law forgets the difference of the different and the otherness of the other and, in this sense, it cannot escape injustice. To say therefore that the law begins as ethics, as the infinite, non-totalizable and non-regulated moment of the encounter with another, sounds counterfactual. But the ethics of alterity is unequivocal; the sense of responsibility, the "internal point of view" that speaks to me and commands me comes from the proximity of one to another, the fact that we are involved and implicated as we are faced and addressed by the other.

A community (and its law) based on justice is therefore double: first, it is an ethical community of unequal hostages to the other and a network of undetermined but immediate ethical relationships of asymmetry, where I am responsible and duty bound to respond to the other's demand. But, second, community also implies the commonality of law, the calculation of equality, and the symmetry of rights. In a community of equals, I too am another like the others and I too am a legitimate claimant and recipient of the other's care. It is on this basis of the "legal as ethical" that we can visualize a politics of law that disturbs the totalizing tendency of the legal system. Such politics would allow the other to reappear both as the point of exteriority and transcendence that precludes the closure of ontology and as the excluded and unrepresentable of political and legal theory. Here we approach the postmodern aporia of justice: to act justly one must treat the other both as equal and as entitled to the symmetrical treatment of norms, and as a totally unique person who commands the response of ethical asymmetry.

Justice is therefore grounded in the ethical turn to the other; it "is impossible without the one that renders it finding himself in proximity...The judge is not outside the conflict, but the law is in the midst of proximity."[33] Judges, lawyers, and law teachers are always involved and implicated, called upon to respond to the ethical relationship by the other. We must compare and calculate, but we remain responsible and always return to the surplus of duties over rights. Injustice would be to forget that the law rises on the ground of responsibility for the other and that ethical proximity and asymmetry overflow the equality of rights. The law can never have the last word. Legal relations are just only if they recognize "the impossibility of passing by he who is proximate."[34] We cannot define justice in advance, we cannot say that "justice is X or Y," because that would turn the injunction of ethics into an abstract theory and would turn the command "Be just" into an empty judgmental statement. Justice is not about theories and truth, nor does it derive from a true representation of just society. If the law calculates, if it thematizes people by turning them into legal subjects, ethics is a matter of an indeterminate judgment without criteria, and justice is the bringing together of the limited calculability and determinacy of law with the infinite openness of ethical alterity.

The indeterminate judgment

The idea of indeterminate judgment refers us to two seemingly unrelated traditions, which have contributed to the history of the common law but have been forgotten in modernity: Aristotelian practical wisdom and casuistry. For Aristotle, practical wisdom is the virtue of praxis. Practical judgments, unlike theoretical statements, do not deal with essences or with necessary and immutable relations. They have a timely and circumstantial character, and they depend on a full and detailed understanding of the contingencies of the situation. The theoretical sciences examine general principles and the formal connections between phenomena, while practical knowledge deals with the changing and the variable and with "ultimate particulars," and tries to grasp the situation in its singularity.[35] Indeed, Aristotle goes as far as to compare the singularity of practical judgment to that of perception *aisthesis*.[36] Thus while the evolving knowledge of the aims of good life forms the horizon of Aristotelian ethics, *phronesis* recognizes that moral norms and values are just that, a horizon. In his discussion of justice, Aristotle argues that equity, *epieikeia*, is the rectification of legal justice, in so far as the law is defective on account of its generalizations. While laws are universal, "the raw material of human behaviour" is such that it is often impossible to pronounce in general terms. Thus "justice and equity coincide, and both are good, [but] equity is superior."[37] Practical judgment is preoccupied with the specificity of the situation and with the perception, understanding, and judging of the singular as singular, and is a major source of inspiration for medieval casuistry.

Casuistry is a church-based form of moral and religious reasoning.[38] Christian casuistry, designed to help priests resolve borderline problems in a principled yet sensitive manner, reached its height of refinement and influence around the sixteenth and seventeenth centuries. Casuistry starts from the position of the unique individual in his or her natural and social environment and attempts to describe this singularity in morally relevant terms. It involves an ordering of cases by paradigm and analogy, appeals to maxims and analysis of circumstances, the qualification of opinions, the accumulation of multiple arguments, and the statement of practical resolutions of particular moral problems in the light of all these considerations. It is based on general maxims, but these are not "universal or invariable, since they hold good with certainty only in the typical conditions of the agent and the circumstances of action."[39]

These maxims were derived from three sources: the Bible; the opinions of the learned who had, in the past, written about moral problems and whose opinion had come to be recognized as authoritative; and, finally, conscience. Conscience, like equity's conception of the term, was not merely individual thoughts or reactions to moral dilemmas and conflict. Conscience depended on individual circumstances, but its judgment was intimately linked with the wisdom of past practices and open-ended principles. The locus of this link is the "case," which brings together the various public and private aspects of the moral dilemma, the concrete persons with their unique histories, the time and place of the action, and the wider considerations involved. Casuistry followed the rhetorical topics and organized its cases as narratives. This allowed as many aspects of the situation as possible to come to bear on its narrative closure which is also the moral answer.

It is evident that one discipline that has taken the injunctions of casuistry seriously for centuries, with only very rare acknowledgments of its close cousin, is the common law. Especially in the jurisdiction of the court of equity, conscience is paramount. For the equity courts, conscience is both principle and individual mental comprehension of the possibility of right action. Like casuistry, the common law has the inherent potential to consider sensitively the specifics of the person before it. But the growth of statutory interventions, the introduction of doctrinalism and of the "textbook tradition," and the postmodern juridification undermined the casuistic method in law. The treasure chest of common-law decisions is full to the brim with cases where the uniqueness of the other person has been disregarded. In theory, the common law has never rejected the working procedures of the case method. Its particularity is to be found in the dialectical relationship between the general principles to be derived from past cases, custom, and statute, and the specific facts involved in any particular dispute. Past decisions are both sources of general but open-ended principle and precedents for future cases and for careful, often lengthy examination of all "relevant" surrounding circumstances, which, in the best judgments, are woven into complete and aesthetically constructed narratives. In recognizing the uniqueness of each case, the common law retains the potential for an ethical application of principles and for the development of a notion of justice that is aware of the requirements of the individual before the court and of the contingency of decision-making.

This analysis can be of great importance for the revitalization of justice in law. We need to develop a new, secular form of casuistic reasoning that will draw from the repressed traditions of case reasoning. The Aristotelian *phronesis* insists on the importance of situation and context but is predicated upon a teleology that does not exist and cannot be re-created. The judge may be the person closest to the classical and casuistical model of the *phronimos* in modernity, but in the absence of a shared universe of value we must envision new ways of giving the other his or her due and of returning law to justice. The morality of legal duty and right produces inevitable and inescapable conflicts and injustices that the legal institution can address only if it returns to the initial intuition of ethics: that practical judgment works only in the context of the good (life). But this universal can no longer be the consensual virtue of the *polis* of classical teleology or the abstract duty to follow divine or state law. At the end of modernity the good can be defined only according to the needs and demands of the other – the person in need, but also the self-defining autonomous person whose request asks for the reawakening of the sensitivity to singularity inherent in the sense of justice. The demand that the other is to be heard as a full person – in other words, the demand for ethics – introduces certain minimum communicative and moral requirements for legal procedure as to the type of hearing to be given to the person before the law and the nature of the interpretation and application of the relevant legal rules.[40] The sense of justice returns the law to the other and the good. But we should repeat that law's inescapable commitment to the rule means that injustice is the inescapable condition of all law.

Postmodern justice

Cases arising from the arrival of refugees exemplify the problems and possibilities of postmodern judgment. Immigration officers in Dover and Heathrow must decide whether the arriving refugee has a valid claim to political asylum that will admit him or her into Britain and allow him or her the protections introduced in international conventions and domestic law. But this administrative decision is occasionally subjected to judicial review to ensure that basic principles of legality, rationality, and natural justice have not been violated in the process of administrative decision-making.

In an important case involving Tamil refugees fleeing the conflict in Sri Lanka, the applications for asylum were refused by the Home Office and the refusals were challenged in the courts.[41] The central legal issue was the correct interpretation of the requirement that refugees should have a "well-founded fear of persecution" that led them to flee their country of origin. The Court of Appeal held that "well-founded fear" was a subjective feeling. A refugee's actual fear, unless it could be dismissed as "paranoid," can ground a claim for asylum. The House of Lords reversed this judgment. An actual and genuine fear was not sufficient. It should have an "objective basis" that could be "objectively determined" by the Home Secretary, the immigration officer, or the judge, by looking not only at the facts known to the refugee but also at "unknown to him facts such as reports, press articles, and information supplied by the Foreign Office." On this basis, the Tamil refugees were refused asylum because the Home Office had concluded that the civil war in the Tamil areas of Sri Lanka did not "on objective grounds" constitute persecution of Tamils.[42]

In this encounter with the refugee, the role of the judge has gradually changed. The judge started as the recipient of the refugee's request, but, in considering the objective but unknown facts, he or she claims to be on the same plane as the refugee. The past pain and the fear of future torture have been translated into an interpretable, understandable reality that, like all reality, is potentially shareable by judge and victim. This translation of fear into knowledge assumes that the judge can occupy the place of the refugee and share the pain. If interpretations create the possibility of linguistically sharing experiences, then pain, death, and their fear bring interpretations to an end. Fear, pain, and death, however, are radically singular; they resist and at the limit destroy language and its ability to construct shared worlds. The refugee suffers fear and violence, first in the hands of the torturer and second in the administrative/judicial claim that this intimate fear can be translated into shareable knowledge. This translation restores law's ability to pass sentences, which was temporarily disturbed by the encounter with reason's other (feeling, pain, death) and law's other (the refugee). When confronted with a traumatic object, the cognitive attitude tries to make it fully transparent, to deny its traumatized and trauma-producing effects, and to translate it into the idiom of an eternal truth.

We can generalize this reading towards a phenomenology of postmodern judgment. Its operation can be compared with the formal structure of performative speech-acts. The performative says and does, saying what it does by doing what it says. I say, "I thee wed," "The meeting is declared open," "War is declared," and so it happens. Similarly, every judgment is implicated with force; the force of the interpretation that turns the singular into an instance of the norm or the particular into a case of the universal, and the physical force that constrains and shapes the body. The "rightness" of the judgment depends on the institutional felicity of the interpretation of law and, in hermeneutical jurisprudence, on its accord with moral principles. But its justice can be judged only according to the way it acts. Its action is neither the continuation of the legal interpretation nor its opposite. In many key respects, discourse and force differ.

The time of justice differs from the time of interpretation. Interpretation turns to the past or measures up to the future as past and future inhabit the ever-present. Interpretation's time is synchronic. The time of action, as violence or justice, is diachronic. This is the time of the event. It addresses the other here and now in each here and now, and answers or denies the call. This is the pure ethical time, the time of what Levinas calls "il y a" – it is happening. Interestingly, the two opposing conceptions of time were discussed by the courts. The Court of Appeal illustrated its subjective definition of fear by means of an allegory. "A bank cashier confronted with a masked man who points a revolver at him and demands the contents of the till could without doubt claim to have experienced a 'well-founded fear.' His fears would have been no less well-founded if, one minute later, it emerged that the revolver was a plastic replica or a water pistol."[43] The House of Lords, however, dismissed the analogy in summary fashion. An "objective observer" of the robbery would accept the cashier's fear as well founded only until he discovered the fact that the firearm was fake. Before that, he could not have been an "objective" observer in any case. While he was still defrauded, he was in exactly the same state as the cashier, possibly in fear but certainly not seeing the truth. The objective observer must reserve judgment until such time as all relevant facts are in. From that position, the Tamil refugees' fears were not "of instant personal danger arising out of an immediate predicament," and the official response should be determined after "examining the *actual* state of affairs in [the refugees'] country."[44]

We can draw a parallel here between the time of fear and pain and the time of justice. When fear, pain, or justice are dealt with as "real" entities that can be verified or falsified according to objective criteria, their time or the time of the response to them is the time of constancy and omnitemporality of descriptions, theories, and institutions. Truth is atemporal and theory is all-seeing. Fear and pain, by contrast, are individual feelings experienced as temporal responses to stimuli. In treating the time of fear as non-instant and non-immediate, the House of Lords is also violating the time of ethics.

Violence or justice can happen only at the moment of their occurrence. They are the performative aspects of the legal judgment. Nothing that happened earlier (a reading of the law or a commitment to principle) and nothing that anticipates the future (a promise or a vision of a happy community) can account fully for or preempt the uniqueness of the response. And, as in the robbery analogy, the response of the person obligated can only be instant and immediate. We can now understand why, for Derrida, the instant of the just decision has an urgency that obstructs knowledge. Justice, like the robber and the fear he created, cannot wait for all relevant facts. Even if the judge had all the information and all the time in the world, "the moment of decision, as such, always remains a finite moment of urgency and precipitation . . . since it always marks the interruption of the juridico- or ethico- or politico-cognitive deliberation that precedes it."[45]

In this sense justice takes again the form of an aporia: to be just, you must both be free *and* follow a rule or a prescription. A just and responsible decision must both conserve and destroy or suspend the law enough to reinvent it and rejustify it in each case. Each case is different and requires a unique interpretation, which no rule can guarantee absolutely. But at the same time there is no just decision if the judge does not refer to law or rule, if he suspends his decision before the undecidable or leaves aside all rules. This is the reason that we cannot say that a judgment is just. A decision may be recognized as lawful, in accordance with legal rules and conventions, but it cannot be declared just because justice is the dislocation of the "said" of the law by the – unrepresentable – "saying" of ethics. "For a decision to be just and responsible, it must, in its proper moment if there is one, be both regulated and without regulation: it must conserve the law and also destroy it or suspend it enough to have to reinvent it in each case, rejustify it, at least reinvent it in the reaffirmation and the new and free confirmation of its principle."[46] Justice seeks the particular at the moment when the universal runs the risk to turn to its opposite, and as such it has the characteristics of a double bind. The action of justice requires an incessant movement between the general rule and the specific case that has no resting place and finds no point of equilibrium. There is a dislocation, a delay or deferral, between the ever-present time of the law and the always-to-come temporality of ethics.

We can conclude that justice has the characteristics of a promissory statement. A promise states now something to be performed in the future. Being just always lies in the future; it is a promise made to the future, a pledge to look into the event and the uniqueness of each situation and to respond to the absolute unrepeatability of the face that will put a demand on me. This promise, like all promises, does not have a present time, a time when you can say, "There it is; justice is this or that." Suspended between the law and the good in-the-face-of-the-other, justice is always still to come or always already performed. But, as the ethical exposure to the other is inevitably and necessarily reduced to the simultaneity of the text, the law and the judge are unavoidably implicated in violence. There is violence in law; the violence of turning the other to an instance of interpretation, but also the physical violence that follows every verdict and judgment. Postmodern jurisprudence has to keep disrupting the law in the name of justice and to keep reminding the law of its inescapable violence. A postmodern theory of justice allows otherness to survive and to become a critical space to criticize the operations of the same. The law is necessarily committed to the form of universality and abstract equality; but it must also respect the requests of the contingent, incarnate, and concrete other, it must pass through the ethics of alterity in order to respond to its own embeddedness in ethics. In this unceasing movement between the most general and calculating and the most concrete and incalculable, or between the legality of form and subjectivity and the ethics of response to the concrete other, law answers the postmodern call to justice.

NOTES

1. Michel Foucault, *Power, Truth, Strategy* (Sydney: Feral Publications, 1979), p. 43.
2. Paul Campos, *Jurismania: The Madness of American Law* (Oxford: Oxford University Press, 1998).
3. Costas Douzinas and Ronnie Warrington, *Postmodern Jurisprudence: The Law of Text in the Texts of Law* (London: Routledge, 1991); Costas Douzinas, Peter Goodrich, and Yifat Hachamovitch (eds.), *Politics, Postmodernity and Critical Legal Studies* (London: Routledge, 1994); Gary Minda, *Postmodern Legal Movements: Law and Jurisprudence at Century's End* (New York: New York University Press, 1995).
4. Alan Hunt and Peter Fitzpatrick (eds.), *Critical Legal Studies* (Oxford: Blackwell, 1987); David Kairys (ed.)., *The Politics of Law: A Progressive Critique* (New York: Pantheon, 1982). Many will disagree with the characterization of the schools of thought listed here as postmodern. Despite their obvious theoretical and political differences, however, they are united in the critique of formalism and rationalism and in the concern with the moral deficit of law, both of which are typically postmodern. This essay's approach is closest to the postmodernism that has dominated the British critical legal movement and has been promoted by the review *Law & Critique*.
5. James Boyd White, *Heracles' Bow: Essays on the Rhetoric and Poetics of Law* (Madison, WI: University of Wisconsin Press, 1985); *Acts of Hope: Creating Authority in Literature, Law and Politics* (Chicago, IL: University of Chicago Press, 1994); Richard Weisberg, *Poethics and other Strategies in Law and Literature* (New York: Columbia University Press, 1992), Maria Aristodemou, *Law and Literature: Journey from Her to Eternity* (Oxford: Oxford University Press, 2000), and Adam Gearey, *Law and Aesthetics* (Oxford: Hart, 2001).
6. Richard Posner, *The Economic Analysis of Law*, 4th edn. (Boston, MA: Little, Brown, 1992).
7. Derrick Bell, *Race, Racism and American Law* (Boston, MA: Little, Brown, 1992).
8. Peter Goodrich, *Oedipus Lex: Psychoanalysis, History, Law* (Berkeley, CA: University of California Press, 1995); David Caudill, *Lacan and the Subject of Law: Toward a Psychoanalytical Critical Legal Theory* (Atlantic Highlands, NJ: Humanities Press, 1997).
9. Herbert Hart, *The Concept of Law* (Oxford: Clarendon, 1979); Dennis Lloyd, *The Idea of Law: A Repressive Evil or Social Necessity?* (Harmondsworth: Penguin, 1978); Ronald Dworkin, *Law's Empire* (London: Fontana, 1986).
10. Hans Kelsen, *The Pure Theory of Law* (Berkeley, CA: University of California Press, 1934).

11. Dworkin, *Law's Empire*, p. 404.
12. James Boyd White, *Justice as Translation: An Essay in Cultural and Legal Criticism* (Chicago, IL: University of Chicago Press, 1990).
13. Jacques Derrida, "Force of Law: 'The Mystical Foundation of Authority,' " trans. Mary Quaintance, *Cardozo Law Review* 11 (1990), pp. 919–1046. This essay, delivered at a Cardozo Law School conference in 1988, became the foundational text of the ethical turn in postmodern jurisprudence.
14. Robert Cover, "Violence and the Word," *Yale Law Journal* 95 (1986), pp. 1601–29.
15. Jonathan Culler, *Framing the Sign* (Oxford: Blackwell, 1988), p. 150.
16. Jacques Derrida, *Of Grammatology*, trans. Gayatri Chakravorty Spivak (Baltimore, MD: Johns Hopkins University Press, 1974), pp. 237–8.
17. Duncan Kennedy, "Form and Substance in Private Law Adjudication," *Harvard Law Review* 89 (1976), pp. 1685–778; "The Structure of Blackstone's Commentaries," *Buffalo Law Review* 28 (1979), pp. 209–382.
18. Gerald Frug, "The Ideology of Bureaucracy in American Law," *Harvard Law Review* 97 (1984), p. 1287.
19. Clare Dalton, "An Essay in the Deconstruction of Contract Doctrine," *Yale Law Journal* 94 (1985), pp. 1002–3.
20. Mark Kelman, *A Guide to Critical Legal Studies* (Cambridge, MA: Harvard University Press, 1987), pp. 16, 245–61.
21. Peter Goodrich, "Contractions," in Anthony Carty (ed.), *Post-modern Law: Enlightenment, Revolution and the Death of Man* (Edinburgh: Edinburgh University Press, 1990), and *Oedipus Lex*, pp. 198–222; Costas Douzinas and Ronnie Warrington, "Posting the Law: Social Contracts and the Postal Rule's Grammatology," *International Journal for the Semiotics of Law* 4 (1991), pp. 115–35; Simon Gardiner, "Trashing with Trollope: A Deconstruction of the Postal Rule in Contract," *Oxford Journal of Legal Studies* 12 (1992), pp. 170–194.
22. G. C. Cheshire and C. H. S. Fifoot, *Cheshire and Fifoot's Law of Contract*, 10th edn. (London: Butterworth, 1981), p. 46.
23. Ibid.
24. Bernard Jackson, *Law, Fact and Narrative Coherence* (Liverpool: Deborah Charles Publications, 1985).
25. John Finnis, *Natural Law and Natural Rights* (Oxford: Clarendon, 1980), pp. 67, 69, 75, 408.
26. Rodolphe Gasché, *The Tain of the Mirror* (Cambridge, MA: Harvard University Press, 1976), p. 136.
27. Lon L. Fuller, *The Morality of Law* (New Haven, CT, and London: Yale University Press, 1964).
28. Roberto M. Unger, *Law in Modern Society: Towards a Criticism of Social Theory* (New York: Free Press; London: Collier Macmillan, 1976), p. 175.
29. Emmanuel Levinas, *Totality and Infinity: An Essay on Exteriority*, trans. Alphonso Lingis (Pittsburgh: Dusquesne University Press, 1969); *Otherwise Than Being or Beyond Essence*, trans. Alphonso Lingis (Dordrecht:, Kluwer, 1991); *Outside the Subject*, trans. Michael B. Smith (London: Athlone, 1993). Jacques Derrida, "Force of Law," in *The Other Heading: Reflections on Today's Europe*, trans. Pascale-Anne Brault and Michael B. Naas (Bloomington, IN: Indiana University Press, 1992).

30. A typical instance of this "generalized other" is found in John Rawls, *A Theory of Justice* (Oxford: Oxford University Press, 1972).

31. Costas Douzinas, *The End of Human Rights* (Oxford: Hart, 2000), chs. 8 and 9.

32. Levinas, *Otherwise Than Being*, p. 158.

33. Ibid., p. 159.

34. Ibid.

35. Aristotle, *Nicomachean Ethics*, trans. J. A. K. Thomson (Harmondsworth: Penguin, 1976), p. 215.

36. Ibid., pp. 219–20.

37. Ibid., p. 199.

38. See generally Albert R. Jonsen and Stephen Toulmin, *The Abuse of Casuistry: A History of Moral Reasoning* (Berkeley, CA, and London: University of California Press, 1988).

39. Ibid., pp. 256–7.

40. Narrative theory can be of great use in this moral envisioning of legal judgment. Paul Ricoeur (*Oneself As Another*, trans. Kathleen Blamey [Chicago: Chicago University Press, 1992], pp. 88–168) and Seyla Benhabib (*Situating the Self: Gender, Community, and Postmodernism in Contemporary Ethics* [Cambridge: Polity, 1992], pp. 121–30) analyse the ethical importance of the narrative construction of life stories. The political imperative of postmodernism is to keep the "tales in motion and circulation, keep interchanging narrators, narratees and narrated, keep making the judge defendant and the defendant judge" (Douzinas and Warrington, *Postmodern Jurisprudence*, p. 110). An ethically aware theory of legal judgment must combine the narrative nature of law with the recognition that a "just" decision responds to the demands of the other as put before the law in the story he or she constructs.

41. R v Home Secretary ex parte Sivakumaran, *All England Law Reports* 1 (1988), p. 193.

42. Ibid., pp. 196, 199.

43. *Weekly Law Reports* 3 (1987), p. 1053. The Court of Appeal, in accepting that the fear is necessarily an individual and unshareable feeling and in responding to it, is in this instance following the principle of justice of the ethics of alterity.

44. *All England Law Reports* 1 (1988), p. 202.

45. Derrida, "Force of Law," p. 967.

46. Ibid., p. 961.

FURTHER READING

Postmodern social theory

Anderson, Perry, *The Origins of Postmodernity* (London: Verso, 1998)

Bell, Daniel, *The Coming of Post-Industrial Society*, 2nd edn. (New York: Basic, 1999)

Bertens, Hans, *The Idea of the Postmodern: A History* (London: Routledge, 1995)

Boyne, Roy, *Postmodernism and Society* (Basingstoke: Macmillan Education, 1990)

Connor, Steven, *Postmodernist Culture: An Introduction to Theories of the Contemporary*, 2nd edn. (Oxford: Blackwell, 1997)

Eagleton, Terry, *The Illusions of Postmodernism* (Oxford: Blackwell, 1996)

Frow, John, *Time and Commodity Culture: Essays on Cultural Theory and Postmodernity* (Oxford: Clarendon, 1997)

Heller, Agnes, and Ferenc Fehér, *The Postmodern Political Condition* (Cambridge: Polity, 1998)

Jameson, Fredric, *Postmodernism, or, The Cultural Logic of Late Capitalism* (Durham, NC: Duke University Press; London: Verso, 1991)

Jenkins, Keith (ed.), *The Postmodern History Reader* (London: Routledge, 1997)

Kellner, Douglas M. (ed.), *Baudrillard: A Critical Reader* (Oxford: Blackwell, 1994)

Kumar, Krishan, *From Industrial to Post-Modern Society: New Theories of the Contemporary World* (Oxford: Blackwell, 1995)

Seidman, Steven (ed.), *The Postmodern Turn: New Perspectives in Social Theory* (Cambridge: Cambridge University Press, 1994)

Turner, Bryan S. (ed.), *Theories of Modernity and Postmodernity* (London: Sage, 1990)

Postmodernism and philosophy

Lyotard, Jean-François, *The Inhuman: Reflections on Time*, trans. Geoff Bennington and Rachel Bowlby (Cambridge: Polity, 1991)

  Toward the Postmodern, ed. Robert Harvey and Mark S. Roberts (Atlantic Highlands, NJ, and London: Humanities Press International, 1993)

Norris, Christopher, *What's Wrong With Postmodernism: Critical Theory and the Ends of Philosophy* (London: Harvester Wheatsheaf, 1990)

Rorty, Richard, *Contingency, Irony, and Solidarity* (Cambridge: Cambridge University Press, 1989)

Vattimo, Gianni, *The End of Modernity: Nihilism and Hermeneutics in Post-Modern Culture*, trans. Jon R. Snyder (Cambridge: Polity, 1988)

Williams, James, *Lyotard: Towards a Postmodern Philosophy* (Malden, MA, and Cambridge: Polity, 1998)

Postmodernism and film

Baudrillard, Jean, *The Evil Demon of Images*, trans. Paul Patton and Paul Foss (Annandale, VA: Power Institute, 1987)

Brooker, Peter, and Will Brooker (eds.), *Postmodern After-Images: A Reader in Film, Television and Video* (London: Edward Arnold, 1997)

Friedberg, Anne, *Window Shopping: Cinema and the Postmodern* (Los Angeles and Oxford: University of California Press, 1993)

Natoli, Joseph, *Postmodern Journeys: Film and Culture, 1996–1998* (Albany, NY: State University of New York Press, 2001)

Postmodern Screen 28:2 (1997)

Postmodernism and literature

Baker, Stephen, *The Fiction of Postmodernity* (Edinburgh: Edinburgh University Press, 2000)

Blasing, Mutlu Konuk, *Politics and Form in Postmodern Poetry: O'Hara, Bishop, Ashbery and Merrill* (Cambridge: Cambridge University Press, 1995)

Brooker, Peter (ed.), *Modernism/Postmodernism* (Harlow: Longman, 1992)

Connor, Steven, *The English Novel in History, 1950–1995* (London: Routledge, 1996)

Conte, Joseph Mark, *Unending Design: The Forms of Postmodern Poetry* (Ithaca, NY: Cornell University Press, 1990)

Currie, Mark, *Postmodern Narrative Theory* (Basingstoke: Macmillan, 1998)

Francese, Joseph, *Narrating Postmodern Time and Space* (Albany, NY: State University of New York Press, 1997)

Gibson, Andrew, *Postmodernity, Ethics and the Novel: From Leavis to Levinas* (London: Routledge, 1999)

Hoover, Paul (ed.), *Postmodern American Poetry: A Norton Anthology* (New York: Norton, 1994)

Jameson, Fredric, *The Cultural Turn: Selected Writings on the Postmodern, 1983–1998* (London and New York: Verso, 1998)

Kucich, John, and Dianne F. Sadoff (eds.), *Victorian Afterlife: Postmodern Culture Rewrites the Nineteenth Century* (Minneapolis, MN, and London: University of Minnesota Press, 2000)

Lucy, Niall, *Postmodern Literary Theory: An Introduction* (Oxford: Blackwell, 1997)

Woods, Tim, *Beginning Postmodernism* (Manchester: Manchester University Press, 1999)

Postmodernism and art

Krauss, Rosalind (ed.), *October: The Second Decade, 1986–1996* (Cambridge, MA, and London: MIT Press, 1997)

Lovejoy, Margot, *Postmodern Currents: Art and Artists in the Age of Electronic Media*, 2nd edn. (Upper Saddle River, NJ: Prentice-Hall, 1997)

Melville, Stephen, *Seams: Art as a Philosophical Context*, ed. Jeremy Gilbert-Rolfe (Amsterdam: Gordon and Breach, 1996)

Sandler, Irving, *Art of the Postmodern Era: From the Late 1960s to the Early 1990s* (Boulder, CO: Westview, 1998)

Postmodernism and performance

Auslander, Philip, *From Acting to Performance: Essays in Modernism and Postmodernism* (London: Routledge, 1997)

Liveness: Performance in a Mediatized Culture (London: Routledge, 1999)

Presence and Resistance: Postmodernism and Cultural Politics in Contemporary American Performance (Ann Arbor, MI: University of Michigan Press, 1992)

Bonney, Jo (ed.), *Extreme Exposure: An Anthology of Solo Performance Texts from the Twentieth Century* (New York: Theatre Communications Group, 2000)

Goldberg, RoseLee, *Performance Art: From Futurism to the Present* (London: Thames and Hudson, 1988)

Performance: Live Art Since the 60s (London: Thames and Hudson, 1998)

Kaye, Nick, *Postmodernism and Performance* (Basingstoke: Macmillan, 1994)

Pavis, Patrice (ed.), *The Intercultural Performance Reader* (London: Routledge, 1996)

Savran, David, *Breaking the Rules: The Wooster Group* (New York: Theatre Communications Group, 1988)

Watt, Stephen, *Postmodern/Drama: Reading the Contemporary Stage* (Ann Arbor, MI: University of Michigan Press, 1998)

Postmodernism and space

Augé, Marc, *Non-Places: Introduction to an Anthropology of Supermodernity*, trans. John Howe (London: Verso, 1995)

Benk, Georges, and Ulf Strohmayer (eds.), *Space and Social Theory: Interpreting Modernity and Postmodernity* (Oxford: Blackwell, 1997)

Ellin, Nan, *Postmodernism Urbanism*, rev. edn. (New York: Princeton Architectural Press, 1999)

Jencks, Charles, *The New Paradigm in Architecture: The Language of Post-Modernism* (New Haven, CT, and London: Yale University Press, 2002)

Lefebvre, Henri, *The Production of Space*, trans. Donald Nicholson-Smith (Oxford: Blackwell, 1991)

Minca, Claudio (ed.), *Postmodern Geography: Theory and Praxis* (Oxford and Malden, MA: Blackwell, 2001)

Smethurst, Paul, *The Postmodern Chronotope: Reading Space and Time in Contemporary Fiction* (Amsterdam: Rodopi, 2000)

Soja, Edward W., *Postmodern Geographies: The Reassertion of Space in Critical Social Theory* (London: Verso, 1990)

Virilio, Paul, *Polar Inertia*, trans. Patrick Camiller (London: Sage, 2000)

Watson, Sophie, and Katherine Gibson (eds.), *Postmodern Cities and Spaces* (Cambridge, MA, and Oxford: Blackwell, 1995)

Postmodernism, science, ecology

Clarke, C. J. S., *Reality Through the Looking Glass: Science and Awareness in the Postmodern World* (Edinburgh: Floris, 1996)

Giblet, Rodney James, *Postmodern Wetlands: Culture, History, Ecology* (Edinburgh: Edinburgh University Press, 1996)

Griffin, David Ray (ed.), *The Reenchantment of Science: Postmodern Proposals* (Albany, NY: State University of Albany Press, 1988)

Haraway, Donna, *Simians, Cyborgs, and Women: The Reinvention of Nature* (New York: Routledge, 1991)

Latour, Bruno, *We Have Never Been Modern*, trans. Catherine Porter (Cambridge, MA: Harvard University Press, 1993)

Myerson, George, *Ecology and the End of Postmodernism* (Cambridge: Icon, 2001)

Oelschlaeger, Max (ed.), *Postmodern Environmental Ethics* (Albany, NY: State University of Albany Press, 1995)

Sassower, Raphael, *Cultural Collisions: Postmodern Technoscience* (New York and London: Routledge, 1995)

Sessions, George (ed.), *Deep Ecology for the 21st Century: Readings on the Philosophy and Practice of the New Environmentalism* (Boston, MA: Shambhala, 1995)

Sokal, Alan, and Jean Bricmont, *Fashionable Nonsense* [in the UK: *Intellectual Impostures*]: *Postmodern Intellectuals' Abuse of Science* (New York: Picador, 1998; London: Profile, 1999)

Spretnak, Charlene, *The Resurgence of the Real: Body, Nature, and Place in a Hypermodern World* (London and New York: Routledge, 1999)

Toulmin, Stephen, *The Return to Cosmology: Postmodern Science and the Theology of Nature* (Berkeley, CA, and London: University of California Press, 1982)

White, Daniel R., *Postmodern Ecology: Communication, Evolution, and Play* (Albany, NY: State University of Albany Press, 1998)

Postmodernism, religion and spirituality

Berry, Philippa, and Andrew Wernick (eds.), *Shadow of Spirit: Postmodernism and Religion* (London: Routledge, 1992)

Griffin, David Ray, *God and Religion in the Postmodern World: Essays in Postmodern Theology* (Albany, NY: State University of New York Press, 1989)

Griffin, David Ray, William Beardsley and Joe Holland, *Varieties of Postmodern Theology* (Albany, NY: State University of New York Press, 1989)

Ingraffia, Brian D., *Postmodern Theory and Biblical Theology: Vanquishing God's Shadow* (Cambridge: Cambridge University Press, 1995)

Lyon, David, *Jesus in Disneyland: Religion in Postmodern Times* (Cambridge: Polity, 2001)

Patton, Kimberley C., and Benjamin C. Ray (eds.), *A Magic Still Dwells: Comparative Religion in the Postmodern Age* (Berkeley, CA: University of California Press, 2000)

Richardson, W. Mark, and Wesley J. Wildman (eds.), *Religion and Science: History, Method, Dialogue* (New York and London: Routledge, 1996)

Scharlemann, Robert P. (ed.), *Theology at the End of the Century: A Dialogue on the Postmodern* (Charlottesville, VA, and London: University Press of Virginia, 1990)

Shepherd, Loraine MacKenzie, *Feminist Theologies for a Postmodern Church: Diversity, Community, and Scripture* (New York: Peter Lang, 2002)

Taylor, Mark C., *Erring: A Postmodern A/theology* (Chicago, IL: University of Chicago Press, 1984)

Ward, Graham (ed.), *The Blackwell Companion to Postmodern Theology* (Malden, MA: Blackwell, 2001)

(ed.), *The Postmodern God: A Theological Reader* (Cambridge, MA, and London: Blackwell, 1998)

Westphal, Merold (ed.), *Postmodern Philosophy and Christian Thought* (Bloomington, IN: Indiana University Press, 1999)

Postmodernism and ethics

Bauman, Zymunt, *Postmodern Ethics* (Oxford: Blackwell, 1993)

Breslauer, S. Daniel, *Toward a Jewish (M)Orality: Speaking of a Postmodern Jewish Ethics* (Westport, CT: Greenwood, 1998)

Critchley, Simon, *The Ethics of Deconstruction: Derrida and Lavinas* (Oxford: Blackwell, 1992)

Ferré, Frederick, *Living and Value: Toward a Constructive Postmodern Ethics* (Albany, NY: State University of Albany Press, 2001)

Kallenberg, Brad J., *Ethics as Grammar: Changing the Postmodern Subject* (Notre Dame, IN: University of Notre Dame Press, 2001)

Madison, Gary B., and Marty Fairbairn (eds.), *The Ethics of Postmodernity: Current Trends in Continental Thought* (Evanston, IL: Northwestern University Press, 1999)

Wyschogrod, Edith, *An Ethics of Remembering: History, Heterology and the Nameless Others* (Chicago and London: University of Chicago Press, 1998)

Ziarek, Ewa Plonowska, *An Ethics of Dissensus: Postmodernity, Feminism and the Politics of Radical Democracy* (Stanford, CA: Stanford University Press, 2001)

Postmodernism and law

Derrida, Jacques, "Force of Law: 'The Mystical Foundation of Authority,'" trans. Mary Quaintance. *Cardozo Law Review* 11 (1990), pp. 919–1046.

Douzinas, Costas, and Ronnie Warrington, *Postmodern Jurisprudence: The Law of Text in the Texts of Law* (London: Routledge, 1991)

Douzinas, Costas, Peter Goodrich, and Yifat Hachamovitch (eds.), *Politics, Postmodernity and Critical Legal Studies: The Legality of the Contingent* (London: Routledge, 1994)

Frug, Mary Joe, *Postmodern Legal Feminism* (London and New York: Routledge, 1992)

Goodrich, Peter, *Oedipus Lex: Psychoanalysis, History, Law* (Berkeley, CA: University of California Press, 1995)

Goodrich, Peter, and David Gray Carlson (eds.), *Law and the Postmodern Mind: Essays on Psychoanalysis and Jurisprudence* (Ann Arbor, MI: University of Michigan Press, 1998)

Litowitz, Douglas E., *Postmodern Philosophy and Law* (Lawrence, KS: University Press of Kansas, 1997)

Minda, Gary, *Postmodern Legal Movements: Law and Jurisprudence at Century's End* (New York: New York University Press, 1995)

INDEX

CAMBRIDGE COMPANIONS TO LITERATURE